CAMBRIDGE TEXTBOOKS IN LINGUISTICS

General Editors: W. SIDNEY ALLEN, B. COMRIE, C. J. FILLMORE
E. J. A. HENDERSON, F. W. HOUSEHOLDER, R. LASS, J. LYONS
R. B. LE PAGE, P. H. MATTHEWS, F. R. PALMER, R. POSNER
J. L. M. TRIM

ENGLISH WORD-FORMATION

In this series:

ENGLISH WORD-FORMATION

LAURIE BAUER

SENIOR LECTURER IN ENGLISH
VICTORIA UNIVERSITY OF WELLINGTON

CAMBRIDGE UNIVERSITY PRESS

CAMBRIDGE
LONDON   NEW YORK   NEW ROCHELLE
MELBOURNE   SYDNEY

Published by the Press Syndicate of the University of Cambridge
The Pitt Building, Trumpington Street, Cambridge CB2 1RP
32 East 57th Street, New York, NY 10022, USA
296 Beaconsfield Parade, Middle Park, Melbourne 3206, Australia

First published 1983

Printed in Great Britain
at the Pitman Press, Bath

Library of Congress catalogue card number: 82-14693

British Library Cataloguing in Publication Data
Bauer, Laurie
  English word formation. – (Cambridge textbooks
  in linguistics)
  1. English language – Word-formation
  I. Title
  422   PE1175

ISBN 0 521 24167 7 hard covers
ISBN 0 521 28492 9 paperback

CONTENTS

Contents

Contents

Contents

Contents

To Winifred

PREFACE

Word-formation is such a confused area of study at the moment that it would not be possible to write an uncontroversial introduction to the subject, and this book accordingly reflects my own beliefs and prejudices. It is my hope that if I cannot convince students and scholars of the correctness of my own point of view, I can at least provide them with a coherent position to argue against. Much of the confusion in word-formation studies is terminological, and one of my aims in this book is to put forward some suggestions for a standard terminology. Most of my proposals (terminological or otherwise) are not, of course, original, and the bibliography will show where they originated.

I should like to thank all those who have given so generously of their time in helping me to prepare this book. My colleagues have all patiently answered innumerable questions on various aspects of linguistic theory and practice. Max Cresswell was particularly helpful with philosophical and semantic issues and Ken Russell with statistical matters. Rainer Bäuerle, Charles J. Fillmore, Janet Holmes, Peter Matthews and Frank Palmer all read the first draft, and their invaluable comments have helped me correct many errors and infelicities. I alone am responsible for those that remain. I must add that none of these people is in any way accountable for the content or argumentation of this book, nor do they necessarily agree with the points made. My greatest debt is to my wife, Winifred, to whom this book is dedicated. Not only has she read several draft versions, but she has also given me substantial help with discussion, comment and encouragement at every stage in the preparation of the book.

Laurie Bauer

I

Introduction

The time of the lexicon has set in.
(Hakulinen, 1978: 325)

1.1 Assumptions and aims

The study of word-formation seems to be emerging from a fallow period. Suddenly word-formation is of central interest to theoretical linguists of all persuasions because of the light it throws on other aspects of language. Unfortunately, there is little agreement on the methodology or basic theoretical background for the study of word-formation, so that the field is currently a confused one.

There is, at the moment, no single "theory of word-formation", nor even agreement on the kind of data that is relevant for the construction of such a theory. This book will not provide a theory, but it will provide an introduction to, and discussion of, some of the basic problems confronting students of word-formation, and draw some conclusions which, it seems to me, must be basic to any future theory. However, given the confusion that reigns at the moment, it should be borne in mind that virtually any theoretical statement about word-formation is controversial, and that this book provides a starting point for discussion more than a body of accepted theoretical dogma.

The basic approach to word-formation taken in this book is synchronic and transformational; but the synchrony is diluted by frequent consideration of diachronic facts, and the way in which the transformational background has been used is untraditional. In particular, ideas and data have been drawn from a wide range of sources, including 'taxonomic' studies as well as transformational ones, and, although the approach envisaged is basically syntactic, other aspects have not been ignored, and phonology, morphology, semantics and pragmatics are all considered.

It is hoped that this book will prove stimulating to scholars with a special interest in word-formation, but that it will also be of value to undergraduates. With this in mind, the book has been presented so that it can be read by someone who has no previous experience of word-formation, or of morphology at all, but a certain amount of background in linguistics has been presupposed. In particular, since word-formation is nowadays rarely studied by students of linguistics before they are familiar with the basics of syntactic theory, a knowledge of transformational grammar as presented in Chomsky (1965) is assumed, not only the general framework of the grammar proposed there, but also notions such as competence and performance and the methodological importance in transformational studies of capturing generalizations. A consequence of this is that much of chapter 2 will be too basic for readers with a broader background in linguistics, and they are invited to skip those sections which are not relevant for them. Chapters 3 and 4 introduce the two main theoretical claims that are made in this book. Chapters 5 and 6 are considerably more technical and specialized. In chapter 7 the range of word-formation processes available in English is considered, and then, in chapter 8 a body of data is considered in the light of the theoretical points that have been made earlier in the book, and the close examination of this body of data leads to further general points of theoretical interest.

1.2   A brief history of the study of word-formation

Interest in word-formation has probably always gone hand-in-hand with interest in language in general, and there are scattered comments and works on the subject of word-formation from the time of Panini, who provided a detailed description of Sanskrit word-formation, right up to the present day.[1] Questions that are still providing difficulties today were asked by scholars in the seventeenth, eighteenth and nineteenth centuries (see e.g. Brekle, 1977; Brekle & Kastovsky, 1977b), and in many ways present-day knowledge shows little advance on Panini's.

Part of the reason for this is that studies in word-formation did not get the boost that linguistics as a whole received in the early

---

[1] For accounts of (various aspects of) the history of word-formation studies see Adams (1973: 4–7), Aronoff (1976: 4–6), Brekle & Kastovsky (1977b), Hakulinen (1978: 325), Lees (1960: xix–xxvi), and the works referred to by Brekle & Kastovsky.

years of the twentieth century. As Adams (1973: 5) points out, this is because the distinction between synchrony and diachrony drawn by Saussure, which has had a profound effect on linguistic studies since 1916, effectively precluded the study of word-formation, where synchrony and diachrony are most fruitfully considered together. Thus, although some scholars like Jespersen (1942) managed to merge synchronic and diachronic approaches in their study of word-formation, most linguists considered word-formation either from a totally synchronic point of view (e.g. Bloomfield, 1935) or from a totally diachronic point of view (e.g. Koziol, 1937).

Simplistically speaking, this was the situation in which word-formation research found itself when linguistics was hit by the "Chomskyan revolution" in 1957. The publication of *Syntactic Structures* (Chomsky, 1957) radically changed the approach to language taken by the majority of the most influential linguists. Whereas phonology and morphology had been the main concerns of American structuralism in the 1940s and 1950s, *Syntactic Structures* took as fundamental the centrality of syntax. American structuralism had not been interested in word-formation because its major interest had been in units smaller than the word (as is pointed out by Adams, 1973: 5), and the word had not been given theoretical prominence in structuralist theory; Transformational Generative Grammar was not interested in word-formation because its major interest was in units larger than the word: the structure of phrases and sentences. Sentences were assumed to be made up not of words, but of morphemes (here Transformational Generative Grammar shows clearly its American structuralist background). Words as such thus played no real role. And even when Lees (1960), working within a Transformational Generative Grammar framework, looked at the generation of words by word-formation, he treated the words he generated not as a separate type of unit, but as a special kind of embedded sentence. This approach is standard in the majority of transformational studies, and very few such studies looked at other problems in word-formation. One exception is Zimmer (1964), who does consider some of the problems that are specific to word-formation.

Lees (1960: xix) dismisses much earlier work on word-formation, including Panini's, as 'taxonomic'. This dismissal has more recently been criticized (Brekle, 1970: 92ff; Brekle & Kastovsky,

3

1977b: 8), particularly as applied to Panini. The term 'taxonomic' was being used in Transformational Generative Grammar at this period as a term of abuse, and it is not clear precisely what Lees means by this.[2] In retrospect, it is not even clear that it matters. The first edition of Marchand's monumental work *The Categories and Types of Present-Day English Word-Formation* (revised 1969) appeared in the same year as Lees's book, 1960, and Lees would probably have termed it 'taxonomic' in that it does not provide any rules which will enumerate (and thus, in the terminology of the time, 'explain') the existing or new forms. Twenty years later, both books are valuable for their theoretical insights, and Marchand's book is perhaps particularly valuable for its data. Both have cast light on the processes of word-formation, and it now seems rather irrelevant to discuss at great length whether either of them is 'taxonomic' and whether they should be. It should also be pointed out that Marchand's book is another exception to the standard approach of treating word-formation exclusively synchronically or diachronically, as its sub-title "a synchronic–diachronic approach" indicates.

The other aspect of language that Transformational Generative Grammar paid particular attention to, especially from about 1962 onwards, was phonology. The culmination of the early work on Generative Phonology is Chomsky & Halle's *The Sound Pattern of English* (1968). Based on an American tradition of morphophonemics, Generative Phonology is mainly concerned with specifying rules which generate all the surface shapes of a morpheme from a single underlying representation: rules are formulated to show, for example, that /naɪf/ and /naɪv/ are both surface forms of the morpheme *knife*, the second form occurring in the plural, or that /dɪvaɪn/ and /dɪvɪn/ are both surface forms of the morpheme *divine*, the second form occurring before -*ity*. This is the closest Transformational Generative Grammar really came to dealing with word-formation between 1957 and 1967. But the phonology is only concerned with determining the phonetic (or phonological) form of

---

[2] The dictionary definition is, of course, "classificatory". If this is all that is implied, it is difficult to see why Lees's approach is not also taxonomic, since he ends up with a classification of traditional examples, according to which of his rules is used in their generation. The discussion in Brekle (1970) and Brekle & Kastovsky (1977b) is not particularly helpful in this respect.

a word from a string of morphemes and boundaries. It has never been concerned with the generation of appropriate strings of morphemes and boundaries to provide the input to the phonological rules: it has always been assumed that this was a problem which the syntactic component would eventually account for.

The study of word-formation became important within the Transformational Generative paradigm with the publication of Chomsky (1970) (which had been available in the USA in manuscript since 1968). It was in this paper that the dichotomy between the "lexicalist" and the "transformationalist" approaches to lexical insertion was set up as one of the major divisions within the transformational school. This dispute brought the data of word-formation into the centre of linguistic interest, although no change was made in the basic assumption that the words formed were special kinds of sentences whose internal shape was determined by the phonology.

Apparently by sheer coincidence, a number of works on word-formation by scholars working outside the Transformational Generative paradigm appeared at about the same time, possibly as a part of a natural swing of the pendulum towards word-formation studies. Among others, the revised version of Marchand's *The Categories and Types of Present-Day English Word-Formation* appeared in 1969; Žepić's rather untraditional work on nominal compounds appeared in 1970; a rather different approach was shown in Brekle (1970); and Adams's *An Introduction to Modern English Word-Formation* came out in 1973. Pennanen's (1972) paper summarizing the general situation should probably be included in this group. The study of word-formation within the Transformational Generative tradition seems to have become more widespread at about the same time, partially inspired by Chomsky (1970), but partially independent of that paper. Examples of such works are Bowers (1969), Giurescu (1972), Gleitman & Gleitman (1970), Lakoff (1970a), Lees (1970), Newmeyer (1970) and Vendler (1968).

In more recent years, word-formation has been considered by various linguists from different points of view: from a phonological point of view (Halle, 1973; Lightner, 1975); from a syntactic point of view (Jackendoff, 1975; Roeper & Siegel, 1978); and from a semantic point of view (Leech, 1974; Lyons, 1977). Whereas many of the linguists working in the field since the late 1950s have used the data provided by word-formation as a grindstone for their own particular theoretical axes, there now also seems to be a growing number of linguists who are interested first and foremost in how word-formation reflects language in general. Such linguists are far more theoretically eclectic than the mainstream Transformational Generative school linguists, which, while a healthy sign itself, means that there is unfortunately very little agreement on theoretical points. An excellent survey of some of these most recent approaches is provided by Brekle & Kastovsky (1977a) (and see also, for a review of their book, Bauer, 1979b).

At the moment, the study of word-formation is in a state of flux. There is no one body of accepted doctrine on the subject, so that researchers are largely having to make up their own theory and procedures as they go along. Theoreticians in the field are in a difficult position because many of the descriptive studies of word-formation available avoid reference to such vital theoretical points as productivity (see chapter 4). Despite these handicaps, the study of word-formation is expanding, and researchers seem to be showing a greater willingness to blend various theoretical viewpoints when dealing with it: to blend synchrony and diachrony, morphology and phonology, syntax and semantics. In fact, it is the "crossroads" nature of word-formation (Kastovsky, 1977), where so many facets of linguistics come together, which seems to be attracting new researchers.

2

Some basic concepts

Morphology is inherently messy.
(Hooper, 1979: 113)

2.1 Introduction

This chapter is mainly an introduction to some of the
terminology required in the study of word-formation. Much of the
terminology used is, in fact, common to all morphological study,
and will help place word-formation in its broader framework. Thus
the notion of inflection will not be dealt with at any length in the
body of this work, but a definition of inflection is necessary in order
to circumscribe derivation, for example. Since a mass of terminology is inevitably confusing, a flow-chart diagram is presented
towards the end of the chapter which summarizes some of the main
information (Figure 2.6, §2.15).

Although this chapter is, in some senses, the foundation stone
upon which the rest of this work is built, the issues raised here are
of interest in themselves, and in some cases provide problems for
general linguistic theory. This is especially true, it seems to me, of
the distinction between inflection and derivation, and of the
postulated zero-morph in conversion.

Because most of this chapter is so introductory in nature and
covers morphology as a whole and not just word-formation, readers
with a solid background in linguistics may find it very elementary.
Such readers are invited to pass swiftly over the bulk of this
chapter, to §2.16, where points more specifically related to word-
formation are dealt with.

2.2 Words and word-formation

Any discussion of word-formation makes two assump-
tions: that there are such things as words, and that at least some of
them are formed. Both these assumptions will be made in this book,
although the term 'word' will be discussed further in §2.4, where

7

the notion will be considerably refined. Much of the book will deal with different kinds of formation and restrictions on them. As an introduction to the whole field, however, some discussion of the existence of words is necessary.

The definition of the word has been, for a long time, a major problem for linguistic theory because, however the term 'word' is defined, there are some items in some languages which speakers of those languages call 'words' but which are not covered by the definition.

Despite the difficulties in providing a definition of a 'word', there are good reasons for operating with such a notion. The first of these is that speakers of a language, even illiterate speakers, have a feeling for what is, or is not, a word. Sapir (1921: 34) reports that speakers of languages that have never been written find no difficulty in repeating a sentence "word for word", for example, while they do have difficulty if asked to divide the 'word' into smaller units. There are some instances where this is not true, as when English speakers argue about whether to write *alright* or *all right*, *alot* or *a lot*, and when Danish speakers are unsure whether to write *simpelthen* or *simpelt hen* 'simply', but in general terms this holds true, and the counter-examples might illustrate a change in progress.

There are other reasons for assuming that the word has some kind of linguistic reality. As Matthews (1972: 99ff) points out, morphological conditioning, when it occurs, takes place within the word. So for example, irregular plural forms in English are determined by the word in question, and only occur with that word: for example, the only word in English that makes its plural by adding *-en* is *ox*, but this *-en* does not affect markers of plurality anywhere else in a sentence in which it occurs. Another argument is that the ordering of elements within a word is frequently independent of, and even compulsorily different from, the ordering of strings of words: for example, in English the genitive can be marked by *'s* or by the separate word *of*; while *'s* is a part of a word and comes after the possessor (*the plane's wings*), *of*, a separate word, comes before the possessor (*the wings of the plane*). The same point can be made with respect to the comparative of adjectives in English: when the comparative is marked by a separate word *more*, this comes in front of the adjective being compared (*more curious*), but when it is marked by *-er*, this comes at the end of the adjective being compared (*curiouser*). Finally, in languages that have vowel harmony (e.g. Finnish, Turkish), its domain is the word, and in languages that have fixed stress (e.g. Icelandic, Polish, Turkish), one of its functions is to delimit the word. In Icelandic, for example, where stress always falls on the first syllable of a word, a stressed syllable is a signal of a new word.

All these factors argue for there being a unit which might be termed a 'word'. However, what the native speaker feels to be a word still differs radically from language to language. In Paiute *wü·to·kuchum·punku·rügani·yugwi·va·ntü·mü* is a 'word' meaning 'they who are going to sit and cut up with a knife a black bull' (Sapir, 1921: 30) (the decimal point will be used in this book to separate the elements of a word where this is an aid to clarity). In Eskimo [aːwlisa·ut·issʔar·si·niarpu·ŋa] is a 'word' meaning 'I am looking for something suitable for a fish-line' (Bloomfield, 1935: 207). In Turkish, *ev·ler·in·de* is a 'word' meaning 'in their house' (Lyons, 1968: 130). In Latin *regebam* is a 'word' meaning 'I was ruling'. In Maori *i* is a 'word' meaning, among other things, 'past tense'. Examples like these could be multiplied. It thus seems that, whatever a word is, it is not the same thing in all languages: it may not be possible to provide, for this sense of 'word', a definition which is valid in all languages except 'a word is what native speakers think a word is' (see Matthews, 1972: §7.5). Such a definition would not be of any great value in linguistic analysis.

Obviously, the rules that must be established for forming words depend on what counts as a word in any given language. 'Words' such as the Eskimo one illustrated above might most suitably be considered as being formed by the rules of syntax. In the Turkish and Latin examples cited, it might be more suitable to consider the formation of the words as being explained not by syntactic rules but by rules which depend on syntactic factors. Neither of these types will be considered under the title of 'word-formation' in this book.

'Word-formation' is a traditional label, and one which is useful, but it does not generally cover all possible ways of forming everything that can be called a 'word'. In particular, the use of the term 'word-formation' is of value when the rules for the formation of words are not identical with the rules for the formation of sentences (as they were in the Eskimo example). Exactly what kinds of things are generally classified as 'word-formation' will be elaborated in this chapter.

As a result, no claim can be made *a priori* about the universality of word-formation processes as they will be discussed in this book. With very few exceptions, word-formation is discussed here with reference only to Indo-European languages, and to a large degree with respect to English alone. It may turn out that in other languages that have the various categories of word-formation set up in this book, the same syntactic and semantic points hold true, and if this is the case, then putative universals may be set up. For the moment, however, conclusions about the universality of the processes involved in word-formation must be fairly strictly limited.

2.3 Examples of inflection, derivation and compounding

The definition of terms such as 'inflection', 'derivation' and 'compounding' is a difficult matter, and relies on the prior definition of a number of other technical terms. In order that the reader should have some idea of what these three mean, they will be exemplified here, and defined later.

The words given below, which differ in their endings, exemplify processes of inflection. The example given here is an Italian **inflectional paradigm** for the present tense of first conjugation verbs:

parl·o	I speak
parl·i	you (sg.) speak
parl·a	he/she/it speaks
parl·iamo	we speak
parl·ate	you (pl.) speak
parl·ano	they speak

Not only tense and person endings, but case and number endings are typically inflectional. Tense, person, case and number can be termed **inflectional categories** in languages which mark them with endings.

The words below, which also differ in their endings, exemplify processes of derivation. The precise nature of the difference between the classes of endings that give rise to inflection and those that give rise to derivation will be discussed later (§2.10), but the distinction is probably fairly clear on an intuitive basis. The example given here is English, and by an extension of the usual sense of the term 'paradigm' can be called a **derivational paradigm**:

> nation
> nation · hood
> nation · al
> nation · al · ize
> nation · al · ist
> nation · al · ist · ic
> nation · al · ity

Compounding, or composition, is, roughly speaking, the process of putting two words together to form a third, as in the following examples:

> oil-paper
> paperclip
> paper aeroplane
> paper thin
> (to) wallpaper
> wastepaper
> wastepaper basket

Such words are called **compounds**, independent of the form class ('part of speech') of the new word, the number of elements involved, whether they are written as one or two words or whether they are hyphenated and so on.

2.4 Word, word-form, lexeme

Consider the unlikely case of a speaker of English coming across a sentence like *This hunter shoots big game* and not understanding the verb. Under these circumstances, he might look it up in a dictionary. But he would not look up *shoots*; he would look up the form *shoot*. Under the entry for *shoot* he would expect to find all the information necessary for the interpretation of not only *shoot* but also *shoots*, *shooting* and *shot*. *Shoot* just happens to be the key member of the inflectional paradigm in which *shoots* occurs. When the 'word' "shoot" is talked about in this sense, it refers not to the particular shape that a word has on a particular occasion, but to all the possible shapes that the word can have. For this sense of 'word' the term **lexeme** will be used. The 'words' *shoot*, *shoots*, *shooting* and *shot* are all subsumed under the lexeme "shoot", and yet each comprises not only the lexeme "shoot" but also the representation(s) of the various inflectional categories attached to the lexeme for use in an utterance on a particular occasion. When it is not the lexeme that is under consideration, but the particular shape that a word has on a particular occasion, the term **word-form** is used.[1] Word-forms have phonological or orthographic shape, while a lexeme is a much more abstract unit. Now consider a statement like "The word 'shot' is a form of the word 'shoot'." In the light of this new terminology, such a statement can be made more precise as "The word-form 'shot' is a form of the lexeme 'shoot'." As a typographical convention, block capitals will be used from now on to distinguish lexemes (e.g. SHOOT), while italics will be used to distinguish word-forms (e.g. *shoots*, *shooting*, *shot*). The statement above can now be made more concise as "*Shot* is a form of SHOOT."

Lexemes can only be said to "occur" by a metaphorical use of the term 'occur' (Lyons, 1963: 12). Since actual occurrences in speech or writing always have phonic or orthographic form, the items that occur are word-forms, and the word-forms represent or **realize** lexemes. The **citation form** of a lexeme is the word-form from the inflectional paradigm of the lexeme which is used when a lexeme is entered in a standard dictionary; thus the citation form of the English lexeme discussed in the last paragraph is *shoot*, and not *shot*, *shoots* or *shooting*. The citation form may be conventionally determined: there is no self-evident reason why the citation form of Latin verbs should be the first person singular of the present tense (e.g. *amo* 'I love') and the citation form of French verbs the infinitive (e.g. *aimer* 'to love') (Lyons, 1977: 19).

There is yet another sense of the term 'word' which needs to be distinguished: the **grammatical word** (also called the **morpho-syntactic word**). This can also be illustrated with the form *shot*, which represents both the preterite of SHOOT (compare *went*, which is the preterite of GO) and the past participle of SHOOT

---

[1] On word-form and lexeme see Lyons (1963: 11, 1968: 196–7, 1970: 21, 1977: 19); Matthews (1972: 161, 1974: ch. 11). One of the clearest discussions of this distinction is to be found in Brown & Miller (1980). In the works referred to, Lyons uses no fewer than three typological conventions to distinguish word-forms and lexemes. The conventions adopted here are those of Lyons (1968, 1970); Matthews (1974).

(compare *gone*). Thus it can be said that the word-form *shot* represents two grammatical words, both of which are in the paradigm of the lexeme SHOOT. Matthews (1972: 161; 1974: 26) uses "word" alone in the sense of 'grammatical word'. This usage will not be followed here for two reasons. Firstly, the notion of grammatical word is of more value in inflectional morphology than it is in word-formation; the use of a complex expression is thus not as unfortunate in discussions of word-formation as in discussions of inflectional morphology. Secondly, it is useful in a study of word-formation (lexeme-formation, to be precise) to keep the term 'word' for another purpose. In discussions of word-formation it is frequently not clear whether it is the lexeme or the word-form that is involved in a given process. For example, in the formations *sarky* < *sarcastic* (or possibly *sarcasm*), and *bottle-feed* < *bottle-fed*, it is not clear whether it is the form of the original that is important or the lexeme involved. In the first case, the fact that the orthographic or phonological sequence *sark* or /sɑk/ is involved seems more important than the fact that the lexeme SARCASTIC or SAR-CASM is involved. In the second instance, it seems to be important that *fed* is a form of the lexeme FEED, and that other forms of the lexeme can be reconstructed from this. On the other hand, the fact that the lexeme involved in the derivation of *sarky* was SARCAS-TIC or SARCASM rather than SARCOPHAGUS or SARCLE may not be unimportant. Not only is it frequently difficult to take a principled decision, but in many cases it is theoretically unimportant whether it is a word-form or a lexeme which is involved (even though the distinction may be crucial on other occasions). The term **word** will be used from now on so as to be deliberately vague between word-form and lexeme. Typographically, words will be treated like word-forms, and will be italicized.

2.5 Morpheme, morph, allomorph, formative

Morphology as a sub-branch of linguistics deals with the internal structure of word-forms. The basic units of analysis recognized in morphology are **morphemes**. Consider, for example, the word-form *untouchables*. This can be segmented to show its constituent elements thus: *un·touch·able·s*. Each of these segments has its own form (or set of forms), its own meanings, and its own distribution. Thus *un-* has the fixed phonological form /ʌn/, a meaning of negation, and recurs in words like *unavailable*, *unbelievable*, *undone*; *touch* has a fixed phonological form and a fixed meaning, and recurs in word-forms like *touched*, *touches*, *touchy*; *-able* sometimes occurs as /ɪb(ə)l/ (*-ible*), has a fixed meaning, and recurs in words like *advisable*, *comparable*, *dislikeable*; *-s* has a range of phonetic forms (/s, z, ɪz/) but a constant meaning of plurality, and recurs in words like *cats*, *boys*, *fishes*. None of the segments *un*, *touch*, *able*, *s* can be further subdivided into smaller segments which function in the same kind of way as they do; each of them represents a morpheme. A **morpheme** may be defined as the minimal unit of grammatical analysis (Lyons, 1968: 181; Matthews, 1974: 11–12).

Now consider sentences (1) and (2) below:

(1)   This cow is eating grass
(2)   These cows are eating fodder

Cows cannot replace *cow* in (1), nor can *cow* replace *cows* in (2). That is, *cow* and *cows* have different distributions, and this difference in distribution is correlated with the fact that *cows* is made up of two morphemes, {COW} and {s}, or {COW} and {plural}, where the braces indicate that the items they contain are morphemes. However, it is possible to substitute the word-form *sheep* for *cow* in (1) to give (1') and for *cows* in (2) to give (2').

(1')   This sheep is eating grass
(2')   These sheep are eating fodder

Although the word-form *sheep* is the same in (1') and (2'), we know, because of the other items in the sentence that agree with it, that *sheep* is singular in (1') but plural in (2'). As a result, *sheep* in (2') can be seen as the product of two morphemes {SHEEP} and {plural} just as *cows* in (2) was, even though *sheep* does not have separate segments which correspond to each of the morphemes. In some languages (e.g. English, Swahili and Turkish) it is fairly usual that an utterance can be analysed into contiguous segments each of which represents one morpheme. In others (e.g. Greek, Italian or Russian) this is very much less usual, if not highly exceptional, because of the frequency with which inflectional categories fail to correspond to separate segments of the word-form (Lyons, 1968: 181–3, 187–92). For example, the Italian word *bell·o* 'beautiful' can be analysed into two contiguous segments as marked, but the second segment represents simultaneously the morphemes {masculine} and {singular}, and there is no way to separate out these two components.

The discussion above has been simplified in that it has been assumed that morphemes occur as forms in a language. Strictly speaking, however, morphemes, like lexemes (and phonemes) do not occur: morphemes are abstract elements of analysis, and what actually occurs is a phonetic (or orthographic) form which realizes the morpheme. When the phonetic (or orthographic) strings which realize morphemes are segmentable, these are termed 'morphs'. Thus in the form *un·touch·able·s* the segmented portions are morphs, each of which represents a morpheme. A **morph** can be defined as a segment of a word-form which represents a particular morpheme (Lyons, 1968: §5.3.4; Matthews, 1974: 83). In the word-form *was*, on the other hand, although the morphemes {BE}, {preterite} and {singular} can be recognized, the word-form cannot be segmented into morphs. By extension of the use of the term, it might be said that *was* is a single morph (and incidentally a word-form) which represents the morphemes {BE}, {preterite} and {singular}, and that the *-o* in Italian *bello* is a single morph which realizes the morphemes {masculine} and {singular}. Although this extended use is employed by Brown & Miller (1980) for example, it is not generally recognized in most of the recent literature on morphology. Hockett (1947) uses the term **portmanteau morph** in such cases.

Besides morpheme and morph, a third term, 'allomorph', is required for morphological analysis. In English, the plural morpheme, in its regular forms, has three different phonological realizations. It is realized as /ɪz/ after sibilant consonants (i.e. /s, z, ʃ, ʒ, tʃ, dʒ/) as in *horses*, *churches*; it is realized as /s/ after any other voiceless obstruent, as in *books*, *deaths*; and it is realized as /z/ everywhere else, as in *bags*, *bones*, *boys*. Which of these forms occurs depends on the phonetic environment, i.e. it is phonetically conditioned. The plural of the lexeme OX, though, is *oxen*. OX is the only lexeme which makes its plural by adding *-en*. This variant of the plural morpheme is conditioned by the lexeme: it is lexically conditioned. Consider now the genitive singular of the definite article in German. With a masculine noun like MANN 'man' or a neuter like KIND 'child', the form of the genitive singular definite article is *des*; with a feminine noun like FRAU 'woman', however, the genitive singular definite article is *der*. The form of the genitive singular definite article is not conditioned by the phonetic shape of the noun or of any other word in the sentence, nor by specific lexemes, but by a grammatical feature of the noun it is used with, namely gender. It can thus be said to be grammatically conditioned. An **allomorph** is a phonetically, lexically or grammatically conditioned member of a set of morphs representing a particular morpheme.

Finally in this section, the notion of 'formative' must be introduced. This is, in some ways, a much wider concept than the others introduced here, and it will be illustrated with two rather different examples which show the range of meaning of this term. The first illustration concerns German compound nouns. In word-forms like *Krankheit·s·zeichen*, *Liebe·s·lied*, *Universität·s·bibliothek* the first and last elements represent the citation forms of the lexemes KRANKHEIT 'illness', ZEICHEN 'sign, symptom', LIEBE 'love', LIED 'song', UNIVERSITÄT 'university' and BIBLIOTHEK 'library'. The *-s-* between these elements, however, does not represent any lexeme, nor any morpheme. As a suffix in German, *-s* can be one allomorph of the morpheme {genitive}, but that particular allomorph could not occur in this position, following nouns which are grammatically feminine. The *-s-* element is an obligatory element in the word-form, but it is not the realization of a lexeme or of a morpheme, and so is not a morph or an allomorph. It is a formative. *Zeichen, Liebe, Lied, Universität* and *Bibliothek*, which realize the morphemes (and lexemes) {ZEICHEN}, {LIEBE}, {LIED}, {UNIVERSITÄT} and {BIBLIOTHEK}, are also formatives (*Krankheit* is made up of two formatives, *Krank* realizing the lexeme KRANK and the derivational affix *-heit*). A **formative** is defined as a distributional segment of a word-form independent of whether or not it is also a morph. (By a 'distributional segment' is understood an element which recurs in the morphological analysis of word-forms.[2]) That is, all morphs are

---

[2] This definition is rather different from that given by, for example, Bazell (1945: 144 fn.) and Matthews (1972: 185, 1974: 11, 41). In some ways it is much closer to the usage of Chomsky (1965). As I understand it, Bazell allows a formative to have no form, whereas for me (as for Matthews) a formative must have phonological (or orthographic) form. Matthews does not include

formatives, but not all formatives are morphs, so that the use of the term 'formative' can avoid the issue of whether a particular element of a word realizes a morpheme or not.

As a second example, showing how this analysis applies to inflections, consider the following analysis of the Italian word-form *finirebbero* (based on Matthews, 1970: 108). *Finirebbero* is the word-form which realizes the grammatical word "the 3rd person plural of the conditional of FINIRE 'to finish'". The arrows in the diagram below show which parts of the word-form realize which morphemes, and the reader will have to accept that these relations can be determined by the analysis of a large number of word-forms. Each of the parenthesized elements on the bottom line is a formative, whether it is part of the realization of three morphemes (e.g. *ro*), of two (e.g. *bb*), of one (e.g. *r*) or of none (e.g. the final *e*).

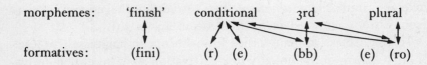

2.6 **Bound, free**

A morph which can occur in isolation (i.e. which can also be a word-form) is termed a **free morph**. A morph which can only occur in a word-form in conjunction with at least one other morph is termed a **bound morph**. Thus in the word-form *blenders*, *blend* can occur in isolation as a word-form, and is a free morph, while *-er* and *-s* can only occur if they are attached to other morphs, and are bound morphs.

In some languages, such as Latin, the morphs which realize lexemes are regularly bound morphs. Thus in *amo* 'I love', the morph which realizes the lexeme AMO is *am-*, and can only occur when bound to another element, in this case *-o*, which is a

---

elements such as *Liebe* which realize lexemes as formatives, only elements which do not realize lexemes. Like Chomsky (1965), I include the realizations of lexemes as formatives, but unlike Chomsky I analyse formatives in utterances, not on the same level as morphemes or lexemes. In the terms of another scholar, Hockett (1947), 'formative' as it is used here covers both 'morph' and 'empty morph', that is, it is a recurrent segment of a word-form, analysed at the morphological level, whether or not it realizes a morpheme.

portmanteau morph realizing the morphemes {1st person}, {singular}, {active}, {present}, {indicative}. The *am-* part is not further analysable. *Am-* is a bound morph which realizes an unanalysable lexeme; bound morphs which do NOT realize unanalysable lexemes are **affixes**. Affixes can be divided into **prefixes**, which are attached before a base (as in *dislike*, where *dis-* is a prefix), **suffixes**, which are attached after a base (as in *freedom*, where *-dom* is a suffix), and **infixes**, which are attached inside a base. Infixation (the use of infixes) is virtually unknown in English (though Eliza Doolittle's *abso · blooming · lutely* qualifies), and comparatively rare throughout Indo-European. For clear examples of infixation it is necessary to turn to non-Indo-European languages. In Bontoc, a Philippine language, for example, *fikas* means 'strong' while *f · um · ikas* means 'he is becoming strong', where the infix *-um-* is added after the initial consonant of the citation form of the lexeme. Similarly, *f · um · usul* 'he is becoming an enemy' derives from *fusul* 'enemy' (data from Gleason, 1955: 29).

In English, as in many other Indo-European languages, prefixation is always derivational while suffixation may be either derivational or inflectional. For example, in the form *un · touch · able · s*, *-able* is a derivational suffix, *un-* is a derivational prefix, and *-s* is an inflectional suffix.

2.7 **Productivity**

Productivity will be discussed at length in chapter 4, but it will be necessary to refer to the notion before that. Basically, any process (and not necessarily just one in word-formation) is said to be **productive** if it can be used synchronically in the production of new forms, and non-productive if it cannot be used synchronically in this way. This can be exemplified from syntax with the Middle English rules of word order. In Middle English it was possible both to put the subject after the verb in declarative sentences, and to put the object before the verb. This can be seen from the following lines:

> To preyere and to penaunce   putten heom monye.
>> (from *Piers Plowman*)
>> If any me blame
> Robert Mannyng is my name.
>> (from *Chronicle of England*)

The rules which allowed this are no longer productive in modern English, so that

>*To prayer and penance put themselves many

and

>*If anybody me criticizes

are no longer acceptable in modern English. Productivity can also be exemplified in word-formation. In modern French the suffix *-ation* can be used to form the nominalization of any verb in *-is·er* (e.g. *marginal·is·er* 'to weaken the effect of [an idea] by making it less central to doctrine' > *marginal·is·ation* 'weakening of effect') and is thus productive. The suffix *-ure*, on the other hand, which was once used to make nominalizations of verbs (e.g. *coiff·er* 'to do the hair of' > *coiff·ure* 'hair style'; *brûl·er* 'to burn' > *brûl·ure* 'burn, scald') can now no longer be used to make new nominalizations, and is thus non-productive (Guilbert, 1975: 178–9). Similarly, the suffix *-eron* which could once be used in French to form a word for the person who carries out an action (e.g. *forg·er* 'to forge' > *forg·eron* 'smith') is now no longer productive, and the suffix *-eur* (e.g. *forg·er* 'to forge' > *forg·eur* 'forger') is used productively in its place (Guilbert, 1975: 178–9).

2.8 Transparent, opaque

A lexeme is said to be **transparent** if it is clearly analysable into its constituent morphs and a knowledge of the morphs involved is sufficient to allow the speaker-listener to interpret the lexeme when it is encountered in context. For example, *coverage* is clearly analysable into *cover* + *age*, and the fact that *-age* shows a nominalization is obvious from other words like *cartage*, *pilotage*, *postage*: *coverage* is thus interpretable from the morphs it obviously contains, and is transparent. In contrast, the word *carriage* is not clearly analysable into *carry* + *age*, although that is the etymology of the word, so it is not transparent but **opaque**. *Airmail* and *blackmail* are both analysable into their constituent morphs, but whereas the meaning of *airmail* is predictable from this information, that of *blackmail* is not, so that *airmail* is transparent, while *blackmail* is opaque. Or consider another example, this time from French. The modern French word *aub-*

épine 'hawthorn' is opaque because it is not possible to see why it should mean 'hawthorn': it is not analysable into morphs, even though *épine* means 'thorn'. But *aubépine* is derived from a transparent Vulgar Latin form *alba spina*, which can be glossed as 'white thorn'. Notice that not all forms which are analysable are necessarily transparent – note *blackmail* discussed above – so that analysability should not be confused with transparency.

2.9 Root, stem, base

'Root', 'stem' and 'base' are all terms used in the literature to designate that part of a word that remains when all affixes have been removed. Of more recent years, however, there has been some attempt to distinguish consistently between these three terms (e.g. Lyons, 1977: 513 fn. 2; Matthews, 1972: 165 fn. 4; 1974: 40, 73).

A **root** is a form which is not further analysable, either in terms of derivational or inflectional morphology. It is that part of a word-form that remains when all inflectional and derivational affixes have been removed. A root is the basic part always present in a lexeme. In the form *untouchables*, for example, the root is *touch*, to which first the suffix *-able*, then the prefix *un-* and finally the suffix *-s* have been added (see Figure 2.1). In a compound word like *wheelchair* there are two roots, *wheel* and *chair*.

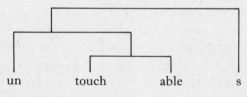

un   touch   able   s

Figure 2.1

A **stem** is of concern only when dealing with inflectional morphology. It may be – but need not be – complex, either in that it contains derivational affixes (as does *govern · ment*) or in that it contains more than one root (as does *red · skin*). Inflectional (but not derivational) affixes are added to it: it is the part of the word-form which remains when all inflectional affixes have been removed. In the form *untouchables* the stem is *untouchable*, although in the form *touched* the stem is *touch*; in the form *wheelchairs* the stem is *wheelchair*, even though the stem contains two roots.

A **base** is any form to which affixes of any kind can be added. This means that any root or any stem can be termed a base, but the set of bases is not exhausted by the union of the set of roots and the set of stems: a derivationally analysable form to which derivational affixes are added can only be referred to as a base. That is, *touchable* can act as a base for prefixation to give *untouchable*, but in this process *touchable* could not be referred to as a root because it is analysable in terms of derivational morphology, nor as a stem since it is not the adding of inflectional affixes which is in question. Matthews (1972: 12 fn. 2) prefers the term **operand** to base, to avoid confusion with other meanings of 'base', but the more traditional term will be retained here.

In Figures 2.2, 2.3 and 2.4 this terminology is applied to the various stages in the build-up of the word-form *untouchables* to show how it is used. In Figure 2.5 it is used in the analysis of the word-form *touched*.

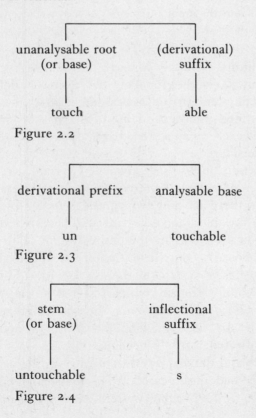

unanalysable root (or base)	(derivational) suffix
touch	able

Figure 2.2

derivational prefix	analysable base
un	touchable

Figure 2.3

stem (or base)	inflectional suffix
untouchable	s

Figure 2.4

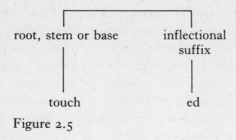

root, stem or base   inflectional
                            suffix

touch   ed

Figure 2.5

2.10 Inflection, derivation

The definitions of lexeme, root and stem above have all presupposed a definition of inflection. This can be theoretically awkward, since definitions of inflection often presuppose a definition of the lexeme, and there is thus the risk of becoming circular. Consider, for example, Lyons's (1977: 521–2) definition of inflection:

Inflection produces from the stem (or stems) of a given lexeme all the word-forms of that lexeme which occur in syntactically determined environments.

This definition delimits, perfectly correctly, those processes which are inflectional, but, depending on how the lexeme is defined, it either runs the risk of circularity or, at best, demands that inflection and lexeme are defined interdependently. The risk of circularity can be avoided, however, when all the characteristics of inflectional morphology are considered.

First of all, inflection "involves relatively few variables in a closed system" (Strang, 1968: 101). For example, in the category of number in English, there are only two values: singular and plural. There are only two variables, and no extra variables can be added to the list without radically changing the entire system. This is what Strang means by "closed". One illustration of the upheaval caused by a change to a closed system is the change in case-marking between Old and Middle English, which resulted in the relatively free word order of Old English becoming the relatively fixed order of Middle English. In Old English all nouns, pronouns and adjectives were inflected, with special endings for nominative, accusative, genitive and dative. By Middle English the accusative and dative endings had disappeared from nouns and adjectives (some traces remain in the pronoun system, e.g. *him*, *them*). This meant a radical change to the case-system of English, and neither before nor after the change was it possible suddenly to add an extra case (say Instrumental) to the paradigm. In contrast, in French (Guilbert, 1975: 182–3), suffixes can be added to a verbal base to produce an action nominalization (*-tion*, *-isation*, *-age*, *-issage*, *-ement*, *-ture*, etc.), an agent nominalization (*-eur*, *-ateur*, *-euse*, *-atrice*, *-oir*, etc.), an adjectivalization (*-ée*, *-ant*, *-atif*, *-able*, etc.), or a new verb (*-ailler*, *-asser*, *-onner*, etc.). For example, *interroger* 'to interrogate' + *ation* > *interrogation*; *interroger* + *-ateur* > *interrogateur* 'interrogator'; *interroger* + *atif* > *interrogatif* 'interrogative'; *rêver* 'to dream' + *-asser* > *rêvasser* 'to muse, dream idly'. There are a large number of such affixes and the classes they form are not closed. It is theoretically possible (though no doubt rare) to add further categories of affixes (for example, an affix to change a verbal base into a preposition might be conceivable); it is quite common for further affixes to be added to particular classes without radically affecting the nature of the system already in use. Thus, for example, Kiparsky (1964) shows how the suffix *-nik* has been borrowed from Russian by a wide range of languages, and Fleischman (1977) shows how the suffix *-age* was borrowed from French into the other Romance languages, and into English. In each case the borrowing language added a new suffix to its range of suffixes, but adjustments to the system of suffixation as such were relatively minor. There are reasons for believing that English is currently gaining two new derivational suffixes *-tician* as in *hairtician* and *-oholic*, as in *drugoholic* (for the latter, see Kolin, 1979). The general rule, then, is that affixes which are members of large classes to which new items can be freely added are not inflectional; those which are members of small classes to which it is not possible to add extra members are inflectional.

The next point about inflection can be discussed in terms of commutability, i.e. substitutability within a syntagmatic frame. If a series of parallel word-forms are considered in isolation from their syntactic environment, and a given affix can be replaced by one or more other affixes wherever it occurs, then it can be said to be highly commutable within the word-form. For example, in a series of word-forms like *bangs*, *calls*, *covers*, *loves*, *tickles*, *walks* the {s} is commutable with {ø} (= 'present tense, but not 3rd person sing.'), {ing} and {ed}, but not with {let} and {ish}, though these affixes can be added to some of the bases. On the other hand, in any given sentence, the possibility of commuting the affixes which are highly commutable within the word-form will tend to be low. For example, in

I am covering the wall with paint

the {ing} cannot commute with {s}, {ed}, {ø}, etc. Inflection can thus be said to be characterized by high commutability within the word-form, but low commutability within the sentence (Bazell, 1953: 69).

It should be noted that this criterion provides a cline of "inflectionality", rather than a yes/no answer to the question of whether a given affix is inflectional. Thus, for example, *-er* can be added to any of the verbal stems listed above to form an agentive nominalization. Although *-er* is usually considered to be a derivational affix (and would be a derivational affix by some other criteria), it shows high commutability within the word-form. Conversely, some affixes which are, by other criteria, inflectional show high commutability within the sentence: thus the {ed} on the end of *walked* in

They walked home from school

shows high commutability within the sentence with {ø}.

It is sometimes claimed (see e.g. Aronoff, 1976: 2) that inflection deals purely with grammatical morphemes. Care is needed with this kind of statement, since if it is meant to be equivalent to a statement that inflection deals with the realization of those morphemes that are specified in a grammatical word (with the exception of the realization of the lexeme) it may be totally circular: morphemes may be listed in the specification of a grammatical word because they are inflectional rather than derivational. However, this claim can be made non-vacuous if it is paraphrased as "Morphs whose form is specified by rules of agreement are inflectional." **Agreement** is here taken to cover both concord and government. **Concord** is the system whereby two (or more) lexemes are obligatorily marked for the same morphological categories to show a specific syntactic relationship between them. Typical examples of concord are the agreement between adjectives and nouns for number, gender and case in many Indo-European languages, and agreement between subject and verb. Consider the following sentences of written French, where concord of morphological categories is shown by the items in parentheses after the glosses:

Le	petit	garçon	est	parti
The	little	boy	has	left
(masc. sing.)	(masc. sing.)	(sing.)	(sing.)	(masc. sing.)
La	petite	fille	est	partie
The	little	girl	has	left
(fem. sing.)	(fem. sing.)	(sing.)	(sing.)	(fem. sing.)
Les	petits	garçons	sont	partis
The	little	boys	have	left
(pl.)	(masc. pl.)	(pl.)	(pl.)	(masc. pl.)
Les	petites	filles	sont	parties
The	little	girls	have	left
(pl.)	(fem. pl.)	(pl.)	(pl.)	(fem. pl.)

Government, on the other hand, is the system whereby one element in a sentence determines which morpheme is added to another element. Typical examples of government are the agreement between the case of a noun and the preposition which precedes it, or between a verb and its direct object in languages like German, Latin or Russian. One instance, which is fairly widespread in Indo-European, can be illustrated by the following two sentences of German:

Er geht in die   Stadt
He walks in the (acc.) town
'He walks into town'

Er geht in der   Stadt
He walks in the (dat.) town
'He walks around the town'

In the first of these two sentences, the preposition *in* governs the accusative case, and the meaning is direction; in the second, *in* governs the dative and the meaning is location.

The difficulty with this criterion as it has been elaborated here is that not all the morphemes which are generally taken to be inflectional mark agreement. For example, the category of tense is usually taken to be inflectional but, except in cases where sequence of tense rules apply, it does not generally mark agreement. Similarly the genitive in

This is that girl's boat

does not really mark agreement, although it does mark syntactic function, and the same might be argued for the comparative in a sentence like:

> She is taller than her brother

Although this criterion fails to include all the morphemes which are generally considered to be inflectional, at least it apparently excludes morphemes generally considered to be derivational. One doubtful case is the use of an adverb to modify an adjective, where the adverbial ending might be determined by government; but if this is government, it is of a rather different kind from that in the examples mentioned above, since it is not determined by individual lexemes but by a grammatical class.

It is sometimes suggested that "where both derivational and inflectional elements are found together, the derivational element is more intimately connected with the root" (Greenberg, 1966: 93. See also Aronoff, 1976: 2; Bazell, 1953: 70; Bloomfield, 1935: 222.) While this is true of English, it is not true of all languages. Thus in *untouchables* the derivational suffix *-able* is closer to the root *touch* than the inflectional suffix *-s*. On the other hand, Robins (1964: 261) cites the example of Welsh, with formations like:

> merch ·   et   ·os
> girl   (pl.) (diminutive)

Ettinger (1974a: 60) cites two examples. The first is from eighteenth-century German, where the inflectional plural morph *-er* often preceded the diminutive derivational morph *-chen*. Ettinger cites examples like *Kleid·er·chen* 'little clothes', *Blätt·er·chen* 'little leaves', *Büch·er·chen* 'little books' and *Ding·er·chen* 'little things'. The construction is still possible in modern German in the word *Kind·er·chen* 'little children'. Ettinger's other example comes from Portuguese, where plural is sometimes marked twice in diminutives. He cites instances like: *animal* 'animal', *animais* 'animals', *animal·z·inho* 'little animal', *animai·z·inho·s* 'little animals', where both the *-i* and the *-s* in *animaizinhos* show the plurality, and the *-z-* is a formative which does not realize a morpheme. (In examples like these, 'stem' as defined above ceases to be a useful concept; in such cases the term 'base' is the only one applicable.)

Now consider **derivation**. Derivation can, to a certain extent, be defined as the converse of inflection. Derivation is the morphological process that results in the formation of new lexemes (Lyons, 1977: 522). It involves, or may involve, many variables in an open class (Strang, 1968: 101). It is characterized by low commutability within the word-form, but a few kinds of derivation are characterized by high commutability within the sentence (feminine forms in -*ess* in English, diminutives and augmentatives in Italian, for example).

One very simple test for derivation has been proposed in the literature.[3] It is that if a form including affixes can be replaced in some of its occurrences in sentences by a simple root form, then that form shows derivation rather than inflection. For example, *frustration* and *writer* in:

> Frustration made him stop writing his book
> The writer received a well-earned prize

can be replaced by *pain* and *boy* respectively, and can thus be said to be instances of derivation. Whereas *kisses* in

> He always kisses his mother goodnight

cannot be replaced by a simple root form, and must thus be considered to be an instance of inflection. Unfortunately, this criterion does not work in highly inflected languages like Russian because in such languages it is so rarely possible to have a simple root as a word-form. And while it might work in written French, this criterion is not even satisfactory in English; in a sentence like:

> They always kissed their mother goodnight

it is perfectly possible to replace the form *kissed* with the simple root *kiss*, and yet one would not wish to say that *kissed* was an example of derivational morphology.

There are two other criteria which, while they do not always give reliable answers, ought to be mentioned in this connection. The first of these can be seen as a consequence of the commutability characteristic discussed above. It is that in derivation there are likely to be large numbers of unpredictable gaps in the system, whereas inflection is much less likely to have such unpredictable gaps. This is sometimes referred to as the **semi-productivity** of

---

[3] Discussed in Matthews (1974: 49–50). Matthews (1974: 58) gives the credit for this criterion to Martinet (1960: §4.35), but Martinet does not make it quite as clear as Matthews does. See also Bazell (1953: 70).

derivational processes (Dik, 1967: 370; Matthews, 1974: 52). For example, although there are forms *regress*, *confess* and *caress*, only *regression* and *confession* are found, not *caression, and although there is a form *session* there is no verb *sess which could form its base. Gaps are, of course, also found in inflectional paradigms, but these are rarer. For example, there are a number of verbs in French which are not found in all persons and tenses (e.g. *gésire*, *frire*, *sourdre*); Halle (1973: 7) lists five Russian verbs (*lazat'* 'to climb', *pobeždat'* 'to conquer', *derzit'* 'to talk rudely', *mutit'* 'to stir up, muddy', *erunit'* 'to behave foolishly') which are not found in the first person singular of the present tense; and modals in English lack, among other things, an infinitive and a past participle.

The second criterion is that the products of inflectional morphology are semantically regular, whereas the products of derivational morphology tend not to be. For example, the relationship between the stem and inflected form in the pairs *car/cars*, *girl/girls*, *shoe/shoes*, is consistent, whereas the relation between the base and the derived form in *impress/impression* 'result of impressing something on something else', *profess/profession*, *suppress/suppression* is not semantically consistent. This point will be taken up in greater detail later (§6.7). There are, however, a number of processes which are usually considered to be derivational and which do display semantic regularity: consider, for example, the formation of English adjectives in *-able* from transitive verbs. This is probably a case where there are no gaps in the derivational paradigm (any transitive verb can act as the base) and the adjectives are all semantically regular, meaning 'capable of being Ved' (where V is the verb in the base). Examples are *exploitable*, *deliverable*, *openable* (Thompson, 1975).

All these various criteria are summarized in Table 2.1.

2.11   Complex, compound

When two (or more) elements which could potentially be used as stems are combined to form another stem, the form is said to be a **compound**. A compound lexeme (or simply a compound) can thus be defined as a lexeme containing two or more potential stems. Since each potential stem contains at least one root, a compound must contain at least two roots. (If one of the potential stems that makes up the compound is itself compound, the

Table 2.1.

Inflection	Derivation
Produces word-forms of a single lexeme.	Produces new lexemes.
Involves few variables in a closed system.	May involve many variables in an open system.
Characterized by high commutability within the word-form.	Characterized by low commutability within the word-form.
Typically has low commutability within the sentence.	Some types show high commutability within the sentence.
Marks agreement.	Does not mark agreement.
In many languages, including English, is marked further from the root than derivation.	In many languages, including English, is marked closer to the root than inflection.
In some languages cannot be replaced by a simple root form in a sentence.	In some languages can be replaced by a simple root form in a sentence.
Typically does not show gaps in the paradigm.	Typically shows gaps in the paradigm.
Typically semantically regular.	Typically semantically irregular.

resultant form may, of course, contain more than two roots, as in *wastepaper basket*.) However, this definition is not quite sufficient, since derivational processes may at times apply to forms containing more than one root (e.g. *school-master·ish*, *super·highway*). In such cases it is said that the base of the derivational process is compound, but not that the whole lexeme is a compound. A compound may therefore be more fully defined as a lexeme containing two or more potential stems that has not subsequently been subjected to a derivational process. It should be noted that while derivation may apply to forms containing more than one root, the presence of two roots is not criterial for derivation as it is for compounding.

It is frequently useful to have a term to cover both the forms produced by derivation and the forms produced by compounding to contrast these with forms produced by inflection and words which are made up of just roots. In this book, the term **complex form** will be used, slightly untraditionally, for this purpose. **Word-formation** can now be defined as the production of complex forms. 'Complex' is used by other scholars to mean 'produced by derivation' (see e.g. Matthews, 1974: 40). In this book a form produced by derivation will be termed a **derivative**. Thus word-formation can be divided, in the first instance, into derivation and compounding (although it will be seen later that there are other categories which do not fit neatly under either of these headings). Word-formation produces complex forms, derivation produces derivatives and compounding produces compounds. It will also be useful to have a term to cover words which are not complex. In this book the term **simplex** will be introduced for this purpose.

2.12 **Endocentric, exocentric, appositional, dvandva**

Compound nouns can be further subdivided into four groups according to semantic criteria. Consider first the examples *beehive, armchair, redskin, highbrow, maidservant*. These can all be divided into a second element, which is the grammatical head (this is the element marked for number, and also, in languages which have grammatical gender, the element which determines the gender of the compound) and a first element which is the modifying element (which is not marked for number and does not determine gender). In the first two examples, the compound is a hyponym of the grammatical head: a beehive is a kind of hive, an armchair is a kind of chair. This type of compound is termed an **endocentric compound**. In the second two examples, the compound is not a hyponym of the grammatical head: a redskin is not a type of skin, nor is a highbrow a type of brow. This type of compound, termed an **exocentric compound** (or sometimes a **bahuvrihi compound**, using the Sanskrit terminology), is a hyponym of some unexpressed semantic head ('person' in both the examples given here). Since the semantic head is unexpressed in such compounds, the compound is frequently seen as metaphorical or synecdochic. Thirdly, *maidservant* is a hyponym of both *maid* and *servant*: a maidservant is a type of maid and also a type of servant. This type of compound is termed an **appositional compound**. The final division of compound nouns is exemplified by *Alsace-Lorraine* and *Rank-Hovis*. Here it is not always clear which element is the grammatical head and the compound is not a hyponym of either element, but the elements name separate entities which combine to form the entity denoted by the compound. This type of compound is normally given the Sanskrit name of **dvandva**, although the English term **copulative compound** is also used to describe them.

These semantic divisions interact with syntactic divisions according to the form class of the whole compound (compound noun, compound adjective, etc.) and the form classes of the individual elements in the compounds, so that *redskin*, as well as being an exocentric compound, is a compound noun made up of an adjective and a noun, and *armchair* is an endocentric compound noun made up of two nouns.

2.13 Class-maintaining, class-changing

A distinction is sometimes made (see e.g. Robins, 1964: 258) between class-maintaining and class-changing derivation. This distinction rests on the prior establishment of form classes such as noun, verb, adjective, etc. A **class-maintaining** process of derivation produces lexemes which belong to the same form class as the base, while a **class-changing** process of derivation produces lexemes which belong to a form class other than the form class of the base. For example, if *-ly* is added to the noun *king*, the adjective *kingly* results. Since a noun has been turned into an adjective, this is a case of class-changing derivation. But if *-dom* is added to the same noun *king*, another noun *kingdom* results, and this is thus a case of class-maintaining derivation. In English, prefixation is typically class-maintaining, and derivational suffixation is typically class-changing.

As Lyons (1977: 521 fn. 6) points out, it is in fact rather misleading to talk of class-maintaining derivation. With the example of *king* and *kingdom* the two lexemes belong to syntactically distinguishable sub-classes of noun, and even with examples like *friendly* and *unfriendly* or *lion* and *lioness*, the class of the new lexeme is not exactly the same as the class of the lexeme used as a base, since the new lexeme is not a base which can undergo the process of derivation by which it was formed. That is, there are no forms **ununfriendly* or **lionessess*. Only in cases where recursive prefixation is permissible (e.g. *meta-meta-theory*) is there genuine class-maintaining derivation in English.

2.14 Conversion

Conversion is the change in form class of a form without any corresponding change of form. Thus the change whereby the form *napalm*, which had been used exclusively as a noun, came to be used as a verb (*They decided to napalm the village*) is a case of conversion.

The exact status of conversion within word-formation is unclear. For some scholars (e.g. Lyons, 1977: 522; Marchand, 1969: §1.2.5) conversion is a branch of derivation, for others (e.g. Koziol, 1937: §618; Strang, 1968: §188) it is a separate type of word-formation, on a level with derivation and compounding. Whether this distinction has any real effect on the structure of a theory of word-formation is not absolutely clear.

Conversion is frequently called **zero-derivation**, a term which many scholars prefer (Adams, 1973: 16; Jespersen, 1942: §6.1; Marchand, 1969: §5.1.1.2). Most writers who use both terms appear to use them as synonyms (although Marchand, 1969: §5.1.1.2 is an exception). However, as Lyons (1977: 523 fn. 7) points out, the theoretical implications of the two are rather different. Gruber (1976: 337f), for example, argues that to treat ordinary derivation and zero-derivation differently in the grammar is to lose a generalization, since both involve changes of form class, but claims that they can only be treated the same way if a zero-affix is permitted. Otherwise, he says, derivation can be treated as a rule-governed process, but zero-derivation cannot be: that is, the relation between *some napalm* and *to napalm* and other similar pairs must be considered to be totally coincidental. Lyons's own view (as noted by Matthews, 1972: 64) is that in cases of so-called zero-derivation, an identity operation can be said to have been carried out between the base and the new lexeme. This means that there is a process linking the two lexemes NAPALM, but that this process defines the form of the derived lexeme as being identical to the form of the base. This is also more or less the line taken by Matthews himself (1972: 190), when he speaks of "a formation involving zero operations". The theoretical dubiousness of speaking of zero affixes in language (see Matthews, 1972: 191; Pennanen, 1971: §7.9 *et passim* and works referred to there) leads me to prefer the theoretical position enshrined in the term 'conversion', especially when this can be given a dynamic interpretation, and that term will be used exclusively from now on in this book. It should, however, be noted that this is an area of dispute in the literature. For a comprehensive review of the literature on conversion and a discussion of the implications of talking in terms of zero-derivation, the reader is referred to Pennanen (1971).

2.15 Summary

Morphology deals with the internal structure of **word-forms** (see Lyons, 1968: 194). In morphology, the analyst divides word-forms into their component **formatives** (most of which are **morphs** realizing **roots** or **affixes**), and attempts to account for the occurrence of each formative. Morphology can be divided into two main branches, **inflectional morphology** and **word-formation** (also called **lexical morphology**: Matthews, 1974: 41). Inflectional morphology deals with the various forms of **lexemes**, while word-formation deals with the formation of new lexemes from given **bases**. Word-formation can, in turn, be subdivided into **derivation** and **compounding** (or **composition**). Derivation is concerned with the formation of new lexemes by **affixation**, compounding with the formation of new lexemes from two (or more) potential stems. Derivation is sometimes also subdivided into **class-maintaining** derivation and **class-changing** derivation. Class-maintaining derivation is the derivation of new lexemes which are of the same form class ('part of speech') as the base from which they are formed, whereas class-changing derivation produces lexemes which belong to different form classes from their bases. Compounding is usually subdivided according to the form class of the resultant compound: that is, into compound nouns, compound adjectives, etc. It may also be subdivided according to the semantic criteria outlined above (§2.12) into **exocentric**, **endocentric**, **appositional** and **dvandva** compounds. Figure 2.6 presents a diagrammatic representation of the basic divisions of morphology as discussed here.

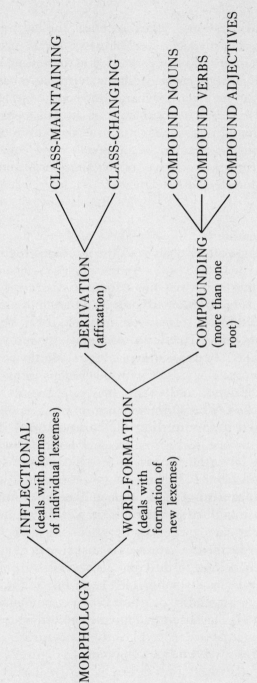

Figure 2.6

2.16 **Lack of clear dividing lines**

So far, it has been implicitly assumed that the various sub-divisions of morphology are discrete, and that it is always possible to make a clear distinction between, for example, compounding and derivation, or derivation and inflection. This is, however, not always true, and a fairer claim might be that morphology presents a cline from clear cases of inflection through to clear cases of compounding, with derivation providing an ill-defined centre part of the scale.[4] All branches of morphology have in common that they deal with the structure of word-forms; inflection and derivation both deal with affixation; and derivation and compounding both deal with the formation of new lexemes. The lack of clear boundaries between these various sub-sections of morphology will be illustrated at greater length below.

2.16.1 *Compounding and derivation*

One of the clearest illustrations of the lack of a clear dividing line between compounding and derivation is the diachronic passage of an element from lexeme to suffix or from suffix to lexeme. The latter case is much rarer than the former, but one borderline instance is presented by the forms *ism* and *ology*. These are now used, especially in the plural, as lexemes in their own right, and there is even a book called *Isms and Ologies*. It is conceivable that lexemes in which these elements occur will soon come to be considered compounds rather than derivatives. A further example comes from the *OEDS*, in one of the citations under *-ese*: "Flee Carlylese, Ruskinese, Meredithese and every other ese." Again, a suffix is used as a full lexeme, although this one shows far less sign of becoming established in usage. Perhaps the clearest example of this process is to be found in linguistic terminology, where a distinction is frequently drawn in terms of 'emic' and 'etic' levels of analysis, where the terms are abstracted from *phonemic* and *phonetic*.

The diachronic passage of a lexeme used as the second element of a compound to a suffix is much more common. This has happened,

---

[4] Many scholars have commented on the difficulty of distinguishing inflection, derivation and compounding, though there is frequently little more than a passing comment. See, for example, Bauer (1978d: §6); Kruisinga (1911: §1700); Koziol (1937: §75); Lyons (1977: 706).

for example to the modern German suffix -*heit*, the modern French suffix -*ment* which is used to form adverbs, and the modern English suffixes -*dom*, -*hood* and -*ly*. German -*heit* and English -*hood* are cognate, and go back to a lexeme meaning 'condition, rank'; French -*ment* is etymologically derived from Latin *mentem* 'a mind'; English -*dom* goes back to Old English *doom* 'judgement'; and English -*ly* as in *courtly* goes back to Old English *lic* 'a body'. This means that at the time English *childhood* was formed, it was a compound, since both elements were lexemes, but at the time *personhood* (Barnhart *et al.*, 1973) was formed, it was a derivative, since -*hood* was a bound morph which did not realize an independent lexeme.

As a possible example of a change from lexeme to suffix which is still in progress, consider the case of *postman*. In *postman* the -*man* element is pronounced with a reduced vowel /mən/, and the form is thus isolated from the lexeme MAN which contains a full vowel /mæn/. Furthermore, at least until a few years ago, the -*man* on the end of *postman*, *chairman* and other such forms appeared to have lost its connection with MAN, 'adult male human', since phrases such as "Madam chairman" were quite possible (the effect of the feminist movement is being felt here now, with the introduction of the form *chairperson*). For these reasons, some scholars (e.g. Quirk *et al.*, 1972: 978) argue that -*man* is losing its connection with MAN, and becoming a suffix with a function similar to that of -*er* or -*ist* (note the equivalent forms *judoman* and *judoist* listed by Barnhart *et al.*, 1973). In French, the loan formative -*man* already acts as a suffix (Dubois & Dubois, 1971: 181). Matthews (1974: 54–5) argues that -*man* in English has not yet achieved suffix status, since a contrast is still made between a *policeman* and a *policewoman* and because the plural of *postman* is still *postmen* (/mən/, just as in the singular) and not **postmans*. Despite the force of these arguments, it looks as if -*man* may be on the way to becoming a suffix. It seems to me that the evidence is rather weaker for considering French *clef* 'key', *modèle* 'model', *pilote* 'pilot', *miracle* 'miracle' as having become suffixes rather than lexemes in forms like *mot-clef* 'key word' *problème-clef* 'key problem', *industrie-clef* 'key industry', etc., but this has also been suggested (Dubois, 1962: 71; Dubois & Dubois, 1971: 178–9), on the grounds that these elements have lost most of the meaning of the respective lexemes and have become "a kind of grammatical tool".

A rather different problem is presented by the Danish word *bomuld* 'cotton'. Here ULD 'wool' is a lexeme in its own right, but *bom-* is a bound form which only occurs in the word *bomuld*. It could be argued that the occurrence of *uld* here was totally coincidental, and that it should not be related to ULD at all, but that BOMULD should be considered a simplex lexeme. There are two factors which argue against this solution, however. The first is the etymology: *bomuld* is a calque on German *Baum·wolle*, 'tree wool', which is a transparent compound. The second is the form of the linking element that *bomuld* takes when it is used in a compound. It is typical of complex forms in Danish that they take an -*s* formative when they become the first elements of compounds. *Uld* alone forms stem + stem compounds, e.g. *uld·kjole* 'woollen dress', but *bomuld* forms stem + *s* + stem compounds, e.g. *bomuld·s·kjole* 'cotton dress'. Thus *bomuld* acts as a complex form. A similar problem is raised by the English bound forms *cran-* and *bil-* in *cranberry* and *bilberry*. These forms seem as if they should be the roots of lexemes, since they are parallel to other roots in words such as *blackberry*, *blueberry*, *goldenberry*, *loganberry* (named after J. H. Logan). Yet other factors cast doubt on their status as roots: they are not forms of any simplex lexemes of English, and they do not take any derivational or inflectional affixes. If they are roots, *cranberry* is a compound; if they are not, it must be a derivative. It might be possible to consider *cran-* and *bil-* and Danish *bom-* as prefixes, but such prefixes would be very much more restricted than most normal prefixes. These words do not fit easily into the category of derivatives, nor into the category of compounds. They seem to be somewhere in between.

Interesting in this connection is the traditional use in French of the term 'composition' to cover not only compounding but also prefixation.[5] This is motivated by the fact that prefixes in French have the same function as prepositions or adverbs used as the first elements of compounds, and in fact some forms (like *entre*, *sous*)

[5] See, for example, Grévisse (1964: §§137–8). The terminological problem is not restricted to French: Marchand (1969: §3.1.1) gives references to scholars who discuss the same problem with reference to English and German. On the situation in French, see also the counter-claim in Martinet (1969: 55).

can be used either as free forms or as affixes. Thus in the phrase *entre nous* 'between us', ENTRE is a lexeme, but in the words *entreprendre* 'undertake' and *entr'acte*, 'between act' = 'intermission' it is not clear whether *entre* should be treated as a lexeme (in which case, these are cases of compounding) or as a prefix (in which case, these are derivatives). In otherwise apparently parallel cases such as *sus · tonique* 'supertonic', *sus · mentionné* 'above mentioned' the *sus* element cannot occur as a lexeme in its own right. The same point holds true in German (Malkiel, 1978: 127). Again, this argues for the lack of a clear distinction between derivation and compounding.

The final problem to be considered in this section depends crucially on a question of definition. Most scholars define a compound as a lexeme made up of two (or more) lexemes (e.g. Adams, 1973: 30; Bauer, 1978d: §2.3.3; Henzen, 1947: 36; Jespersen, 1942: §8.1.1; Rohrer, 1967: §6.2). This gives rise to problems with such forms as Danish *cigar · mager* 'cigar maker', *vold · tægt* 'violence taking' = 'rape', English *war · monger*. In all these cases the first element is a free morph, that is it realizes a lexeme, but the second element, although it is morphologically transparent, is not found in isolation. It is, however, commutable with a form which is found in isolation. That is, although **mager*, **monger* are not found as independent lexemes, FABRIKANT 'maker', and SUPPORTER are, and the forms *cigarfabrikant* and *war supporter* are perfectly acceptable. So although *cigarmager*, *voldtægt*, *warmonger* and forms like them are parallel to other forms which are compounds, and are felt to be compounds by native speakers, they do not fit under the definition of compounds as lexemes formed by the conjunction of two other lexemes.

However, a compound in this book has been defined as a form containing two potential stems, not two lexemes (see above, §2.11). It is certainly true that *mager*, *tægt* and *monger* when they occur take the inflectional suffixes required by the linguistic context: *cigarmagere* (pl.), *voldtægten* (definite), *warmonger's* (genitive). By the definition given here, therefore, these forms are compounds. The definition of compounding adopted, and hence the solution chosen to the problem presented by the examples above, is presumably fairly arbitrary. But the fact that the border between compounding and derivation can be moved in this way by a minor terminological adjustment shows, in itself, how unstable the borderline between the two is.

Consider also a form like *Anglophobe*. There is no lexeme *ANGLO, nor is there a lexeme *PHOBE. *Anglo* is not a stem either, since inflectional affixes cannot be added to it directly (although they can be added to *phobe* in *Anglophobe*). It is arguable, however, that *Anglo-* and *-phobe* are bound roots, which occur in *Anglia*, *Anglic*, *phobia*, *phobic*. That is, given the present definition of a compound, *Anglophobe* does not count as a compound. (Exactly what kind of word-formation is involved here will be discussed at greater length in §7.3.) But if a compound were to be defined as a form containing two roots, then *Anglophobe* could be classified as a compound. Again, it is of interest to note the traditional French usage which labels as compounds all lexemes formed by such neo-classical processes of word-formation, words like *autobiographie*, *discothèque* (see e.g. Grévisse, 1964: §§145–9). Since *auto* and *thèque* are not roots in French it is only by considering their status in the classical languages that words of this type can really be called compounds according to the definition provided here. This is, of course, not to deny that they might have some things in common with compounds, not only in French, but also in English (Adams, 1973: 31–2; below, §8.3).

2.16.2 *Derivation and inflection*

Just as it was found that there are elements which have changed from lexeme status to affix status with the passage of time, and thus have given rise to a change from compounding to derivation, so there are elements which, viewed diachronically, have changed from derivational to inflectional elements. Matthews (1974: 53) cites the example of what appears to have been an inflectional affix in Indo-European, namely *-*sk*-, which was used to form an inchoative form in the present tense of verbs. In Latin, the etymologically derived form -*sc*- appeared in a few verbs like MATURESCO 'to ripen', COGNOSCO 'to get to know', but although it still had its inchoative meaning, it was used to form new lexemes, and not as a regular form in a verbal paradigm. In modern Italian, the etymological descendant -*sc*- (variously pronounced) is an inflectional form appearing in the conjugation of one subclass of verbs. One element has thus gone from being inflectional, to being derivational, and back to being inflectional again.

Jespersen (1924: 42) points out that a distinction between inflection and derivation is bound to be artificial in some cases. He cites French, where the doubling of an *n* and the addition of an *e* provides an inflectional change from masculine to feminine in the case of *bon/bonne*, but a derivational change from masculine to feminine in the case of *paysan/paysanne*. It seems counter-intuitive that the same formal and semantic modification should be classed now as inflection, now as derivation, although this has to be the case if the criteria discussed above (§2.10) are applied.

One of the tests given above (§2.10) for derivation was that a derivative could be replaced by a simple root form in sentences. But consider a sentence such as *It's getting colder*. Here, *colder* could be replaced by *cold*, and the sentence would still make perfect sense. By this test, therefore, the comparative ending must create new derivatives. On the other hand, consider the same form *colder* in a sentence like *Siberia is colder than Denmark*. Here, *colder* could not be replaced by a simple root form. It seems, then, that the same test provides conflicting results with a single form, which should be considered derivational in some sentences and inflectional in others. While this conclusion is clearly unsatisfactory, it does illustrate that the comparative cannot be unambiguously assigned to either inflectional or derivational morphology.

It was pointed out above (§2.10) that inflection produces new forms of a single lexeme, while derivation produces new lexemes. This gives rise to a problem with the status of English past participles. Every English verb (except the modals and a very few defective verbs) has a past participle, which is a form of the verbal lexeme used in particular grammatical circumstances. Thus, the past participle is an inflectional form of the verb in English. But almost any past participle of English can be used as an adjective in that it can be used attributively to modify a noun: *a married man*, *the destroyed building*, *a heated argument*. Some past participles have even more adjectival traits, in that they can be modified by *very* (*his very reduced circumstances*, but not **his very shot comrade*) or form the base of an adverb in *-ly* (*heatedly*, but not **destroyedly*). Again, since the ending *-ed* (or the other morphs that replace *-ed*) can be used to create lexemes which are then used as if they belong to a different word-class from the word-class of the base, it appears to be derivational in nature. Thus the same ending, producing the same word-form, is simultaneously inflectional and derivational. Matthews (1974: 53–4) considers this particular problem in greater detail.

3
Lexicalization

Irregularity is a manifestation of an important regularity of language: change.
(Hudson, 1974: 224)

Patterns of synchronic alternations, however clearly discernible they may be, are merely reflections of past historical developments.
(Hsieh, 1976: 15)

3.1 Reconstruction of the history of a vocabulary-item

When a word first appears in a language, whether as a loan or calque, or as a nonce formation (i.e. a new complex word coined on the spur of the moment), it appears that speakers are aware of its newness, that is they are aware that they are exploiting the productivity of the language system (see in greater detail below, chapter 4). Thus, in modern journalistic language the word is often put in inverted commas, a phrase is added such as "what has been called", "as it is termed" and so on, or a complete gloss is provided.[1] The large amount of written evidence for this awareness of novelty is a fairly recent phenomenon, since it is only in the twentieth century that vast numbers of dailies and periodicals have become commonplace, but it may be assumed that the awareness of innovation is not as recent as that, and that earlier generations put intonational "inverted commas" round the term, and provided oral glosses in the same way. In literary language, where new forms are often produced specifically to provide effect, such marking does not take place, and the form is most frequently left to speak for itself; but it should be remembered that, statistically speaking, literary

---

[1] Consider, for example, some of the entries in Barnhart et al. (1973), of which the following are fairly typical: "But Nader contended that automakers should build 'crashworthy' cars . . .", "The employment of 'incaps' (i.e. incapacitating chemicals) will be bound to cause widespread deaths . . .", "E. T. Pengelly and K. H. Kelly from the University of California, Riverside, . . . have named this faculty a 'circannian' rhythm." Similar examples may be found in other dictionaries of neologisms, e.g. Dansk Sprognævn (1978) for Danish and Giraud et al. (1974) for French.

language is the exception rather than the rule in linguistic behaviour.

Whether or not the new term gains currency will depend upon a number of factors. One of these is the status of the person who used the term – Adams (1973: 2) cites the example of *triphibian*, which may have been helped into currency by the fact that it was apparently first used by Winston Churchill – or, in journalistic terms, the status and circulation of the newspaper involved. But although this is a factor which is frequently mentioned (see Ljung, 1977: 177; Pennanen, 1966: §8.7), whether or not a word is accepted and used seems frequently to depend on the attitude to the word evinced by society as a whole (Guilbert, 1975: §1.3.2). Society's stamp of approval in turn frequently depends on there being a need for the form in question. In the clearest cases this means that there is a new object or construct which needs a name (for example, *television, liquidizer*, and in linguistics such terms as *Chomsky adjunction* or *the category squish*), but frequently it is simply a matter of a known concept being required in a part of speech in which it has not previously been used.

In other cases there may not be an obvious need for a new word. For example, there is no obvious need for Danish *TV*, French *charter* and German *Fernsprecher*, given the prior existence of the synonymous forms *fjernsyn, affrété* and *Telephon*. In such cases, the new word may arise for reasons of prestige. In other cases, new complex words may be used to gain an effect, to save space (especially in newspaper headlines) or simply because the speaker cannot remember the usual lexeme used for the required concept. An example of the first of these is *dontopedology* 'putting one's foot in one's mouth', which has a humorous effect because it is a scientific-sounding label for something rather trivial; an example of the second is the recent use in headlines of *press freedom* in place of the more normal *freedom of the press*; and an example of the third (though one which may be gaining ground) is *equalitarian*[2] for *egalitarian*. It would also be possible to speak of "needs" in these instances, since in each case the existing list of lexemes fails to give immediate satisfaction in the speaker's search for an expression, but

[2] R. Brown & A. Gilman, 1968. The pronouns of power and solidarity. In J. Fishman (ed.), *Readings in the Sociology of Language*. The Hague: Mouton, p. 263.

43

this would be a rather looser use of "need". For further discussion of "need" in such contexts, see Bernard & Delbridge (1980: 192ff). Even when there is a clear need for one, it is well-known that society does not just painlessly absorb a new term. It is most frequently at this stage, while a new form is on the brink of being accepted by society, that people write letters to the editor complaining about the use of the new form on aesthetic, etymological, grammatical or semantic grounds, as well as for reasons of "vulgarity" (see Adams, 1973: 2; Quirk, 1962: 120ff).

When a term is actually accepted by society, it becomes assimilated and used in exactly the same way as other lexemes of the language. The speaker–listener forgets why the word has the form that it does, and considers it merely as the appropriate label for the concept in question, even if the form is perfectly transparent. Very few speakers of contemporary English think of a *hedgehog* as a pig which lives in a hedge, or of a *handlebar* as a bar which provides or is used as a handle. Derwing (1973: 124 fn. 2) notes that his daughter "was nearly four years old before she noted (to her delighted surprise) that even 'oranges' and 'orange juice' had anything in common!" It would seem that new learners of a language may never consider the underlying motivation of complex forms, and yet use those forms perfectly satisfactorily. In such cases speakers appear to treat complex forms as though they were monomorphemic, although there is always the possibility that they will at some stage realize that the label is in fact analysable. That is why linguists would almost always treat such forms as analysable, although Wheeler & Schumsky (1980) report that in an experimental situation, subjects frequently failed to isolate even the affixes *-ship, -dom* and *-er* in English words. In some cases, an unanalysable form is treated as analysable, and this is when cases of **folk etymology** occur, for example when *asparagus* is re-analysed as *sparrows' grass*.

Once the point is reached where a form is treated as unanalysable, it is free to diverge from the original by sound change or semantic change, so that it no longer has any obvious connection with the original formation. Thus the modern English word *nice* originally comes from Latin *nescius*, where *ne* is equivalent to 'not' and *scius* is related to *scire* 'to know'. But the semantic change did not take place until all feeling of negation had been lost (in this case, not until the lexeme had been borrowed into English from French). Modern English *nest* goes back to two Proto-Indo-European roots meaning 'sit' and 'down', but the phonological shape of the word has changed so that neither element can now be recognized in it. It is also possible that the process of word-formation by which the new lexeme was formed could cease to be productive, and the lexeme then becomes morphologically isolated, either as a single form or as part of an isolated series.

3.2 Terminology

These diachronic facts are relatively uncontroversial. They create, however, descriptive problems in a synchronic grammar, since at any given moment lexical items will exist in a language at every one of the stages described above. This has led to a certain amount of confusion in the literature, and in particular to very confused terminology. A terminology will be suggested here which seems to fit with majority usage, at least to the extent that the terms used in the literature are given precise definitions or have definitions which may be deduced with precision from the contexts.

3.2.1 *Nonce formations*

A **nonce formation** can be defined as a new complex word coined by a speaker/writer on the spur of the moment to cover some immediate need. This definition admits new words as nonce formations even when they are totally regular, and even if they go on to become accepted in the language community: not all scholars would necessarily agree with a definition cast in such broad terms. It is perfectly conceivable that the same form should be coined by different speakers, either at different times, or very close together in time (as when some new object appears which requires a name) without affecting the item's status as a nonce formation. A form ceases to be a nonce formation as soon as the speakers using it are aware of using a term which they have heard already: that is to say, virtually immediately. Despite this fact, there are large numbers of nonce formations which are used on very few occasions (perhaps no more than once) and, in the cases where they do appear more than once, they are used by different speakers, so that their status as nonce formations is not affected. Typically this is the case where the "immediate need" which gives rise to the formation is unique or extremely rare. Consider, for example, the following (attested) formations: the Danish *kitteldeflorationssyndrom* 'white coat defloration syndrome', the French *épaules façon bouteille Perrier* 'shoulders [in the] shape [of a] bottle [of] Perrier [water]', and the English *garden shed flatlet*.

One fact about nonce formations that is not sufficiently appreciated is how large a proportion of complex forms that are heard everyday are nonce formations. Thiel (1973: 379) discovered that in a corpus of 1331 compound nouns from a 1970 issue of the German magazine *Die Zeit*, 37·9 per cent were listed in dictionaries while 62·1 per cent were not. Although not all of the 62·1 per cent were necessarily nonce formations by the definition given here, and although it might be expected that a larger proportion of the derivatives in such a corpus would be listed in dictionaries, the figures are still suggestive.

One point that is very characteristic of some kinds of nonce formations considered in isolation is their potential ambiguity. This is particularly true of compounds and of nominalizations of verbs. As an example of a compound, consider *world-sky*. According to Hornby (1974), WORLD has eight meanings:

(1)   the earth
(2)   extending over the earth
(3)   time, state or scene of existence
(4)   the universe; everything
(5)   the material things and occupations of life
(6)   human affairs
(7)   persons, institutions etc. connected with a special social class
(8)   average society, fashionable society, their opinions, customs etc.

and SKY has two:

(1)   where we see the sun, moon and stars
(2)   climate

A larger dictionary would no doubt give a more subtle division of meaning, and more meanings for each lexeme, but these are sufficient for the illustration. Given the appropriate context, virtually any combination of these meanings would make sense, so that the compound *world-sky* should have 16 possible meanings, be 16 ways ambiguous – or more if exocentric readings are also considered. This is what is meant by the potential ambiguity of a nonce formation. In context, of course, the range of meanings is severely limited. This particular nonce formation was attested in Richard Dimbleby's commentary on the lying-in-state of George VI: "the twilight of his death has dimmed the whole world-sky" (cited by Vos, 1952: 34). The meaning of SKY is limited to (1) above, and the meaning of WORLD is limited to (2) or (6). The compound is still ambiguous, but much less so than it would be out of context.

As an example of the potential ambiguity of nominalizations consider CONDEMNATION. This has (at least) two meanings, which can be roughly glossed as 'the act of condemning' and 'the fact of condemning' as in the following two sentences:

> His condemnation of the government lasted hours
> His condemnation was a bitter blow for the government

This point will be considered in greater detail in §6.7.

While this potential ambiguity is probably most easily seen in nonce formations where the reader/listener has no expectations as to the meaning of the form, it can also be illustrated by established lexemes or series of lexemes. Thus Lyons (1977: 538) points to the ambiguity of *London train* as illustrated by the sentences:

> Has the London train left yet?
> Has the London train arrived yet?

and contrasts this with *London taxi* which means 'a taxi which operates in London' rather than 'a taxi bound for London' or 'a taxi coming out of London'. Lees (1960: 116) points to the varying analyses of *flour mill* vs. *windmill*. Bauer (1978d: §3.4.2) mentions pairs such as *man trap* vs. *The Baby Trap* (the title of a feminist book).

It is the existence of data of this kind that has led to the postulation of a large number of contrasting verbs in the deep structures of compounds, which it is then claimed are neutralized on the surface (see Lees, 1960; Motsch, 1970; Rohrer, 1967; Vendler, 1968), and in the generation of nominalizations, to the postulation of deep structure semantic markers such as 'Act' and 'Fact' (Fraser, 1970; Newmeyer, 1970) to distinguish the various readings of a nominalization. Such deep structures will be considered in greater detail in chapter 6.

3.2.2 *Institutionalization*

The next stage in the history of a lexeme is when the nonce formation starts to be accepted by other speakers as a known lexical item. Typical of this stage (especially for compounds) is that the potential ambiguity is ignored, and only some of the possible meanings of the form are used (sometimes only one). Thus, for example, there is nothing in the form *telephone box* to prevent it from meaning a box shaped like a telephone, a box which is located at/by a telephone, a box which functions as a telephone, and so on. It is only because the item is familiar that the speaker-listener knows that it is synonymous with *telephone kiosk*, in the usual meaning of *telephone kiosk*. In Meys's terms (1975), *telephone box* has gone from being **type familiar** to being **item familiar**: it is not just the construction which is recognized, but the particular lexeme. The term has become **institutionalized**.[3] Any institutionalized lexeme will be transparent.

Institutionalization applies not only to the formation of new lexemes by word-formation, but also to the extension of existing lexemes by metaphor. Leech (1974: 227) cites the example of *fox*, which can be used to designate a cunning person but not, for instance, a person with a pointed nose, although pointed noses and cunning are both standard attributes of foxes.

3.2.3 *Lexicalization*

The final stage comes when, because of some change in the language system, the lexeme has, or takes on, a form which it could not have if it had arisen by the application of productive rules. At this stage the lexeme is **lexicalized**.[4] Lexicalization can

---

[3] Leech (1974: 226); Lyons (1977: 524); Matthews (1974: 193). Bauer (1978a,d) uses the term 'received'; Gleitman & Gleitman (1970: 90) use the term 'frozen'.

[4] The term is no doubt unfortunate because of its other technical meanings (see e.g. Leech, 1974: 191; Lyons, 1970: 138, 1977: 549). Nonetheless it seems to have currency in studies of word-formation in approximately the sense in which it is being used here (see e.g. Basbøll, 1975a: 49; Bauer, 1978a, 1978d; Brekle, 1975: 27; Brekle & Kastovsky, 1977b: 15; Downing, 1977: 819; Ettinger, 1974a: 66; Guilbert, 1975; Kiefer, 1972: 42; Lewicka, 1963: 132; Lipka, 1977; Motsch, 1970: 213, 1977: 184; Teleman, 1970: 20; Tietze, 1974: §4.3; Warren, 1978: 46). Leech (1974: 226) and Lyons (1977: 536) prefer the term 'petrified' to 'lexicalized'. Another term frequently met in the literature is 'idiomatized' (see e.g. Clark & Clark, 1979: 804; Fleischer, 1975: 13; Lipka, 1977; Ljung, 1977) which is sometimes distinguished from 'lexicalized'.

come about (and be traced) at every level of linguistic analysis, and this will be illustrated more fully in the next section. It should be noted that although many lexicalized forms are opaque (i.e. they cannot be analysed in terms of synchronic morphemes, e.g. *nest* discussed above), opacity is not a necessary pre-requisite for lexicalization. Some lexicalized forms, especially forms which are lexicalized because of a change in the morphological system of the language, may remain perfectly transparent. Thus although *warmth* can be analysed to give *warm · th*, the suffix *-th* cannot be added synchronically to an adjective to provide a noun; this can be seen from the impossibility of using new adjectives to provide nouns of this type: **cameoth*, **funkyth*, **maxith*, **psychedelicth*, **surrealth*. *Warmth* is analysable but lexicalized. Similarly, suffixation in *-ment* does not appear to be productive (new words using this suffix do not appear to be being coined), so that a word like *involvement* must be lexicalized.

The discussion so far has tended to imply that items are either lexicalized or not. Some scholars, however, suggest that it is more satisfactory to list items as being phonologically or morphologically or semantically lexicalized (Basbøll, 1975a: 50; Lyons, 1977: 528ff). Then if all the phonological behaviour of a lexeme is predictable by the general rules governing phonological behaviour, but the semantics of an item is unpredictable, the item can be marked as having an irregular semantic form (being lexicalized semantically) without implying anything about its phonological behaviour. That means that the phonological behaviour of this particular item will not be accounted for first in the rules and then in the lexicon, and so a saving is made. This is the view that will be taken here. For a view of possible lexical entries incorporating this approach, see Lyons (1977: 528ff) and below, §6.8.

Lyons (1977: 547) has an extra term which is apparently equivalent to lexicalization. This is "fossilization" (see also his use of "petrification" for lexicalization). Forms are said to be "fossilized" if "the rule by which they are derived from the simplex lexemes of which they are composed is no longer productive in the present state of the language system." As examples, *pick-pocket* and *turn-coat* are cited. It is, however, not clear that "fossilized" formations really form a group that is separate from "petrified" ones. Both fall under the definition of lexicalization given here, though Lyons obviously feels that "fossilization" is an extreme form of "petrification". On the other hand, it is doubtful whether *edible*, which Lyons lists as a case of institutionalization, could be productively derived from *eat* "in the present state of the language system". Lyons seems to be using "petrification" for the institutionalization of compounds, whereas "institutionalization" is reserved for derivatives. "Fossilization" is then lexicalization applied to compounds. It must then be decided whether it is useful to make a terminological distinction between derivation and composition in this way. It would seem that such a distinction can only be justified if it can be shown that derivatives and compounds act differently with respect to the whole process of the diachronic shift from nonce formation to apparently arbitrary and unmotivated lexeme. I know of no evidence that would point to this being the case. Accordingly only three terms will be distinguished here: 'nonce formation', 'institutionalization' and 'lexicalization'. It will, however, be useful in later discussion to have a term which subsumes both 'institutionalized' and 'lexicalized'. The term **established** will be used in this book with that meaning.

3.3 Types of lexicalization

Lexicalization, as it has been described here, is essentially a diachronic process, but the traces it leaves in the form of lexicalized lexemes have to be dealt with in a synchronic grammar. If it is assumed, as it is here, that a lexical item can be lexicalized in a number of different ways, then the entry for each item in the lexicon must have a slot for showing each possible kind of lexicalization. In the remainder of this chapter, a number of illustrations will be provided showing how items can be lexicalized. Each one of these, accordingly, necessitates a suitable section in the lexicon where the idiosyncrasy (i.e. irregularity, unpredictability) can be noted. A full theory of the lexicon will have to take this kind of data into account.

3.3.1 *Phonological*
3.3.1.1 Prosodic features

The most common prosodic feature to show lexicalization is stress. It is frequently the case that stress patterns for particular complex forms are different from the stress patterns for simplex lexemes, and once a form is institutionalized it is free to undergo changes of stress so that it receives a pattern which would not be possible if the item were formed productively. This can be illustrated with Danish nominal compounds of the form (A(BC)) (Bauer, 1977, 1978a). These receive primary stress on the A element, but secondary stress is on the B element in productive forms (e.g. *'perle · ˌhals · bånd* 'pearl neck band' = 'pearl necklace'), but on the C element in lexicalized forms (e.g. *'lomme · tør · ˌklæde* 'pocket dry cloth' = 'pocket handkerchief'). Similarly, English derivatives in *-ic* normally have the stress on the syllable preceding the suffix (*syn'chronic, pho'netic*), but there are some forms (e.g. *'Arabic, 'chivalric, 'choleric*) which are, or may be, stressed on the first syllable.

In Danish there is another prosodic element which can show lexicalization, namely the *stød* (glottal catch). Basbøll (1975b) points out, for example that *under · lig* /onʌli/ 'strange', *under · fuld* /onʌfulʔ/ 'wonderful' are exceptions to the productive rule that *under* /onʔʌ/ 'wonder' always keeps its *stød*, even when it is a base for the formation of a complex form. He also comments that *troende* 'believing' need not have a *stød* when it is being used in its religious sense, although as a regular participle it does have a *stød*.[5] It is thus lexicalized in its religious meaning, but not as a participle.

3.3.1.2 Segmental features

There are at least two different factors which can cause lexicalization in segmental features. The most obvious of these is a sound change which, for whatever reason, affects a morph either only in isolation or only when it appears in combination with other morphs. The second is that prosodic features may cause a change in the segmental features of a morph when it appears in some specific combination.

As far as the influence of prosodic elements is concerned, there are examples like the days of the week in English which in some dialects are normally pronounced with the *day* element reduced to

---

[5] The Danish *stød* or glottal catch, which I have transcribed [ʔ], is not a full glottal stop, and since its position in the word is always predictable from stress and segmental information (although it is not predictable whether any given word will carry a *stød*) it is best treated as a prosodic phenomenon like tone (with which it is closely related) rather than as a segmental phoneme.

/dɪ/ because of the strong stress on the first element. Normally, /eɪ/ either does not reduce (as in *payday*) or reduces to /ə/ (as in the rather different example of *famous* as opposed to *infamous*), so that reduction to /ɪ/ (except in specific places like French loan words: *ballet* can be /bæleɪ/ or /bælɪ/) is an irregular feature.

Examples abound where a form has become isolated due to the process of phonetic change in the language system. Jespersen (1909: §4.34ff, 1942: §8.17) lists literally dozens of examples. For instance, *lammas* derives from Old English *hlāf·mæsse* 'loaf mass', but the *lam* part can no longer have been felt to be connected with the word for 'loaf' at the time of the sound change which gave the form *loaf*, because if it had been the first element of *lammas* would have undergone the same vowel change. Another example is *husband* from Old English *hūs·bonda* 'house master' where the *hus* element has been isolated from the free morph *house* by the application of the Great Vowel Shift to HOUSE, and so on. Basbøll (1975b) illustrates a similar case in modern Danish: *stål·tråd* 'steel thread' = 'wire' is pronounced with an irregular short /ɔ/ in the first element, although *stål* in isolation and in the first element of nonce compounds is pronounced with a long /ɔ:/. In this particular example transparency is not affected, since long ~ short alternation is a familiar and productive phenomenon in Danish (e.g. *på* (with /ɔ:/) ~ *på·begynde* (with /ɔ/)).

Changes of this type, which lead to opacity, provide a problem for a theory of word-formation. Consider, for example, the form *husband*. Should this be listed, in a synchronic grammar of English, as a compound form with phonological and lexico-semantic idiosyncrasies, or should it be listed as a simplex lexeme? Presumably each case has to be judged on its own merit. In this particular case, it seems likely that the most satisfactory solution will be to consider *husband* as a simplex lexeme. In the case of *ståltråd* discussed above, it might be better to list the variant /sdɔl/ of STÅL in the lexicon, in the way suggested by Lyons, since the *tråd* element is perfectly regular here. It is not clear that there is (or should be) a single once-and-for-all solution to this kind of problem.

In some cases the language community seems to react to the opacity brought about by sound change, and remotivates a lexeme phonologically. This is what happens in the case of so-called

spelling pronunciations of the type /weskət/ > /weɪstkəut/, /hʌzɪf/ > /hauswaɪf/, /fɒrɪd/ > /fɔhed/.

3.3.2 *Morphological*
3.3.2.1 Linking elements

It is suggested by Bauer (1978a: §2.2) that every stem in a language like Danish which forms compounds of the form stem + linking element + stem, should be listed in the lexicon with one and only one linking element. This linking element (which may be zero, to account for stem + stem compounds) is then added to the stem in question every time that stem is used to form the first element of a nonce compound. This means that it is synchronically predictable what the form of any compound with a given first element will be. The linking element may, however, change diachronically. For example, in Luther's day German compounds with first elements in *-keit* were formed without any linking element (stem + stem compound, zero linking element) whereas today all words in *-keit* add *-s* when they are used as the first element of a compound. Thus, what for Luther was *Gerechtig·keit·liebe* 'love of justice' is in modern German *Gerechtig·keit·s·liebe*. Lexemes which were institutionalized before such a diachronic change in linking element either (a) all change their linking element as well, as is the case with the German example quoted above, or (b) retain their old forms and thus become lexicalized, since the form in which they appear in the language could not be generated by contemporarily productive rules. For example, new formations with a first element in *jord* 'earth' in Danish contain no linking element (*jord·bank* 'earth-bank', *jord·fordeling* 'earth distribution') but in *jord·e·liv* 'life on earth', *jord·e·moder* 'earth mother' = 'midwife', *jord·e·rig* 'earth kingdom' = 'the earth' there are forms with a linking *-e-*. Such forms cannot be generated synchronically and are thus lexicalized.

It is quite possible for the same two lexemes to form compounds at two different periods and with two different linking elements in which different facets of the potential ambiguity of the compounds have become institutionalized. Such compounds can then provide apparent minimal pairs where a difference in linking element is the only formal difference between two compounds which differ widely in meaning. Consider, for example, German *Kind·es·liebe* 'love

53

given by a child' vs. *Kind·er·liebe* 'love for children' OR 'love given by a child'; *Wasser·not* 'drought' vs. *Wasser·s·not* 'flood'. However, not too much weight should be given to such coincidences, since they are generally no more than that, although there are rare cases where a difference in linking element reflects a consistent semantic difference: one example is Danish *mands-* vs. *mande-*, where the latter consistently means 'man-sized, worthy of a real man' (Bauer, 1978b).

3.3.2.2 Roots

In a language like English, which has a large learned vocabulary based on languages from different branches of Indo-European (Greek and the Romance languages, and especially Latin), and which borrows words freely, there are innumerable examples of derivatives which are closely related semantically, and possibly also etymologically, but which have different roots. For example, there are *eat* and *edible, legal* and *loyal, opus* and *operation, right* and *rectitude, sound, sonar* and *sonic*, and so on. To such forms can be added alternants that have arisen because of sound changes in English, with no borrowing involved. In this class belong /tu/ and /tʌ/ in *two, tuppence*, /haʊs/ and /hʌz/ in *house, husband* (see above, §3.3.1.2) and /dɪvaɪn/ and /dɪvɪn/ in *divine, divinity*.

In many cases only one member of these sets of roots continues to be productive in current English. Thus, for example, it does not seem to be possible to create new lexemes in English by adding suffixes to the roots *ed* (as in *edible*), *intellig* (as in *intelligible*: a new form with *intellig* would probably be seen as being related to *intelligent*, if any were found), /tʌ/ (as in *tuppence*) and so on. Other roots remain productive. For example *son* gives rise to *sonication, sonochemistry*; *oper* gives rise to *operand, operon* (examples from Barnhart *et al.*, 1973). Those morphemes that have two productive roots must have that information listed in the lexicon, along with information about when the different roots are used. Where only one root is productive, forms with the non-productive root are lexicalized and must be specially marked. In the case of *edible*, for example, either the form *ed·ible* is listed with the extra information that this is equivalent to EAT + *-able*, as suggested by Lyons (1977: 533), or it is marked under EAT that EAT + *able* →

(optionally) *edible*. The optionality here is because of the parallel form *eatable* which is regularly derived from productive forms of morphemes, but does not exist for those speakers who make a semantic distinction between *eatable* and *edible* such that all food is by definition edible, though if it has been burnt it may no longer be eatable. For such speakers a semantic environment will have to be added to the above rule in place of the "optionally".

3.3.2.3 Affixes

Just as linking elements and roots can cease to be productive, so too can affixes. For example, the affix *-ment* which was used to form nominalizations of English verbs (*derailment, achievement, assignment*, etc.) is now dead or at least moribund. Of the ten words in *-ment* listed in Barnhart *et al.* (1973), six represent new uses of an old form, three are loans directly from French, and only one, *Englishment* 'rendering into English, anglicization' may illustrate a productive use (although it sounds like a very idiosyncratic formation, and perhaps it ought not to be given too much weight). This does not of course mean that English can no longer form nominalizations: other nominalizing suffixes are still productive; but it does mean that forms in *-ment* are all lexicalized. Similarly, all nominalizations from adjectives which end in *-th* (*warmth, length, width*) are now lexicalized (most of them also have unproductive root forms).

3.3.3 *Semantic*

Semantic lexicalization is not a unified phenomenon, and it is not clear how it is best classified, or even whether it can be successfully classified at all. Several classifications have been proposed in the literature, but none of these is entirely satisfactory.

For example, Lipka (1977) provides a classification of instances of semantic lexicalization in which the basic division is between lexicalization brought about by change in the cultural background and that brought about by a change in the language. An example of the former is German *Schreib·feder* 'writing feather' = 'pen', where the cultural background has changed in that quills are no longer in general use; an example of the latter is *mincemeat*, where *meat* once meant all food and not just flesh – note the expressions "meat and drink" and "one man's meat is another man's poison" where, although it is not clear to all speakers of modern English, the 'food' meaning is preserved. This classification of Lipka's, however, has the disadvantage of being a diachronic one, and it is not necessarily obvious synchronically which of these two processes has applied.

A second, and more widely accepted classification, is into lexicalization that is the result of the addition of semantic information, and lexicalization that is the result of the loss of semantic information (Leech, 1974: 226; Lipka, 1977; Lyons, 1977: 535ff). For instance, *understand* provides an example of lexicalization due to the loss of semantic information, since it contains, in current English, none of the meaning of *under* and none of the meaning of *stand* (Lipka, 1977: 160). Conversely, *wheel chair* and *push chair* are examples of lexicalization due to the addition of semantic information (Leech, 1974: 226). You can push a wheel chair, and a push chair has wheels on it, so that the names *per se* do not seem to distinguish between the two sets of denotata. And yet there is no overlap in the sets of real-world objects which can be referred to using these words. It does seem to be the case that *wheel chair* has an extra semantic marker of the type 'for invalids', contrasting with a marker 'for young children' on *push chair*.

While this classification is, on the surface, much more appealing, there turn out to be so many problems associated with it that it becomes almost impossible to apply. In view of the wide influence that Leech's discussion of the topic has had, it is perhaps worth mentioning some of these problems. Firstly, as Lipka (1977: 160) points out, there are some words which simultaneously illustrate both the loss of semantic information and the addition of semantic information. Lipka cites the example of *playboy*, where there is extra semantic information in the *play* element, since playboys "play" in a very special way, but loss of semantic information in the *boy* element, since a playboy is a male, but not a non-adult male.

Secondly, there are many words which do not appear to fit the classification at all. Consider, for example, the word *bedstead*. The *stead* element is etymologically related to the *stead* in *homestead, in his stead, instead, stand somebody in good stead*, but none of these is helpful in interpreting *bedstead*. Should it then be said that *bedstead* is a case of loss of semantic information because it has lost all the information about 'place' that is normally in *stead*, or should it be said that it is a case of the addition of semantic information, because the meaning 'frame' has been added? In this instance, and generally in cases where one element of a word has disappeared or virtually disappeared from common usage, the classification seems to break down completely.

Thirdly – and I shall consider this problem at greater length – it is not clear what the "addition of semantic information" should be taken to include. Consider, for example, a word like *typewriter*. The information in the word is that some entity writes and that this is connected in some way with type. It so happens that most typewriters have key-boards, shift-keys, platens, the symbols for the numbers on the top line, and so on, but none of that information is included in the word. To what extent, then, is it fair to say that all this is additional semantic information? Notice that it is not even specified in the word that a typewriter is a machine and not a person: indeed, at the end of the last century the word *typewriter* was used to denote the person as well as the machine (see the entry in the *OED*). The most obvious answer might be to include under the heading of "additional semantic information" only such information as is obligatory for the appropriate use of the word in referring, but the person/machine problem with *typewriter* suggests that even this is excessive.

Consideration of exocentric compounds such as *egg head, redskin* and *waxwing* gives rise to particular problems in this context, since the unexpressed semantic head is frequently conventionally fixed (i.e. is established), and might be said to be additional semantic information. This is the point of view taken by Jackendoff (1975: 657), for example. He claims that unless these compounds are individually listed in the lexicon there will be no way to tell that "a *redhead* is a kind of person, but that a *blackhead* is a kind of pimple". But consider the form *redskin*. This has two institutionalized semantic heads, a person and a potato, though many speakers know only one. Suppose a person who knows only the 'person' sense of *redskin* meets the following utterance:

> I'm not a great potato-eater, but I do like redskins, especially when they're new

Such a person is still not likely to think that the utterer is a cannibal. Such reinterpretations are possible because there is generally enough information in the context to show pragmatically what the head of the compound must be. That is why nonce exocentric compounds can be interpreted, and why institutionalized exocentrics can be reinterpreted in different contexts. Consider:

> Granny Smith was rude to all lesser breeds, but particularly to Mr Mackintosh. "You redskins", she would sniff, "You're all alike: no firmness of character."

That such a reinterpretation is possible was confirmed for me recently when I saw the word *redskin* used in an advertisement for an apple orchard. It would not be surprising to find *redskins* used of plums or, in an appropriate context, anything else that has a red skin. Thus Jackendoff's conclusion that exocentric compounds must be listed in the lexicon is clearly deficient, and it seems that the interpretation of such forms must be explained by reference to the pragmatics of the situation. That being the case, even the quite considerable amount of information that can be accounted for by the unexpressed head of an exocentric compound cannot fairly be included as "additional semantic information" for present purposes, since such forms are not lexicalized.

While the classification of semantic lexicalization, and even the possibility of classifying semantic lexicalization, may be in doubt, the fact of semantic lexicalization seems to be well established. In the literature (e.g. Aronoff, 1976) it is frequently discussed in terms of lack of **semantic compositionality**, i.e. the meaning of the whole is not predictable from the meanings of the parts. As the discussion of forms like *redskin* above has shown, there are cases where I would not wish to speak of semantic lexicalization despite the fact that the meaning of the whole is not predictable from the meanings of the parts – and such cases arise particularly, though not exclusively, with compounds. The line between semantically lexicalized and non-lexicalized is thus not clearly drawn at the moment, but it is plain that there are examples which must be taken to be lexicalized, e.g. *blackmail, butterfly, mincemeat.* A few further examples which might be considered for inclusion under the heading of semantic lexicalization are listed below, with the reasons for their being considered.

Firstly consider some compound examples: in some kinds of

English, *boy-friend* can be used only in a romantic or sexual context (although the same is not true of *girl-friend* in American English, for example); although *lady-killer* denotes a person who does something to ladies, he does not usually kill them – at least not in the most literal sense; in New Zealand a *town house* is a semi-detached house with a very small garden, and not just any house in a town – this can be contrasted with the traditional British English sense of *town house* with its implications of secondary residence. As examples of derivatives, consider *inspector* which, as it is applied to policemen, bears very little relation to inspecting; and *unquiet* is certainly not the negation of *quiet*. In extreme cases, such as *gospel* from Old English *gōd spel* 'good news', a word might have become so semantically (and phonologically) lexicalized as to be best treated as a simplex word.

3.3.4   *Syntactic*

One of the most vexed questions in word-formation studies in recent years has been what the proper place is for dealing with word-formation in a grammar (see e.g. Brekle & Kastovsky, 1977b; Motsch, 1977; Stein, 1977). Interestingly enough, while derivation has frequently been relegated to the phonological component, compounding is more frequently dealt with as a matter of syntax (see e.g. Giurescu, 1972; Lees, 1960; Rohrer, 1967; Žepić, 1970). The answer to the question of what counts as syntactic lexicalization will depend largely on the attitude taken to the role of syntax in word-formation. If it is felt that word-formation is (at least partially) describable in terms of syntactic processes – which is the general approach taken in this book – then it will be possible for one of those syntactic processes to fall into disuse, and for words formed using that syntactic process to become lexicalized. This might be termed syntactic lexicalization internal to the complex form. Whether or not it is accepted that syntax plays a role in word-formation, the syntactic behaviour of a complex form may or may not be predictable from general principles and/or the root(s) and affix(es) involved. If it is not predictable from this information, then it is possible to speak of syntactic lexicalization external to the complex form, meaning lexicalization which shows up in the way the complex form interacts with other items in the sentence.

3.3.4.1 Internal to the complex form

In many cases, what is considered as an instance of syntactic lexicalization internal to the complex form will depend upon the way in which the grammar is formulated. However, there are some examples where this does not seem to be a relevant consideration. One of these is English exocentric compounds made up of a verbal stem and a noun which can be seen as the direct object of that verb: that is, forms like *pickpocket, scarecrow, spoilsport, telltale, wagtail*. The precise way in which these forms are (or were) generated does not really matter, since it seems that it must somehow be specified that such forms include a verb and a noun which could appear as the head noun in the direct object of that verb, and this is a syntactic fact about each verb. While this type remains extremely productive in French and the other Romance languages (Coseriu, 1977), it is only of very marginal productivity – if productive at all – in English (Lyons, 1977: 547–8; see also below, §7.2.1.2). It thus seems likely that English compounds on this pattern are syntactically lexicalized.

3.3.4.2 External to the complex form

This type can be illustrated with the lexeme DIS-BELIEVE. There are several verbs, coined by prefixing *dis-* to a verb base, which behave syntactically in the same way as the base verb: for instance, *obey* and *disobey* can both be used transitively and intransitively, both take noun objects rather than sentential objects, and both take the same classes of objects. But whereas *believe* can take a sentential object, as in

> I believe (that) the pound has devalued again

disbelieve can only be used with a noun object or (for some speakers) followed by the preposition *in*:

> *I disbelieve (that) the pound has devalued again

Similarly, *believe* but not *disbelieve* can take an accusative with infinitive complement:

> I believe him to be the most important linguist present
> *I disbelieve him to be the most important linguist present

Such behaviour on the part of the derivative cannot be predicted from the base verb *believe* or from the fact of prefixation with *dis-*.

This type of lexicalization is also found in idioms. Consider, for example, *out of the way* 'isolated' which, despite its form as a prepositional phrase, functions as an attributive adjective: *a very out of the way little place.*

3.3.5 *Mixed*

Most of the examples that have been cited in this section have been mentioned as examples of only a single type of lexicalization. It would, however, have been possible to use many of the examples to illustrate more than one type. For instance, it was mentioned in §3.3.2.3 that words like *length* and *width* are lexicalized not only because they contain an unproductive suffix, but also because the roots which appear in these forms are unproductive. In §3.3.2.1 the Danish example *jord·e·moder* 'earth mother' = 'midwife' was given as an instance of a compound which is morphologically lexicalized because of the form of the linking element; but since any connection with 'earth' has been lost and a midwife is not necessarily a mother, *jordemoder* is also semantically lexicalized. *Arabic*, cited in §3.3.1.1 as an example of supra-segmental phonological lexicalization, is also a case of syntactic lexicalization, since the collocations in which it occurs as an adjective are limited by the existence of *Arab* and *Arabian*. Similarly *lammas*, cited in §3.3.1.2 as an example of segmental phonological lexicalization, is also an example of semantic lexicalization because all notion of 'loaf' has been lost.

Such examples of forms which are lexicalized in more than one way are far from exceptional. Indeed, it rather seems that once a form is lexicalized in one way it is easier for it to become lexicalized in others. This can eventually lead to the complete demotivation of a form, so that it has to be treated as a simplex lexeme – this may be true of *gospel, nest* and *nice* discussed above (§§3.1, 3.3.3). The point at which it becomes more economical to treat a lexeme as simplex in a synchronic grammar will probably have to be decided in each individual case. It is no doubt this tendency for lexemes to become lexicalized in several ways which has led some scholars (e.g. Bauer, 1978d) to suggest that a word is either lexicalized or not lexicalized, without recognizing that it might be lexicalized in only one way.

4
Productivity

> Though many things are possible in morphology, some are more possible than others.
>
> (Aronoff, 1976: 35)

> The linguist who neglects this particular factor [productivity] will be counting "dead souls" as live people.
>
> (Marchand, 1969: 5)

4.1 Preliminaries
4.1.1 The existence of productivity

So far it has been implicit that word-formation is productive, but this position has not been argued for. In fact, it is probably not controversial to claim that it is productive: most authorities in the field make this assumption.[1] Nevertheless, productivity remains one of the most contested areas in the study of word-formation, and several articles and books have been written specifically on this area.[2] This is not because there is dispute over whether particular processes of word-formation are productive; the dispute concerns the extent to which word-formation can be said to be productive in general. It is to this dispute that the major part of this chapter will be devoted.

It is worth reiterating that certain processes of word-formation, at least, are clearly productive. In German, any infinitive can be used as a noun, independent of whether it has previously been used that way or not. In English, -er can be added to any new verbal base to give a new lexeme which means 'the person who carries out the action of the verb'. Also in English the suffix -ful can be added to the name of any container to provide a noun: canful, pocketful,

---

[1] Adams (1973: 12–13); Jespersen (1942: §8.1.5); Lees (1960: xviii); see also the works referred to in Bauer (1978d: §2.1.2).

[2] Bauer (1978c); Burgschmidt (1977); Guilbert (1975); Leitner (1977); Rose (1973); Thompson (1975). Productivity is also discussed in almost any work on word-formation: e.g. Aronoff (1976); Beard (1977); Ljung (1977); Quirk et al. (1972: 976).

skipful, etc. The productivity of word-formation has, over the centuries, been a major factor in providing the huge vocabulary of English, and the fact that the process of creating new lexemes with new forms has not faded out can be seen by consulting a dictionary of neologisms, such as Barnhart *et al.* (1973). New forms also occur regularly in the press (particularly in headlines and advertisements), and letters to the editors of such prestigious journals as *The Times* often show just how aware the reading public is of new forms and new uses of old forms. In this sense the productivity of word-formation can be taken as a fact which any theory of word-formation will be called upon to explain.

4.1.2 *Productivity and creativity*

Following Lyons (1977: 549), a distinction will be drawn here between **productivity** and **creativity**. Productivity is one of the defining features of human language, and is that property of language which allows a native speaker to produce an infinitely large number of sentences, many (or most) of which have never been produced before. It is assumed that productivity is to be accounted for by the rules of a generative grammar. Creativity, on the other hand, is the native speaker's ability to extend the language system in a motivated, but unpredictable (non-rule-governed) way.

To take an example from word-formation, the invention of a form *headhunter* to designate a member of a tribe which keeps and preserves the heads of its human victims is a case of productivity: the form is produced according to fixed rules which, in this particular case, could be syntactically specified. The metaphorical extension of the term *headhunter* to mean 'one who recruits executives for a large corporation', on the other hand, is a case of creativity. In retrospect it may be perfectly clear that the two kinds of headhunters have a lot in common, but, given that *head* does not have the meaning 'executive', there is nothing in the form *headhunter* to show it could be used with this second meaning, and nor could it be predicted that precisely this form would be extended with this kind of meaning.

Both productivity and creativity give rise to large numbers of neologisms, but in what follows it is only rule-governed innovation, that is, productivity, which will be discussed. This is because it is impossible to make any worth-while generalizations about creativity because of its unpredictability, although it would no doubt be possible to provide a taxonomy of types of creativity.

4.1.3   *Synchronic and diachronic productivity*
There is great danger, when discussing word-formation, of confusing productivity from a diachronic point of view with productivity seen purely synchronically (see Gunter, 1972: 1). This is because productivity in word-formation is frequently considered to mean no more than the invention of new lexemes which then become a part of the language system. Statements to the effect that "DONTOPEDOLOGY is a lexeme of English that was first used by H.R.H. the Duke of Edinburgh", or that "HEADHUNTER is a lexeme of English that was formed according to regular principles" are implicitly diachronic. They consider the emergence of a new lexeme in a language, and, implicitly, the difference this makes to the language: it is only after the emergence of DONTOPEDOLOGY that the speaker has the choice between using that and the phrase *to put one's foot in one's mouth.*

On the other hand, there are innumerable nonce formations in any language which never become established. Yet they are formed according to specifiable rules in exactly the same way as those formations which, quite by chance, later become established. The native speaker has the ability at any time to form a new word, just as he has the ability to form a new sentence. That is, there must be rules in the language-system which allow the formation of nonce words in a synchronic grammar. The subsequent fate of nonce words formed by these rules is a matter of diachrony.

This fact is of particular relevance in discussions of back-formation. Back-formation is the formation of a new lexeme by the deletion of a suffix, or supposed suffix, from an apparently complex form by analogy with other instances where the suffixed and non-suffixed forms are both lexemes. Thus *laze* is actually derived from an earlier form *lazy*, possibly by analogy with such pairs as *craze/crazy*. It has frequently been stated that back-formation of this kind is purely a diachronic phenomenon (Pennanen, 1966: 10; Quirk *et al.*, 1972: 977 fn. b; Tietze, 1974: §4.1.1).[3] But this can be seen not to be true. While it is true that now the paradigms:

---

[3] These all seem to refer back to the first edition of Marchand's *Categories and Types* . . ., where it is stated that back-formation "has diachronic relevance

meddle	peddle
meddler	pedlar

sound identical, and it is not possible to tell that the second was a case of back-formation, at the time the form *peddle* was first used as a lexeme, there must have been some synchronic process which allowed the analogy. Whether this can actually be called a 'rule' of back-formation, or whether it is a simple analogy (always supposing that the two can be distinguished: see Bauer, 1979b; below, chapter 9) is irrelevant. Back-formation must be allowed for in a synchronic grammar if it is still a current method of forming lexemes. In current English, back-formation does still thrive, as is witnessed by the existence of back-formations such as to *lech* < *lecher*, to *eutrophicate* < *eutrophication* recorded in Barnhart *et al.* (1973). Thus there must still be a rule which allows this kind of formation in English, even though, should speakers of the future have both *to lech* and *lecher* it will seem to them that the pair *lech*: :*lecher* is entirely parallel to *love*: :*lover*.

4.2 **Syntactic and morphological productivity**[4]
Lyons (1977: 527) states that:

there appears to be no difference of kind, pre-theoretically, between the productivity of what are universally regarded as syntactic processes and the productivity of at least some derivational processes.

On the other hand, Motsch (1977: 195) claims that:

Neologisms obviously do NOT arise following general rules independent of concrete constructions. (my translation, my emphasis, LB)

In this section the evidence for these two conflicting viewpoints will be considered, to see to what extent morphological productivity can be said to be identical or similar to syntactic productivity. If the two are identical, then it may be assumed that word-formation should

---

only". In the second edition, this statement has been modified to read that back-formation "has OFTEN diachronic relevance only" (Marchand, 1969: §1.2.4; my emphasis). Although the modification was not made for the reasons outlined here, it seems to me that it is important to realize that back-formation can have synchronic implications. For more details on back-formation, see below, §7.7.

[4] This section is an expanded version of Bauer (1978c), and owes much to the discussion of that paper at the Fourth Scandinavian Conference of Linguistics.

be dealt with by (a part of) the syntactic component. If the two do not share anything in common, then it will be reasonable to assume that word-formation has nothing to do with syntax.

At least three statements about productivity are commonly found in transformational literature as applied to sentences:

1.   speakers of a language have the ability to produce and understand new sentences of that language (Chomsky, 1966a: 3–31);

2.   there is no such thing as the longest sentence of a natural language (Chomsky, 1957: 23; Lyons, 1968: 221);

3.   the statistical probability that any given utterance has been heard/produced previously by the speaker-listener approaches zero (Chomsky, 1957: 16–17; 1966a: 12 fn. 20)

(Statement 3 is in effect a much stronger version of 1, but it will be useful to keep the two separate here.) The applicability of each of these three statements to word-formation will be discussed below.

4.2.1 *Production of new forms*

This has already been discussed above (§4.1.1), and requires very little further comment. A glance at any etymological dictionary should be enough to convince anyone of the diachronic fact of the production of new forms, and science-fiction stories often provide good sources of contemporary material (see, for example, Brian Aldiss, *Hothouse*, London: Faber & Faber, 1962). When word-formation is said to be productive, it frequently means no more than that native speakers can produce and understand new words (see, for example, Pennanen, 1972: 292). On this criterion, productivity in sentence formation and productivity in word-formation are identical.

4.2.2 *Existence of a longest form*

In discussing whether there is such a thing as the longest word in a language, it will be useful to consider compounding and derivation separately.

4.2.2.1 Compounding

In the Germanic languages, at least, there is no such thing as the longest compound. This has been pointed out by, for example, Lees (1960: 117), Teleman (1970: 18) and illustrated with an infinitely extendable compound in Danish by Bauer (1978c: appendix). Indeed, quite serious formations sometimes take on dimensions which might only be expected in jocular compounds. Consider, for instance, the German *Über·see·reich·weiten·fern·seh·richt·funk·verbindung* 'over sea reach distance [i.e. range] distant see [i.e. TV] direction radio connection' cited by Fleischer (1975: 82).

Of course, as is the case with sentence formation, limitations on short-term memory may affect the length of compounds in actual use, but this does not affect the theoretical grammaticality of these formations. Thus:

> His great-great-great-great-great-great-great-great-great-great-great-great-great-great-great-great-grandfather was killed in a Viking raid on Holy Island

and

> This is the malt that the rat that the cat that the dog that the cow tossed worried caught ate

might both be so complicated that pencil and paper would be required to work out exactly what they mean, but they have equivalent status with respect to grammaticality (see Chomsky, 1965: 11ff).

4.2.2.2 Derivation

In the case of derivation the facts are far less clear-cut. One of the main pieces of evidence here is recursiveness, and the evidence is not totally unambiguous. As far as prefixation in English is concerned, there are some cases where it is clearly recursive. Forms such as *re-remake, meta-meta-theory* and *semi-hemidemisemiquaver* can be found, even if they are rarely listed in dictionaries. Here it seems perfectly correct to say that there is no theoretically defined limit to prefixation, since there is no non-*ad hoc* way of allowing *meta-meta-theory*, for example, as grammatical, but excluding, say, *meta-meta-meta-theory*. There are, however, practical limits determined by such pragmatic factors as the amount of abstraction or degree of musical division a speaker is prepared to discuss: that is, *hemidemisemihemidemisemiquaver*

67

must be assumed to be grammatical, even though no musician is likely to want to use one.

On the other hand, not all prefixation is recursive in this way. Contrast, for example, the acceptability (and, by implication, the grammaticality, though see Aitchison & Bailey, 1979, for some discussion) of the following sentence pairs:

(1a)   This is not likely
(b)   This is unlikely
(2a)   This is not unlikely
(b)   *This is ununlikely

Negative prefixation does not appear to be recursive at all in English, the only possible examples being forms like *undisfigured*, and even these are rare.

Furthermore, it is not even clear that recursive prefixation is possible in all cases with those prefixes where it is attested. While *re-remake* is perfectly acceptable, and *re-remarry* seems acceptable to me, I find *re-retype* slightly less acceptable, *re-repaint* (a house) odd, and *re-reclimb* (a mountain) distinctly unusual. Note, moreover, that this is not a pragmatic limitation on the number of times that a house can be painted or a mountain climbed, such as would make *re-redigest* unacceptable. Consider also *re-reshoot, re-rebury, re-reappear, re-reborn*. As is pointed out by Stein (1977: 225), constructions of this type usually yield to forms with syntactic paraphrases, in this case *re-bury again*, and so on.

It is also noteworthy, finally, that English appears to show great reluctance in combining prefixes at all. While *pseudo-formalization, semi-formalization* and *crypto-formalization* might all be coined in appropriate circumstances, it seems totally unlikely that a form *pseudo-semi-crypto-formalization* would be coined, although it would be comprehensible if it were found. While examples like *re-undo* are found (Stein, 1977: 225), which shows that the stringing of prefixes is not ungrammatical in English, it does not seem to be a very productive method of word-formation: an attested, if jocular, example like *psychosociopseudohistorian*[5] sounds rather exaggerated. It is interesting to note in this context that Ljung (1970: 13) comments that the maximum number of

[5] C. Harrison. 1975. *How to be a Pom*. Palmerston North: Dunmore Press, p. 26.

prefixes he found strung together in English, even in quite a large corpus, was three.

As far as prefixation is concerned, then, the evidence seems to be contradictory. On the one hand, examples like *re-remake* suggest that the productivity of words is identical to the productivity of sentences, but on the other, examples like **ununlikely* suggest that there is a marked difference.

Where suffixation is concerned the picture is also confused, but for different reasons. It is quite easy to illustrate that the rules for the addition of suffixes must be formulated in such a way as to allow for recursiveness. Consider, for example, the following sets of data:

A. *-ation* (1) occurs before *-al*   (2) *inspir·ation·al, revel·ation·al*
   -al (2)   ,,   ,, *-ize*   (3) *industri·al·ize, palat·al·ize*
   -ize (3)   ,,   ,, *-ation* (1) *idol·iz·ation, organ·iz·ation*

B. *-ic* (1)   ,,   ,, *-al*   (2) *con·ic·al, poet·ic·al*
   -al (2)   ,,   ,, *-ist* (3) *education·al·ist, herb·al·ist*
   -ist (3)   ,,   ,, *-ic*   (1) *atom·ist·ic, monarch·ist·ic*

Both of these sets of data are generable according to rules of the following general form:

$$\text{base } x + \text{suffix } 1 \rightarrow \text{base } y$$
$$\text{base } y + \text{suffix } 2 \rightarrow \text{base } z$$
$$\text{base } z + \text{suffix } 3 \rightarrow \text{base } x$$

and these rules are recursive by virtue of the fact that base x appears both to the left and the right of the arrows as an eventual rewrite of itself. What is more, the circuit involved here is actually exploited by the language, so that the following words can be found in dictionaries:

$1 - 2 - 3$ (*denominationalize*); (*classicalist*)
$2 - 3 - 1$ *formalization*;   *nationalistic*
$3 - 1 - 2$ *civilizational*;   *egoistical*

(where those in parentheses may not be genuine examples, since the *-ation/-ic* could be analysed as part of the root). The problem is whether there is a restriction on these rules such that their inherent recursiveness may not be used to allow the same suffix to recur in a single word. It is in fact extremely difficult to find examples of the recursive use of the same suffix listed in dictionaries. The best I can offer are *rationalistical, syndicalistic* (where the first *-al/-ic* could be analysed as part of the root) *institutionalization* and *professionalization.*[6] However, it was noted in relation to recursive prefixation that words containing the same prefix twice were precisely the kinds of words which did not appear to be frequently listed in dictionaries, despite their acceptability, and the same may be true of suffixation. So given a verb *comput·er·ize* or *contain·er·ize*, it seems to me to be perfectly acceptable to add a further *-er* to give *computerizer, containerizer*, and so to exploit the recursiveness of suffixation, even though these words are not listed in dictionaries.

As with prefixation, however, it is clear that such recursive suffixation is not possible across the board. The kind of reduplication of the same affix that was found with prefixes (*meta-meta-theory*) is not possible with suffixes (**containerizeize*), and there are many suffixes which in practice do not appear to occur in long strings of suffixes. In the study already mentioned, Ljung (1970: 13) notes that in his corpus the largest number of suffixes he attested strung together was four.

This is not all there is to be said on the subject of suffixation in this context, however. For even if it is taken that the number of suffixes and the combinations of types of suffix are limited, there is evidence that, at least in some languages, the base from which a derivative is formed may not be limited in length. For example, in Finnish it is apparently possible to form an agentive nominal on the basis of almost any sentence, so that the equivalent of *on one foot stander* is derived from the sentence equivalent to *he is standing on one foot, in wet snow roller* from *she is rolling in wet snow*, and so on (Bauer, 1978c: 334; Hakulinen, 1978: 328). Thus in Finnish the number of possible bases for suffixation, and the maximum length of a base for suffixation, must be equivalent to the number of possible sentences and the maximum length of sentences. It must thus be theoretically impossible to create a longest derivative in Finnish. A similar conclusion is called for by such English examples as "I feel particularly *sit-around-and-do-nothing-ish* today" and

---

[6] There is dispute in the literature as to whether *-ation* should be treated as a single suffix, with an allomorph *-ion*, or as a sequence of two suffixes *-at·ion*. This dispute, while interesting in its own right, does not affect the argument here, since *-ion* appears recursively in these two examples under either interpretation. A clearer example is *sensationalization* given by Miller (1978: 114), but I have not been able to find this listed in a dictionary.

"This is definitely a blower-upper, not a *leave-it-where-it-is-er*".[7] Another type of example from the Germanic languages that calls for the same conclusion is the type where a derivational affix is added to a compound base, as in *brain-drain·er, crashworthi·ness, pop art·ist* and *tomboy·ish*. In these established examples it so happens that the compounds are composed of only two elements, but it has been shown that compounds are theoretically limitless (see above, §4.2.2.1) so that it would appear that such examples also have theoretically limitless bases, and correspondingly that there is no longest possible derivative.

The general conclusion would seem to be that, while there are pragmatic restrictions on the length of words, and while some derivational procedures are more severely limited than others (either pragmatically or in a theoretically motivated way), derivatives on the whole cannot be said to be limited in length, and that parallel to the statement that there is no theoretically possible longest sentence of a language, it must also be said that there is no theoretically possible longest derivative, at least in the languages under discussion.

4.2.3 *Probability of occurrence*

The greatest difference between the productivity of sentences and the productivity of complex lexemes shows up when the probability of occurrence of a specified item is considered. As far as sentences are concerned, it can be taken that the probability of occurrence of a given item is effectively zero (Chomsky, 1957: 16–17; 1966b: 34–6). Many practical applications of linguistics depend on the same not being true of lexemes. For example, frequency dictionaries depend on lexemes occurring different numbers of times in a corpus: that is, lexemes differ in their probability of occurrence. There is a theory of sound-change which predicts that sound-changes will take place first in frequent lexemes (see e.g. Hooper, 1976b): this assumes that lexemes have different probabilities of occurrence, and probabilities of occurrence that are not equal to zero. There are no frequency dictionaries of sentences, or theories about sound changes in frequent sentences. Dictionaries list the lexemes of a language (non-exhaustively, it is true), but any

---

[7] Both attested, the former in conversation, the latter in a recent repeat broadcast of an old *Hancock's Half Hour* radio programme.

attempt to list the sentences of a language would just be ridiculous. In foreign language teaching, Cloze tests have been developed where every (say) tenth word in a text is deleted and the student has to reconstitute the original text; no tests are given where every tenth sentence is deleted, since the reconstitution of the original sentences is not expected to be feasible.

The problem comes in interpreting this difference in probability of occurrence in theoretical terms. Beard (1977: §3.2) points out that the difference should not be surprising. Given a language with forty phonemes, he says, there will be more than forty possible arrangements of those phonemes, and so more than forty possible lexemes. This is true even after all the phonotactic restrictions on the stringing together of phonemes are taken into account. Similarly, he says, if there is a language with n lexemes, there will be more than n possible arrangements of those lexemes into sentences, even when the syntactic (or semantic) restrictions on the stringing together of lexemes have been taken into account. Thus it is inevitable that sentence formation should be more productive than word-formation, but Beard suggests that the difference is a difference in quantity only: the numbers involved are different, but the general type of productivity remains the same.

Some idea of the vast difference in productivity can be gained by trying to put figures to the number of possible arrangements of phonemes and lexemes in a language. In general this can be thought of in terms of choices and places. Consider first the very simple system in which there are two items a and b. Suppose further that all the allowable constructions containing these items are exactly two items long. This means that there are two positions in each construction. In the first position either a or b can be chosen, and in the second position, there is also the same choice between a and b. Thus *aa, ab, ba, bb* are the acceptable constructions. In general there are (number of choices in position 1) × (number of choices in position 2) × . . . × (number of choices in position n) acceptable constructions. Thus in the example above the number of acceptable constructions is $2 \times 2 = 4$. The number of acceptable constructions can be increased either by increasing the number of items, which increases the number of choices, or by increasing the number of positions in which there is a choice. If there is a choice of three items in each of two positions, then the total number of acceptable constructions is $3 \times 3 = 9$; if there are three positions in which there is a choice between two items, then the number of acceptable constructions is $2 \times 2 \times 2 = 8$. If constructions with three choices in each position can be either three or two positions long, the total number of acceptable constructions is $3 \times 3 \times 3$ ($=27$) $+ 3 \times 3$ ($=9$), i.e. 36.

If this type of operation is extended to the phonemes of a language like English, then an approximate figure for the number of arrangements of phonemes (i.e. number of lexemes) can be worked out. It must be approximate, because it is not possible to be precise about the number of choices available in each position, nor about the number of positions. However, assumptions can be made which will produce a rough approximation. For instance, it can be assumed, for ease of working out, that there are forty phonemes in the language, half of which are consonants and half of which are vowels. If it is taken that in the first position there are forty choices and that there are twenty choices in every subsequent position this will make some allowance for the fact that there are restrictions on sequences of phonemes and will provide a rough estimate. The length of the unit is difficult to decide on, but in most cases it may be said that words are not longer than twenty phonemes (although examples have been cited in this book of words longer than that). If there are twenty positions with forty choices in the first position and twenty in the other nineteen, then the total number of acceptable constructions is $40 \times 20 \times 20 \times 20 \times 20 \times 20 \times 20 \times 20 \times 20 \times 20 \times 20 \times 20 \times 20 \times 20 \times 20 \times 20 \times 20 \times 20 \times 20 \times 20 = 2097152 \times 10^{20}$. This figure does not allow for words of 19, 18 . . . 1 phonemes in length.

Enormous as this number is, it fades into insignificance beside the number of possible combinations of lexemes. Even quite modest dictionaries of English, which list only established lexemes, have word-lists round about the 50,000 mark (e.g. Hornby, 1974). If it is assumed that the choice in any position is limited to one-fifth of these and that sentences are limited to fifty lexemes in length (which is certainly far from true), then the number of possible sentences comes out as 1×10^{200}, and this number is probably extremely conservative, given how long some sentences can be and the fact, established earlier, that a language like English has a potentially infinite vocabulary (up to the beginning of this parenthesis there were seventy-four words in this sentence, which shows how conservative the fifty word limit is). Again, this figure does not take account of sentences that are 49, 48, . . . 1 lexemes long.

Thus it seems fair to conclude, as Beard does, that the difference in probability of occurrence of lexemes and sentences can probably be attributed entirely to this difference in the number of possible arrangements of the elements. In practical terms, lexemes recur frequently enough to be given some kind of positive figure for their probability of occurrence because, even though the number of possible arrangements of phonemes (i.e. number of lexemes) is enormous, the number in regular usage is finite and, comparatively speaking, fairly restricted. Sentences, on the other hand, are members of a set which is so large that even for practical purposes it is meaningless to talk in terms of probability of occurrence for them, although it would, of course, be possible (if unrewarding) to compute a positive probability of occurrence for sentences over any finite corpus.

One result of the difference in productivity between lexemes and sentences is that it allows what Meys (1975) calls "item-familiarity" with lexemes, but rarely with sentences. That is, the speaker–listener feels that he knows individual complex words in a way that he does not feel that he knows individual sentences. This difference is frequently attributed to a difference in type of productivity between lexemes and sentences. It has been argued here that such a conclusion is ill-founded.

4.2.4 *Syntactic vs. morphological productivity*

To summarize, it can be said that syntactic and morphological productivity seem to have more in common than they have to distinguish them. In fact, if one accepts the conclusion that the difference between the productivity of sentence formation and word-formation is a quantitative but not a qualitative one, then the two are so similar that it becomes virtually obligatory for the analyst to attempt to deal with sentence formation and word-formation in the same component of the grammar. There may, however, be other factors in the way of this. One that is often mentioned is the problem posed by semi-productivity in derivation. This will be considered at greater length in §4.4.

4.3   Remarks on "Remarks . . . "[8]

4.3.1   *A problem for studies of productivity*

It is no longer possible to claim that word-formation is a productive process without taking into account Chomsky's very influential article, "Remarks on nominalization" (Chomsky, 1970), where the contrary claim is made. Chomsky argues that nominalizations cannot be treated transformationally (i.e. cannot be treated as being generated productively by fixed rules) because they are too irregular. In what follows I shall review Chomsky's arguments against a transformational approach to nominalization, and consider their force.

Chomsky terms his position the "lexicalist" position, and contrasts this with the "transformationalist" position taken by others, notably Lakoff (1970a). The lexicalist position, as outlined by Chomsky, is that all nominalizations (and, by implication, all compounds and derivatives) are listed independently in the lexicon, i.e. they are treated as if they were fully lexicalized or simplex lexemes. This position is also taken by, for example, Jackendoff in subsequent publications. The transformationalist position, as characterized by Chomsky, represents the other extreme, namely that no nominalizations (and by implication, no compounds or derivatives) are listed in the lexicon, but all are derived by the transformational syntactic component of the grammar.

Although Chomsky does mention the possibility of a compromise position between these two extremes, almost all the discussion in Chomsky's article is formulated in terms of proving the extreme transformationalist position to be incorrect. It is implicit that once this view is rejected an espousal of the lexicalist position will automatically follow. While this all-or-nothing kind of approach may have been justified in terms of the polemical argumentation between the opposing camps of linguists in the late 1960s, it is the source of much of the criticism which can be levelled at the article. It will be argued below that, in fact, a compromise position gives a more accurate picture of the true state of affairs in word-formation.

Chomsky has three main arguments against a transformationalist approach to nominalization. Firstly, nominalization is not "productive" (this term is used rather idiosyncratically by Chomsky);

---

[8] This section is a revised version of material which first appeared as Bauer (1978e).

secondly, derived nominals have the internal structure of noun phrases, not of derived sentences; and finally, derived nominals are idiosyncratically related in terms of both morphology and semantics to their corresponding verbs. I shall consider these points in turn.

4.3.2   *"Productivity" in Chomsky (1970)*

By "productivity", Chomsky does not mean that there is no derived nominal corresponding to some verbs, but that the derived nominal cannot always replace the verb (or adjective) to which it corresponds in a given sentence. For example, he cites (1970: 188–9):

(3a)   John is certain to win the prize
(b)   John amused the children with his stories
(4a)   *John's certainty to win the prize
(b)   *John's amusement of the children with his stories

though he notes:

(5a)   John is certain that Bill will win the prize
(b)   John was amused at the children's antics
(6a)   John's certainty that Bill will win the prize
(b)   John's amusement at the children's antics

Chomsky claims (1970: 191) that the deep-structure relationships between the verb and its arguments are different in the cases (3)–(4) and (5)–(6). In (3a) *It* is certain, whereas in (5a) *John* is certain; in (3b) *the children* were amused, in (5b) *John* was amused, and he suggests that the difficulty of expressing this in transformational terms should lead to the abandoning of the transformationalist hypothesis.

However, further consideration of the examples quoted reveals the following facts. *Certainty* is lexicalized, representing a loan from Old French, not a case of productive word-formation (see Marchand, 1969: §4.55.7). It would thus not really be surprising if its sense were as restricted as its form. But even if this were not the case, 'the state of being certain' could only be predicated of an animate being, and not of a pro-form *it*. *Amusement* is also lexicalized: *-ment* no longer seems to be productive (see above, §3.3.2.3). The *OEDS* lists no new words in *-ment* since the turn of the century either under A (1884–1964) or under N (1884–1976) (representing the extremes of the supplement at the time of writing). Further, at the time when this suffix was productive (especially the nineteenth century) the meaning 'state of being Ved' was a particularly common one associated with it (Marchand, 1969: §4.65.5). Semantically there is another generalization which Chomsky misses here. It seems to be the case that a noun in the genitive modifying a derived nominal (including here cases of conversion) from a verb (or adjective) expressing emotion, must show the experiencer of the emotion: compare, for example:

(7a)   John shocked the Victorians by his immorality
(b)   *John's shock of the Victorians by his immorality
(8a)   John was shocked at the Victorians' immorality
(b)   John's shock at the Victorians' immorality

4.3.3 *Internal structure*

There is also a syntactic problem involved in generating derived nominals in a sentence, and attempting to equate the acceptability of the sentence with the acceptability of the nominal. Chomsky (1970: fn. 11), referring to Lakoff, points out that *John's beliefs* cannot be derived from *What John believes* because of the existence of such sentences as *John's beliefs are not mutually consistent*, and nor can it be derived from *The things that John believes* because of the existence of sentences like *I respect John's beliefs, John's beliefs are intense*. Chomsky sees in this an argument against the transformationalist hypothesis. But given the notion of the transformational cycle, this is not necessarily so, since the cycle, applying to the lowest S first, will provide the derived nominal by the time the matrix sentence comes under consideration, if a tree like (9) is presupposed.

(9)

```
                NP
        _____|_____
       /        |        \
     Det        N        Pl
                |
                S
               /_\
         . . . believe . . .
```

The S that forms the nominalization may not need to contain any further information than that it is to be nominalized (possibly by a marker in the same category as sentence-type markers such as Q and Imp, as suggested by Tietze, 1974) and that it contains the verb *believe*.[9] This would also solve two problems raised by Chomsky later in his article.

Firstly, Chomsky claims (1970: 193) that the acceptability of (10), which contains a gerund, as opposed to the non-acceptability of (11), which contains a nominalization, supports the lexicalist hypothesis:

(10)   His criticizing the book before he read it
(11)   *His criticism of the book before he read it

This is because (a) he assumes that the gerund is derived from an underlying verb (i.e. (10) is derived from the same string as would underlie *He criticized the book before he read it*) while the nominalization is not, and (b) *before he read it* is a VP modifier, and can thus modify a verb as in (10), but cannot modify an NP, as in (11). But in a derivation which included a tree like (9), it would still be impossible for *before he read it* to modify *criticism*, even though *criticism* would be derived transformationally. This is because the N node in (9) has no sister which can be an adverbial.

Chomsky's second problem concerns phrases such as *sudden refusal, obvious sincerity*. These could be derived from relative clauses in structures like (9), but with an extra embedded S as a sister of N (see Chomsky, 1965: 107, vii). Chomsky (1970: 195) suggests that these phrases, in a transformationalist account, must be derived from strings underlying sentences containing adverbials (*refused suddenly, was obviously sincere*), but this is not necessarily true, and is thus not necessarily a problem for a transformationalist account.

Thus Chomsky's objection that derived nominals (unlike gerunds, which have the structure of verbs in full sentences) have the structure of NPs cannot be taken as an argument against a transformationalist position. Instead, different transformational sources may account for the two kinds of nominal: gerunds can be derived from sentences, as Chomsky suggests, while nominalizations can be derived from configurations like (9).

---

[9] Exactly what the embedded S contains besides the verb will be discussed in chapter 6. The point is not crucial at this stage, though the structure suggested here is controversial.

4.3.4 *Idiosyncrasy*

The relationship between the derived nominal and the corresponding verb is often idiosyncratic. This is true both in morphological terms (Chomsky, 1970: 190) and in semantic terms (ibid.: 189).

4.3.4.1 Morphological idiosyncrasy

To consider the morphological point first, it is clear that part of the difficulty is that Chomsky is dealing with the full range of English derivational suffixes, and not just with the productive ones. He quotes (1970: 189), among other examples, *laughter*, which seems to be the only word in English with a *-ter* nominalizing suffix (with the possible exception of *slaughter*), as well as *marriage* where the suffix does not seem to be productive (see Marchand, 1969: §4.4), and *belief*, which fits into the lexicalized *sheath/ sheathe, advice/advise* series. If only suffixes which are productive were considered, it seems likely that the situation would be much simplified, though I do not know of a study that has considered the problem from this point of view. A look at productive nominalizations in Danish supports this point of view. There are in Danish, as in English, several analysable nominalization suffixes, yet in 1968–9, new nominalizations in Danish used only two endings *-ning* and *-(er)ing* (Dansk Sprognævn, 1972) and the distribution of these was entirely predictable on phonological grounds, so that nominalizations from that period were completely regular in Danish.

4.3.4.2 Semantic idiosyncrasy

The semantic idiosyncrasy can be partially explained in the same terms. *Trial*, which Chomsky (1970: 189) also lists, is one case where the established meanings of the nominalization do not correspond to all the established meanings of the verb, and the main meaning of the nominalization is specialized to one, not very common, meaning of the verb. As for examples like *doubt* and *residence* 'place where one resides', they are French loans, and thus not necessarily subject to productive rules.

But there is a further point to be considered here. Many – if not most – derived nominals listed in dictionaries are ambiguous, and possibly several ways ambiguous. For example, *qualification* can mean:

(i)   a quality suiting one for office
(ii)   a required condition for holding office
(iii)   the act of qualifying
(iv)   the state of being qualified
(v)   modification, limitation or restriction
(vi)   an instance of (v)

(Definitions modified from Hanks, 1971.) And *residence* is also six ways ambiguous.

Two possibilities may be considered here, and the two are not necessarily mutually exclusive. The first is that only some of the meanings are productive (e.g. (iii) and (iv) above) and that a derived nominal is lexicalized in other meanings but productive in this limited number of meanings. The second possibility is that the semantic relationship of the derived nominal to its corresponding verb is not in fact fully specified. Instead only the grammatical relationship of verb-nominalization is specified, and the semantic relationship is pragmatically determined. There is some evidence that this must be the case for nominal compounds (see Bauer, 1978d: §§3.4, 3.5) and it would not be very surprising if the same mechanism were used in other parts of word-formation. This would explain the ambiguity of words such as Danish *container·is·er·ing*, which in isolation can be understood in two ways ('the containerization of goods' vs. 'the containerization of transport') but which are uniquely interpretable in context. This point will be considered again in §6.7. Either of these proposals would have the effect of considerably reducing the amount of apparent semantic irregularity Chomsky notes in nominalizations.

4.3.5   *Complements*

There is one further point which Chomsky raises, and that is the question of the form of the complement of the verb or nominalization. He says (1970: 190):

The fact that *refuse* takes a noun phrase complement or a reduced sentential complement and *destroy* only a noun phrase complement, either as a noun or as a verb, is expressed by the feature structure of the 'neutral' lexical entry . . .

(where "'neutral' lexical entry" means a lexical entry unspecified for whether a noun or a verb will be the surface realization of the morpheme: this is how Chomsky relates a nominalization to its verb in his grammar). While this is a perfectly possible solution, the problem can be solved just as neatly using a transformationalist approach. There is a generalization here that in productive series, if a verb takes a specific preposition, its derived nominal will take the same preposition, and if the verb takes a direct object, then *of* will be inserted between the nominalization and the underlying object. Although the occurrence of this *of* could be stated by some kind of redundancy rule in Chomsky's framework, a transformational analysis would seem to be just as natural. The lexicalized cases where this does not work, for example *hope* (contrast *We hope for a miracle* and *?our hope for a miracle*), *desire* (contrast *We desire peace* with *our desire for peace* and **our desire of peace*, especially since *we are desirous of peace* is acceptable) provide as big a problem for Chomsky as they do for a transformationalist analysis which takes no account of lexicalization, as it was discussed in chapter 3.

4.3.6 *Conclusion*

It would seem that if an all-or-nothing approach to the question of the transformationalist vs. the lexicalist hypotheses is resisted, and the concept of lexicalization is introduced, then Chomsky's "fairly substantial" evidence in favour of the lexicalist hypothesis ceases to be as substantial as it first appears, and that Chomsky's arguments do not rule out the possibility of a generative approach to word-formation. But even if Chomsky's conclusions were accepted in full, a generative approach to word-formation would not necessarily be excluded. This is because Chomsky deals entirely with nominalizations, and points which are true of them are not necessarily true of all types of word-formation. Adjective formation in *-less* and *-able*, noun formation in *-er* and *-ness* seem to me to be processes which are not subject to any of the objections that Chomsky makes. While there are scholars who disagree (e.g. Matthews, 1979: 27–31, on the subject of *-ness*), it seems to me that they do so because they do not distinguish between possible forms and established forms in word-formation. The forms which become established are never more than a small proportion of the possible forms (see e.g. Williams, 1965, on some attested formations in *-ness* to contrast with Matthews's position). This forms the topic of the next section.

4.4 Semi-productivity

There was a very brief discussion earlier (§2.10) of semi-productivity, which, it was stated, is usually taken as being typical of derivation as opposed to inflection. Semi-productivity can be illustrated with the following example from Marchand (1969: §4.55). Marchand notes that both *-ness* and *-ity* can be added to bases in *-able* to provide nominalizations. It seems, however, that it is not the case that either affix can be added freely to any base, since speakers show marked preferences for one or the other in particular cases. On the basis of the entries in the *OED*, Marchand gives the following instances of acceptable and unacceptable formations:

serviceableness	*serviceability
*certainness	certainty
suitableness	suitability

Thus it seems that the two suffixes are not freely added to any base in *-able*, are therefore not completely productive, but only semi-productive. The phenomenon of semi-productivity has led some scholars (e.g. Adams, 1973: 6; Leitner, 1977: 152; Stein, 1977; and many others) to argue that derivation should not be seen as a productive process in the same way as sentence formation at all. It was argued above that this conclusion is not really tenable.

The opposing view is held by such scholars as Zimmer (1964: 18). He claims that if the rules of word-formation are allowed to apply in a completely free manner many of the forms produced will be "grammatical but non-occurring" rather than ungrammatical. The reasons for their non-occurrence may be totally irrelevant to the language system as such (others who take this point of view include Bauer, 1978c; Lees, 1960; Rose, 1973). In support of this view, it can be pointed out that despite Marchand's asterisk assignment reproduced above, *certainness* and *serviceability* are both listed in Geddie (1968), and must thus be considered both grammatical and acceptable.

Moreover, it should be noted that sentences could also be said to be "grammatical but non-occurring" in the same kind of way. Just as there is no lexeme MAGPIE-BRAKE because there is nothing in the real world that is denoted by such a lexeme, and no lexeme METAPHORICALIST because it so happens that there is no group of people for this lexeme to denote, so the sentence:

> Peter wrote the Lord High Executioner a letter in invisible ink on the back of a live bullock

is probably non-occurrent because of the unlikelihood of the event which it describes taking place. Such factors are not generally considered relevant in the discussion of the productivity of sentence formation, and there does not seem to be any cogent reason for believing that they are any more relevant in discussions of word-formation. I therefore suggest that the phenomenon of semi-productivity should not be assumed to make any difference in principle between the productivity of sentence formation and that of word-formation.

There is one further point which deserves mention in support of this stance. It is that there are a number of limitations on the productivity of word-formation which are, at present, poorly defined and ill-understood. Some of these limitations will be discussed in the next section. Some of them will turn out to be of a grammatical nature. These regular restrictions on word-formation are equivalent to restrictions imposed by such things as agreement in sentences. Since one does not usually talk of semi-productivity in sentences for such grammatical reasons, neither should one speak of semi-productivity in word-formation.

Bowers (1969: 522) points out that it is only if one speaks of "grammatical but non-occurring" forms that one can be said to be discussing competence and not performance, which is the aim of a generative theory of word-formation. Motsch (1977: 191) complains that all too often restrictions on productivity are written off by scholars of word-formation in this way; but given a grammatical framework in which the distinction between competence and performance is consistently and crucially drawn, this must be a permissible strategy and, indeed, a necessary consequence – at least as far as the "grammatical but non-occurring" forms are concerned. I would, however, agree with Motsch in as much as it is meaningless to talk of performance factors here unless the competence factors are also understood: there is a real danger that 'performance' will become a rag-bag category, used to explain all variation that is not neatly captured by the theory of a particular analyst.

It should be noted that the discussion above has been in terms of grammaticality rather than in terms of acceptability. This is a corollary of talking in terms of competence rather than performance. Dik (1967: 372) claims that speaking of grammaticality in such cases is inevitably circular, since the intuitions of the speaker (= the analyst) form part of the input to the writing of the grammar which, in the final analysis, is supposed to represent the intuitions of the speaker (= the analyst). However, since the intuitions of the analyst can be left to one side and the productive patterns that are observed (or tested, see Basbøll, 1975a: 48; Whitaker & Whitaker, 1976: 267–8) can provide the sole data on the basis of which the grammar generates new grammatical forms, the circularity which Dik sees here can be short-circuited. It thus seems to me justifiable to distinguish between grammaticality and acceptability in discussions of word-formation.

Against a background of these views, it makes no sense to discuss the productivity of individual morphological processes without first having considered at least some of the limitations on word-formation. This will be done in the next section.

4.5 Some restrictions on productivity

For ease of exposition, a distinction will be drawn here between those restrictions on productivity (or on word-formation as a whole) which are purely syntactic, and those which are not syntactic. At this stage in the proceedings, the distinction may seem purely arbitrary and rather artificial, but I believe that it is a useful distinction for the discussion. The syntactic restrictions will be dealt with at some length in chapter 6. In this section only non-syntactic restrictions will be handled. A syntactic restriction can be provisionally defined as one affecting the rules, configurations and/or features which lead to the generation of a string made up of a base and an affix or (in the case of conversion) process marker, or which, in the case of compounding, lead to a string made up of two (or more) stems, and marked as forming a compound.

4.5.1 *Pragmatics*

In recent years, a number of researchers have come independently to the conclusion that pragmatic factors must be appealed to if a satisfactory account of word-formation is to be given (e.g. Bauer, 1978d: §§3.4, 3.5; 1979a; Clark & Clark, 1979; Downing, 1977; Geckeler, 1977: 80; Karius, 1976; 1977; Leitner, 1977: 142–3; Lipka, 1977: 159; Ljung, 1970: 73; 1977: 170; Rose, 1973: 546; Thompson, 1975; Warren, 1978: 7). **Pragmatics** can here be defined in a wide sense as the influence of knowledge and beliefs about the structure of the real world, in contrast to knowledge about the language-system. Some of the ways in which word-formation is influenced and limited by pragmatic factors are discussed below. For more details, see the works referred to above.

4.5.1.1 Requirement of existence

As a general rule, a word will not be formed to denote an item/action/quality which does not exist. Lipka (1977: 161) deals with this under the heading of **hypostatization** ("Hyposta-sierung"). Of course, "existence" has to be interpreted in a very wide sense here, to allow for fictional and mythological "existence" as well as observable existence in the world as the speaker knows it, but the general point is clear. Thus it was mentioned above (§4.4) that there is no word *magpie-brake* because there is nothing in the real world which can be thus described. But this is a fact about the real world, and not a fact about language. If a fairy story were written in which flying pumpkins were brought to a standstill by having magpies to pull against them, then the word *magpie-brake* would become perfectly acceptable. The reader can no doubt think of further contexts in which this would be an acceptable word. And if a group of people made a dogma of seeing everything as an allegory on something else, they could well be denoted by the term *metaphoricalist* (note the established word, *literalist*). This is important, because the lack of existence[10] of a given form (or interpretation of a form) is often used as an argument against the

---

[10] Although the discussion is usually carried out in these terms, it is very dangerous to say that a particular compound or derivative "does not exist": by consulting dictionaries some kind of guess can be made about whether a word is established or not, but not about whether it exists or not. All that can be said is that the writer has not attested a particular formation.

productivity of word-formation. Thus, for example, Jackendoff (1975: 655) argues that

> Part of a speaker's knowledge of the English lexicon is the way in which the meanings of compounds are related to the meanings of their constituents: thus we would say that somebody did not know English if he (seriously) used *garbage man* to mean 'a man made out of garbage', by analogy with *snowman*.

But this does not mean that *garbage man* with that meaning should be blocked by the grammar. Consider, for example, the following plausible context:

> In the back street where I grew up, everybody was poor. We were so poor that we never went on holiday. Our only toys were the garbage cans. We never built sandcastles, only garbage men.

The institutionalized meaning of *garbage man* might make this odd, but it is not ungrammatical. It simply depends on there being some item in the speaker's (vicarious) experience which can sensibly be denoted by the word. The fact that *lickability* is not listed in Lehnert (1971) – and thus not in the *OED* or *Webster's* – does not mean that suffixation of *-ability* is non-productive, but merely that people have not needed to refer constantly to the lickability of lollipops, candy-floss or stamps.

4.5.1.2 Nameability requirement

Not only must a lexeme denote something which the speaker feels to be real, it must denote something which is nameable. Thus Rose (1973: 516), for example, points out that "we would not expect to find regularly derived denominal verbs in any language with the meaning 'grasp NOUN in the left hand and shake vigorously while standing on the right foot in a $2\frac{1}{2}$ gallon galvanized pail of corn-meal-mush'." Rose sees this as being because the relationships which can be expressed derivationally are simple and general. He also implies that they are possibly universal. If this is true, it is a very significant fact about word-formation, because it is well-known that different languages mark different aspects of reality in their structure (for example, Hopi can mark repetitive or vibratory action much more easily than English can: see Whorf, 1936) and one might expect that such differences would also appear in the derivational systems of languages. Independent of whether the relationships which can be expressed in derivation are universal, it is clear that new derivational markings can be introduced in a language to express new meanings if the need is present. Consider, for example, the modern use of the suffix *-nik* in English to denote 'a person who rejects standard social values' (see Barnhart *et al.*, 1973: 317). To this extent at least, whether or not a thing is nameable must be considered a pragmatic feature.

On the other hand, nameability in complex words must also be subject to more general rules governing the permissibility of lexical items, such as those mentioned by Chomsky (1965: 29): objects described by nouns must meet "a condition of spatiotemporal contiguity", and so on. Chomsky postulates that such restrictions are universal, and they must apply as filters on complex as well as simplex lexemes.

4.5.2 *Blocking*

Blocking is the name given by Aronoff (1976: 43) to the phenomenon of the non-occurrence of a complex form because of the existence of another form.[11] The form which causes the blocking may itself be complex or simplex. For example, Bolinger (1975: 109) points out that, despite the productivity of *-er* suffixation in English, there is no word *stealer* because of the prior existence of the word *thief* which carries the appropriate meaning;[12] the existence of forms like *bad* and *small* blocks the formation of **ungood* and **unbig*; the prior existence of *enlist* prevents the use of *list* as a verb with that meaning (Clark & Clark, 1979: 798).

This can be seen as an extension of the pragmatic factor discussed in §4.5.1.1: not only does there have to be something for a lexeme to denote, there also has to be a need (in a fairly loose sense) for a new lexeme to denote that something before a new lexeme will be produced and accepted by the linguistic community. Since the acceptance by the linguistic community is an important

---

11 Also termed the "Regel der besetzten Stelle" ('rule of the filled slot') (Burgschmidt, 1977: 43) and "preemption by synonymy" (Clark & Clark, 1979: 798). See also Motsch (1977) and Rose (1973).

12 This is actually not quite accurate, as a glance in the *OED* shows. However, *stealer* appears to be used only when the object stolen is also mentioned, while *thief* can be used without any such mention.

part of the process, it can be seen that blocking prevents not so much the coining of nonce complex forms as their institutionalization: *stealer* might be said by an individual on a single occasion, but would not become established unless the lexeme were used to denote some specific new subgroup of thieves or robbers (or, as can be seen from the *OED*, with a different meaning altogether: "the ten stealers" was used by Shakespeare to mean 'the fingers').

Aronoff (1976) develops the notion of blocking further than this. He lists a number of nominals related to adjectival bases in *-ous* such as:

various	–	variety
curious	–	curiosity
glorious	glory	*gloriosity
furious	fury	*furiosity

where the presence of a nominal like *glory* or *fury* can be said to block the generation of an *-ity* form, but then he points out that a *-ness* nominalization is possible in every case. For further evidence on this point, if any is needed, see Williams (1965), who lists large numbers of attested *-ness* formations which correspond to lexicalized nominalizations of other types. Aronoff suggests that this is possible because *-ness* nominalization is fully productive, with the result that the linguist need list no such nominalization in the lexicon. Thus there is an inverse relationship between productivity and institutionalization/lexicalization such that the most productive patterns are not lexicalized, and fully lexicalized processes are not productive. This leads to the view, which will be taken up again below (§4.5.8) that productivity is not an either/or phenomenon, but presents a cline.

4.5.3 *Limitations on the bases that may undergo processes*
It is a well-known phenomenon that there are some bases which, because of some aspect of their make-up, do not provide a suitable input to a given rule of word-formation. Different types of restriction on the base will be discussed and exemplified below.

4.5.3.1 Phonological
In some cases the segmental phonological shape of the base can decide whether the base may be used as the input to a rule of word-formation. For example, Hasselrot (1972: 13) gives the

example that in French the diminutive suffix -*ette* is not added to a base which ends in /t/ or /d/. Although this seems to be absolutely true with regard to the /t/, Hasselrot himself lists three possible non-established exceptions to the rule about /d/: *rid·ette* 'little wrinkle', *bastid·ette* 'little countryhouse' and *stud·ette* 'a small studio'. He lists no non-established forms where -*ette* is added to a base in /b/.

In English it feels very clumsy to add the adverbial suffix -*ly* to adjectives which end in -*ly*. Thus, although the *OED* does list *friendlily* and *sillily*, these tend to be avoided, and -*ly* is not productively added to -*ly* adjectives to give *elderlily, *miserlily, *sisterlily, *worldlily.

Malkiel (1978: 134) presents a slightly more complicated case from Latin. There the suffixes -*alis* and -*aris* are in complementary distribution: -*alis* is the basic form, but -*aris* occurs after a base which includes an /l/. Thus *nav·alis* illustrates the basic form, and *consul·aris* and *salut·aris* illustrates the -*aris* variant arising after /l/, even if the /l/ is not at the end of the base. The exception comes when an /r/ follows the /l/ in the base, when -*alis* is used, as in *sepulchr·alis*.

Restrictions of this kind are exceedingly common, and many more examples can be found in the literature (see e.g. Ettinger, 1974a: 64–79). One very interesting case is discussed by Ettinger (1974b). It is the case, which Ettinger believes to be a common one, where two synonymous suffixes are in partial complementary distribution, depending on the segments in the base. He illustrates this (1974b: 75–6) with the German diminutive affixes -*chen* and -*lein*. After final -*l(e)* only -*chen* is found: *Bällchen* 'little ball', *Schälchen* 'little scarf', *Spielchen* 'little game', and after final /x, ŋ, g/ only -*lein* is found: *Bächlein* 'little stream', *Ringlein* 'little ring', *Zweiglein* 'little branch', but after bases ending in other consonants, the two are free variants, so that either member of the pairs *Briefchen/Brieflein* 'little letter', *Häuschen/Häuslein* 'little house', *Tischchen/Tischlein* 'little table', is equally possible. He also (1974b: 90) illustrates the same point with relation to Italian.

As well as segmental restrictions on the bases that can undergo particular processes, there may also be suprasegmental restrictions. These can be illustrated from English with reference to the infixation of -*bloody*-, -*bloomin(g)*-, -*fuckin(g)*- and other such forms into the middle of words, to give forms like *absobloominlutely*.

This process is a very unusual one in English morphology because it is the only case of productive infixation in English (there seems to be no reason to call it anything other than infixation, see McMillan, 1980), and because the infixes are potential word-forms and not bound morphs, unlike most other English affixes. It is also unusual in that the words produced by this infixation never seem to become established; this seems to be because of the high productivity of the process, which in some ways makes it look as if it might be a rather more inflectional process than others discussed in this chapter. It is, however, generally assumed that this infixation is derivational (see e.g. Aronoff, 1976: 69; McMillan, 1980: 167), and the process will accordingly be included here despite this possible objection.

In the vast majority of cases, these infixes occur immediately before the syllable of the base that bears the lexical stress: thus while *licketyfuckingsplit*[13] is acceptable, **lickfuckingetysplit* is not. Other examples which fit the standard pattern are *albloodymighty*, *imfuckingpossible*, *kangabloodyroo* and *propafuckingganda*.[14] *Handibloodycap*,[14] *dimfuckingwit* and *atmosfuckingphere*[15] are rather odd because they tend to require the re-assignment of stress to the final syllable, although it would normally fall on the first syllable of the base. Even in these cases though, the syllable after the infix would normally bear a secondary stress. As McMillan (1980: 167) points out, it is very difficult to add such infixes to words which are stressed on the first syllable and do not have a subsequent subsidiary stress, words like *solid* and *criminal*. Thus the stress of a lexeme is crucial in deciding whether it may act as a base for this infixation.

Not only are infixes like *-fucking-* limited by stress to where they can occur in the word, they are limited by syllable pattern. Since *-fucking-* is an infix the minimal form in which it can occur is a disyllable with stress on the second syllable. This accounts for forms like *urfuckingbane*.[16] But the most common pattern is for this

---

[13] William Goldman. 1976. *Magic*. London: MacMillan, p. 12.
[14] All cited by McMillan (1980).
[15] William Goldman, *Magic*, pp. 233, 167.
[16] William Goldman, *Magic*, p. 196.

infix to appear in words of three or more syllables: *imfuckingpossible, ecofuckingnomics, incanfuckingdescent, confronfuckingtation, unbefuckinglievable,*[17] *guaranfriggintee.*[18]

In other cases of English word-formation where there might be a restriction to polysyllabic bases, an alternative analysis is that the affix in question is used only with classical bases. An example is the formation of nouns with the prefix *mal-*, where it appears that the base is always of more than one syllable. Similarly, the suffix *-ize* is added predominantly to bases of more than one syllable (though there are exceptions here, e.g. *filmize* and *Grecize*).

4.5.3.2 Morphological

It is a well-known feature of morphological systems that borrowed or learned words and formatives often behave differently, both morphologically and phonologically, from native non-learned words and formatives. Thus, neither Czech nor German can normally mix native bases with foreign affixes or foreign bases with native affixes, so that a German word **Sterb·ation* parallel with English *starv·ation* would be quite impossible (Mathesius, 1975: 27). In English it is necessary to mark formatives as [± latinate] to account for such phenomena as velar softening, which only occurs in latinate words: *critic* gives /krɪtɪsaɪz/, but if a form were created meaning 'to turn into a barracks' it would have to be /bærəkaɪz/. Aronoff (1976: 51–2) points out that there are some suffixes which can only be added to bases which are [+ latinate], and others which can only be added to bases which are [− latinate]. As an example of the first group he quotes *-ity* (with the exception of *oddity*), and as an example of the second group he quotes *-hood*. He further points out that such features are not purely etymological, since words etymologically derived from Latin can be accepted as native, as is shown by the existence of *priesthood* and *statehood*. *Personhood* (Barnhart *et al.*, 1973) can be added to this list. Exactly what factors influence this diachronic shift in status is not clear, but it also occurs in other places: the set of adjectives which can be used as the first element of adjective + noun compounds is a restricted set consisting largely of (mainly monosyllabic) adjectives of Germanic origin – examples are *blackboard, busybody, highroad, hothouse,*

---

[17] Ibid. pp. 29, 34, 106, 168, 196. There are many more examples in this book.
[18] J. Goldman. 1965. *Waldorf*. London: Michael Joseph, p. 82.

longstop, quickstep, redhead, stronghold and so on; however, this group also contains a number of adjectives which etymologically are early Romance loans, but which are treated for these purposes as being of Germanic origin – *doubletalk, grandfather, nobleman, tenderloin.*

Having made the point that a feature such as [± latinate] is needed, Aronoff (1976: 52) goes on to argue that since *readability* is attested, the latinate feature must also be attached to *-able*, and that it must be the feature marking of the last morpheme which is important, rather than the feature marking of the root.

Suffixation can be sensitive to specific suffixes already present in the base in other ways, too. Ettinger (1974b: 366) points out that in German it is not possible to form a diminutive from a base which contains the feminine derivational marker *-in*; that is, *lehrer·chen* 'little teacher' would be possible in an emotive sense, but not **lehrer·in·chen*. A similar example is that in English no suffix can be added to a base that already ends in the same suffix; that is, forms such as **joy·ful·ful, *helpless·ness·ness, *duke·dom·dom* are impossible. It is not the fact of previous suffixation which blocks these forms, as the existence of *help·less·ness* proves, but the identity of the two suffixes. Note that this is not a restriction on the function of the suffixes, since two nominalization suffixes can be conjoined, as in *provis·ion·ment*, but **environ·ment·ment* is not possible.

Aronoff (1976: 53–4) also shows that the make-up of the base can play a role. He gives the example of adjectival forms in *-al* derived from nouns in *-ment*. If the *-ment* is an affix added to a verbal root, then there is no *-al* adjective. If the *-ment* is a part of the root, then there is an *-al* adjective.[19] Thus:

*orna	ornament	ornamental
employ	employment	*employmental.

Thus rules of word-formation have to be sensitive to the difference between a base which is a root, and a base which is more than a simple root. The morphological class of a base can also be important. Ettinger (1974a: 7) cites the example of the Latin

---

[19] Aronoff mentions two counter-examples: *governmental* and *developmental*. Note that in the appropriate sense, *government* is not only morphologically, but also semantically lexicalized.

diminutive suffix -(c)ul-. The presence or absence of the -c- is conditioned by the declension of the base, such that -c- is not added to first and second declension nouns, but is added to third, fourth and fifth declension nouns.

4.5.3.3 Lexical

Certain word-formation processes are triggered or limited by the individual roots. Lightner (1975: 633) points out that the ending -ric only occurs in conjunction with *bishop* in English. This is an extreme example, which would probably be more economically captured by listing BISHOPRIC as a lexicalized lexeme, but there are other examples which work by similar processes. Aronoff (1976: 40) gives the example of the formation of -ity nominalizations from adjectival -ous bases. In some of these, the -ous becomes -os-, as in, for example, *curious, curiosity*; in others it is deleted, as in *voracious, voracity*. Aronoff says that there is no way to predict which pattern will be used, and that the patterns must thus be listed in the lexicon along with the various roots. This is presumably to say that the less productive pattern (at least) is only found in lexicalized words.

4.5.3.4 Semantic

Semantic limitations on the base in derivation are also very common, and many examples can be found in the literature. The examples collected together here should be seen as random ones, symptomatic of a much more widespread phenomenon.

One example where a specific semantic feature is a necessary prerequisite to a process of word-formation has been widely discussed in the literature (Beard, 1976; Hirtle, 1969; Hudson, 1975; Ljung, 1970, 1976; Stein, 1976). It is the case of adjectives ending in -ed like *blue-eyed, three-legged, red-roofed*. The claim is that the base in question must be inalienably possessed by the head noun that the adjective modifies. Thus *a two-carred man or **a black-shoed lady* are not possible, since cars and shoes are possessed alienably. The restrictions are not quite as simple as this implies, and much of the discussion centres on what other factors are involved, and how inalienable possession is to be defined. Nevertheless, the main point for present purposes, namely that a semantic property is necessary for word-formation, seems reasonably clear. What is perhaps surprising, is that it would seem to be a semantic property of the head noun, rather than of the base of the adjective: that is, it seems intuitively speaking to be something to do with men that they inalienably possess eyes, legs, etc., but not cars, rather than a property of eyes and legs that they are inalienably possessed by men. From a linguistic point of view, it is easier to list the things that a man possesses inalienably, than to list for every item those entities which inalienably possess it, since the first is a finite list, the second an open list. Thompson (1975: 346), citing a paper by Givon, provides an example which goes in the expected direction. She points out that the suffix -*ship* is added to a base which denotes 'position, office or title', and she gives as an example a nonce form *overseership*.

A slightly more abstract example is provided by Zimmer (1964: 15), who points out that "negative prefixes are *not* used (in English) with adjectival stems that have 'negative' value on evaluative scales such as 'good-bad' . . ." A more neutral way of expressing this point would be to say that only the unmarked term in a pair of graded antonyms can take a negative prefix (see Lyons, 1968: §10.4.4 on marking in graded antonyms). Thus someone can be said to be *unwell*, but not **unill*; *unhappy* but not **unsad*; *uncheerful* but not **unsorrowful*; *unoptimistic* but not **unpessimistic*.

Finally, Ettinger (1974b: 389–90) provides a very interesting example from Italian augmentatives. He states that although the adjective *grande* can be used to modify nouns which are [+ Count, + Concrete, − Man-made], no augmentatives can be formed on this class if the object denoted is larger than a human being. Thus, words denoting large natural objects, such as *fiume* 'river', *lago* 'lake', *vallata* 'valley', *piano* 'plain' do not have augmentatives, though there are augmentatives corresponding to words denoting smaller objects: *pietrà* 'stone', *sasso* 'stone', *fiore* 'flower', *ciòttolo* 'pebble'. Man-made objects which are larger than human beings do not provide the same restriction, so that *canale* 'canal' gives rise to *canalone*, *piazza* 'square' to *piazzone*, *strada* 'street' to *stradone* and so on.

4.5.4 *Restrictions on stem collocations in compounds*

The claim is made in Bauer (1978d: §3.4.4) that the determining element in an endocentric nominal compound always

denotes the primary defining characteristic of the subgroup denoted by the compound as a whole. Thus in *policedog* the primary
defining characteristic of the member of the group of dogs under
discussion is its connection with the police; the primary defining
characteristic of an *armchair* is seen as being its arms, although it
may also be upholstered, etc. Given this, it is to be expected that
there should not be any genus-species compounds like **human-
man*, **animalhorse*, **placemoor* where the determining element is
implicit in the head element. As a general rule, this is true, but it is
not without exceptions. Bauer (1978d: §3.4.4) cites *vegetable
marrow*, where the information in the modifier is pragmatically
non-redundant, to separate it from *bone marrow*. Downing (1977:
831–2) also mentions that apparently redundant formations are
acceptable if they can be given a non-redundant reading. Note,
however, that species-genus compounds, which might appear to be
equally redundant, are far more common: *cod fish*, *beech tree*,
puppy dog, *palm tree*, *boy child*. This fits with the primary defining
characteristic features mentioned above, but not with any desire to
eradicate redundancy.

4.5.5 *Semantic coherence*

Aronoff (1976: 388f), following Zimmer (1964), claims
that the more productive a process is, the more easily can its
semantic effect be specified. Aronoff illustrates this with nominalizations in *-ness* and *-ity*. The meanings of the *-ness* nominalizations can be stated in terms of a choice between three operations on
the verb; *-ity* nominalizations, on the other hand, provide nominalizations which are semantically far more complex. The process is
correspondingly less productive. This correlates with lexicalization
and institutionalization. Institutionalized or lexicalized lexemes can
be semantically unpredictable, nonce formations cannot be. Very
productive suffixes, when they are being used productively, must
have a predictable meaning. As Aronoff (1976: 39) remarks, "Com-
monsensically, the correlation is perfectly reasonable: the surer
one is of what a word will mean, the more likely one is to use it."

4.5.6 *Analogy*

There are occasional examples of complex forms being
produced which are either unique or extremely limited in produc-

tivity – possibly limited to two or three forms. Motsch (1977: 187) cites the German example of *zweisam*, formed on the pattern of *einsam* 'one some' = 'lone·some, lonely' (*-sam* is also found in other words of German, e.g. *gleich·sam* 'identical some' = 'almost', *gemein·sam* 'common some' = 'mutual', but the pattern must be provided by *einsam* which is the only established form to contain a numeral). *Dreisam* 'three some' might just be conceivable, but **drei·hundert·neun·und·sech·zig·sam* 'three hundred nine and sixty some' would be impossible. Here some of the explanation may be pragmatic, in that *zweisam* might be seen as a nameable quality, but whether or not this is a sufficient explanation, the result is a paradigm with only two members and no clear productivity,[20] even though *zweisam* is a relatively recent nonce formation.

In cases like these it is necessary to speak not of rules of word-formation but of analogy in word-formation. By an **analogical formation** will be meant a new formation clearly modelled on one already existing lexeme, and not giving rise to a productive series. That is, following Thompson (1975: 347), a distinction is drawn between productivity and analogy. This does not preclude the possibility, of course, that an analogical formation will provide the impetus for a series of formations: this is presumably what happened in the case of formations in *-scape*, based on *landscape*, then an analogical formation *seascape* giving eventually a productive series including not only *cloudscape*, *skyscape* and *waterscape* but also *dreamscape*, *winterscape* and *wirescape* (Aldrich, 1966). There are also forms which appear to be coined because of a chance phonetic resemblance. Examples chosen at random from Barnhart *et al.* (1973) are *ambisextrous*, *medichair* and *wargasm*. These are genuine analogical formations which cannot be accounted for by any kind of rule. It should be noted that this definition of an analogical formation is much narrower than the one usually implied in diachronic studies and is, in a sense, as closely related to creativity as to productivity.

---

[20] Note the difficulty in deciding what is acceptable in this paradigm: if *dreisam* is acceptable, what about *fünfsam, achtsam, zehnsam, zwölfsam*? Is there any non-arbitrary way to decide where the cut-off point comes? I suspect that there is not.

4.5.7 Other restrictions

One further linguistic restriction on productivity would seem to be the existence of a form with a lexicalized meaning other than that which would be assigned to it productively. For example, there is no commonly used nominalization from *ignore* in English, although it would be useful to have one: *ignorance*, which would be suitable, is lexicalized with a different meaning, and is thus unavailable; *ignoration*, which is listed in the *OED*, strikes many people as being unsuitable. Similarly, there is no nominalization in *-eur* from *voler* 'to fly' in French (note English *flyer*) because of the prior existence of an homophonous form *voleur* meaning 'thief'. This restriction should not be appealed to too readily, however. Clark & Clark (1979: 800) claim that *spring* and *fall* are not used as verbs in the same way that *summer* and *winter* are (*They summered/ wintered in the country*) because of the prior existence of the homophonous strong verbs *spring* and *fall* which would prevent *They springed/falled in the country*. In fact, this cannot be the only reason for the non-existence of *fall* with this sense, since British English does not have *They autumned in the country* despite the fact that *autumn* has no homophonous verb with which it might be confused.

There are also a host of non-linguistic factors which restrict productivity. These can be seen operating in the rejection of some lexical innovations by some speakers on aesthetic grounds such as *The Daily Chronicle*'s assertion in 1909, that "you could hardly think of a worse word" than *aviation* (cited in Adams, 1973: 2): presumably such factors would prevent those speakers from coining that particular term, and they might well prevent all speakers from coining some forms. Even though these factors are, by their very nature, idiosyncratic, and thus impossible to take into account systematically in a grammar of word-formation, they must be mentioned as adding an extra filter to word-formation processes.

4.5.8 Productivity as a cline

It appears from much that has been said above that productivity is not so much an either/or phenomenon as a cline (see also Hakulinen, 1978: 328). Some processes are more productive than others. And this is true even when other limitations have been taken into consideration (see Aronoff, 1976: 36).

This is linked crucially with lexicalization, for several reasons. One is that, as was mentioned above (§4.5.5), semantic coherence correlates with productivity, and lack of semantic coherence has to be listed in the lexicon. Another is that the longer a process of word-formation has been used productively, the more likely it is that an appreciable number of the bases to which the process can be applied will yield institutionalized lexemes. There are accordingly fewer bases available for the process to apply to productively, and hence the process is less productive. In fact, the inter-relation of productivity and lexicalization is very complex, and there is not necessarily influence in one direction only. I shall do no more than note the complexity of the situation.

However, even when other factors are taken into consideration, it would seem that word-formation often operates according to some kind of variable rule. At least in some types of formation, a morphological process seems to show a preference for one kind of application over another kind. For instance, the suffix *-ee* seems to be added productively to intransitive and to transitive verb bases (this will be discussed at greater length in §8.2.1). In the first case the result is forms like *resignee*, in the latter, forms like *huggee* (examples from Foster, 1964). But although the affix can be added productively to either kind of base, there is a marked preference for it to be added to a transitive verb base. In fact, the number of *-ee* formations with an intransitive verb base, established or nonce, is really extremely low: *escapee* and *infiltree* are the established ones, and there are a few more nonce formations.

Another example is provided by the suffix *-eer*. This suffix shows a clear preference for bases that end in *-t* as in *profiteer*, *racketeer*, etc. (Adams, 1973: 162; Jespersen, 1942: 244). That this is no more than a preference, however, is shown firstly by a large number of formations on bases that end in *-n* (*sloganeer*, *motioneer*) and secondly by occasional formations such as *Municheer* (Adams, 1973: 175ff). A third example has already been discussed (§4.5.3.1), and that is the preference for the infix *-fucking-* to be put in a base of three or more syllables.

Precisely how such a variable rule is to be expressed is of no immediate concern here, but the fact of preferred productivity types is very important when productivity is being described, in particular because it shows clearly that productivity is not merely an either/or choice.

4.5.9 *Restrictions acting in unison*

In most of what has been said in this chapter, it has been assumed that any potential formation is checked against a list of restrictions for that type of formation, and if it goes against the specifications provided in any one of these the potential formation is rejected. Although it would be extremely difficult – if not impossible – to find a set of data which could prove conclusively exactly how these restrictions function, I suspect that this way of viewing the matter is considerably oversimplified. It seems likely, rather, that some of these restrictions (or tendencies) may, on occasions, be ignored, but that there comes a point when too many restrictions would be broken if a particular word were formed, and so the potential formation is blocked by a cumulation of factors: that is, the restrictions do not all work independently but in unison when a potential formation is considered. Ideally, it might be possible to speak in terms of the weightings of different restrictions and a threshold level below which restrictions can be ignored, but in the present state of our knowledge this can remain no more than speculation.

4.6 **Productivity summarized**

In the light of the discussion of this chapter, it is now possible to attempt a definition of productivity. The basic way in which an affix is said to be productive (as noted by Ljung, 1970: fn. 7) is that a productive affix can appear in new words. These words may never develop beyond being nonce formations, or they may, in the course of time, become established.

A non-productive affix, on the other hand, is one whose distribution can be accounted for only in terms of a list of the bases with which it occurs (Gruber, 1976: 324). It is not necessarily the case, however, as is claimed by Gruber (1976: 346) that only non-productive affixes allow assimilation or change the stress pattern of the base.

Within the group of productive affixes, some are more productive than others. The degree of productivity varies according to the strictness of the limitations on the base, but also according to other factors, many of which are less open to measurement: the need for new lexemes of a particular kind, preferences and, one which has not been specifically mentioned, although it comes under the general heading of aesthetic reactions, euphony.

The limiting case of productivity at the lower end is presented by analogy, where only one new form may exist. The upper limit is vague. It is unlikely, however, that there is any word-formation process which has absolutely no limitations, in the sense that there is an affix which can be added to absolutely any base in the language. That is why the usual definition of "full" productivity is like that given by Gruber (1976: 322): "To be fully productive, an affix must be usable with all [bases] definable by some semantic, syntactic, or possibly phonological property." Even in this sense it is doubtful that any process can be said to be fully productive, as the prior existence of other lexemes often provides some kind of curb.

So-called semi-productivity may be one of two things. Usually it is non-productivity, with lexicalized forms being used as a corpus over which generalizations are sought. The other, less likely, possibility, is that it is productivity with very heavy restrictions on it. In neither case is semi-productivity given independent status as a theoretical construct in this book.

In summary, a morphological process can be said to be more or less productive according to the number of new words which it is used to form.

5
Phonological issues in word-formation

Natural phonology, but unnatural morphology.
(Skousen, 1974: 327)

5.1 Introduction

Although many of the examples used in the preceding chapters have been taken from English, the points made have had a much wider application, as has been shown by the number of examples from other languages. In this chapter, and the rest of the book, attention will be concentrated far more upon English, and examples from other languages will be correspondingly rarer. With respect to phonology, this has some quite important implications. English is a relatively complex language phonologically speaking, with a large number of phonemes, and a large amount of phonological variation and alternation. As a result, the problems that will be discussed with relation to English may not occur in other languages. For example, in §5.2 the stress patterns on compounds like *peanut butter* ($^{--\,'--}$ or $^{'----}$) will be discussed. I know of no other language where precisely this problem is relevant. In French, for example, stress is always predictable over the phonological phrase, so that the problems discussed in §5.2, and also those discussed in §5.3, just do not occur in French. In Danish and German stress assignment in compounds is also relatively straightforward, although it is suggested in Bauer (1978b) that there are corresponding morphological difficulties in those languages, concerned with the form of the linking element (the -*s*- in Danish *moder·s·mål* 'mother tongue' from *moder* + *mål*; the -*en*- in German *Tief·en·struktur* 'deep structure' from *tief* + *Struktur*). On the other hand, there are, of course, many problems in English phonology which have counterparts in the phonologies of other languages. For example, the stress shift between Danish *vio'lin* and *violi'nist* is comparable in theoretical terms to the stress shift between English *'auction* and *auctio'neer*; the consonant change in

French *grec* 'Greek' and *Grèce* 'Greece' (/gʀɛk; gʀɛs/) is theoretically comparable to the consonant change in English *vine* and *wine*.

The restriction to English does, however, rule out of consideration a number of problems which do not arise in English because of the nature of the language. The most obvious of these are prosodic features. In Danish, for example, the presence of the *stød* ('glottal catch') can depend on word-formation: *dag* 'day' is pronounced with a *stød* on the vowel (/daʔ/), but there is no *stød* on *dag·lig* 'daily' (/dauli/). In tone languages and tone accent languages tone can also be bound up with word-formation. In Swedish, for example, the verb 'to hear' is *hö'ra* with the complex tone 2, while 'to interrogate' is *för·hö'ra* with the simple tone 1. In many cases, the theoretical problems involved in the description of such phenomena will be similar to those involved in the English phenomena discussed below. Nevertheless, the restrictions imposed by looking only at one language should be borne in mind.

Stress in English will be discussed first, in relation to compounds and then in relation to derivatives, and then segmental variation in English will be considered.

5.2 Compounds and stress

One of the main controversies concerning compounds and stress in English is whether a particular stress pattern should be seen as a criterion for a compound. This has mainly been discussed in the literature with reference to noun + noun compounds, and those are the ones upon which the discussion will be centred here.

5.2.1 *The assumption of consistency in stress-patterning*

The first point to be noted is that it will be assumed here, as it generally is in the literature, that any given speaker will be consistent in assigning a stress pattern to a given compound. That is, it is assumed that a speaker who assigns different stress patterns to *tea cup*, *bow window* and *headmaster* on one occasion will also do so on any subsequent occasion, and will do so in a consistent manner. Furthermore, it is assumed that such consistency will be found not only in the individual speaker, but in the entire speech community. This kind of assumption is almost always implicit in the literature on compounding, as well as in dictionaries: see, for example, Hornby (1974), where stress patterns are marked for such compounds.

It must be remembered that what is important is the pronunciation of the form in isolation. If the forms are attested as parts of utterances, there is likely to be quite a lot of variation in stress assignment. There are several reasons for this. One common one is emphasis. Thus '*underwriter* and '*undertaker* are both normally pronounced with stress on the first syllable; but in the sentence *Are we talking about undertakers or underwriters now?* the stress is likely to be on *take* and *write* (Kingdon, 1958: 147). Similarly, in isolation '*bow* '*window* is normally pronounced with two stresses as marked. The same is true of '*dormer* '*window*, and also of '*lattice* '*window*. However, if I read all three aloud as a list, I stress '*bow window*, '*dormer window* and '*lattice window* with only one emphatic stress on each name (Bauer, 1977: 330). In a few cases, the position of a word in a sentence may also cause a different stress pattern. For example, I might very easily say *Would you like a* '*milk* '*shake?*, using the same stress pattern as I would use in isolation, but *An ice-cold* '*milk shake is just what I need*, with only one stress on *milk shake*. This kind of variation is perhaps particularly common with compound adjectives, which can change in stress pattern depending on whether they are used attributively or predicatively: *She was wearing a* '*peacock blue dress*; *Her dress was* '*peacock* '*blue*. Such variation is not restricted to noun + noun or adjectival compounds (consider *after'noon* but '*afternoon tea*), nor even to compounds (consider *conti'nental* but '*continental* '*breakfast*). It seems that a principle of stress shift which applies more generally just happens to affect the stress of compounds at this point.

Despite the provisos introduced by the consideration of such factors, the assumption that speakers are consistent in their stress assignments is a very dangerous one. Very little work appears to have been done on this topic, but what little has been done (see Bauer, to appear; Pennanen, 1980; Vos, 1952; and works referred to there) suggests that, both in actual use and under experimental conditions, speakers are far from consistent. It seems that not only is there disagreement between speakers as to the stress patterns on given items, but that individual speakers pronounce the same compound with different stress patterns on different occasions. If this were true only of items like *ice cream* and *peanut butter* where there are recognized alternative stress patterns, this would not be a theoretical problem, but it seems that there is general vacillation, even when the items are presented in isolation in an attempt to rule out the extra variation imposed by sentence prosody. This conclusion may be over-pessimistic (indeed, in many ways it is to be hoped that it is!): the data and discussion in Bauer (to appear) are far from conclusive, and it may very well be that when more accurate measures of stressing and a number of other factors are taken into account, the intuitions of the majority of linguists and lexicographers will be vindicated, and it will turn out that there is genuine consistency in the speech community.

If there is no consistency in such matters in the speech community, then the point that is made in the next section will remain true, though it may be uninterestingly true. If, as is generally believed, there IS consistency in the speech community in the stressing of compounds, then the argument in the following section becomes substantive. In either case, the argument presented here can be seen as an answer to those scholars (e.g. Lees, 1960; Marchand, 1969) who have seen stress as criterial to compounding.

5.2.2   *Why stress is not criterial for compounds*

It will therefore be assumed in this section that there is consistency in stress-patterning for compounds, even if it is difficult to support such a view experimentally. Bearing that assumption in mind, consider the two lists of forms below:

(a)	'bankrate	(b)	'bank 'holiday
	'carbon-paper		'carbon di'oxide
	'garden party		'garden 'city
	'paper-clip		'paper 'tiger
	'strip-show		'strip-'poker
	'trade name		'trade-'union
	'wing-span		'wing-com'mander

All the examples in these lists are established, and the stresses are as marked in Hornby (1974). In each case, the items in list (a) have only one major stress on the leftmost element, while the items in list (b) have two major stresses (and if these items are said in isolation, the second stress will sound more prominent because of the influence of intonation). It should be noted that the spelling does not provide an accurate guide to which list an item will appear in, since although none of the items in list (b) is written as one orthographic word (i.e. with no gap between the elements), in list (a) there are three spelling variants: one orthographic word, hyphenated and two orthographic words, and yet they are all pronounced with only one stress. Moreover, occasionally an item can be found which has all three spelling variants, e.g. *wordformation*, *word-formation* and *word formation* or *girlfriend*, *girl-friend* and *girl friend*.

The controversy surrounding compounds turns on how many of the items should be considered compounds, and how many should be considered syntactic phrases. Some scholars (e.g. Bloomfield, 1935: 228; Lees, 1960; Marchand, 1969: §2.1.20) take stress as criterial to the compound, and say that only those items listed in (a) are compounds, while those listed in (b) are syntactic phrases. Others (e.g. Adams, 1973; Bauer, 1977, 1978d; Downing, 1977; Hatcher, 1960; Kingdon, 1958; Warren, 1978) consider that all the items in the lists (a) and (b) are compounds independent of stress, and that for this particular subset of compounds it is the collocation of two nouns which shows that the construction is a compound. In what follows, I shall try to motivate this second view-point.

Those scholars who wish to motivate a distinction between compounds and syntactic phrases in this way, usually suggest that the compound is more "word-like" than the syntactic phrase. Criteria for judging the "wordness" of an item (in English, but also in other languages) include positional mobility (the word can be used in different places in the sentence), uninterruptability (items cannot be inserted between formatives within a word) and internal stability (formatives cannot be reordered within the word) (Lyons, 1968: §5.4.10). It will be shown, however, that these criteria do not distinguish between items like those in (a) with single stress, and items like those in (b) with double stress.

As far as positional mobility is concerned, both single and double stressed noun + noun constructions behave in exactly the same way: both can play different roles in the sentence such as subject, object, etc., and both can be moved by movement transformations such as passivization and pseudo-clefting:

> The 'wing com'mander saw the 'strip-show.
> The 'strip show was seen by the 'wing com'mander

If a noun phrase including a noun + noun collocation is moved, then both parts of it must be moved together, independent of whether the collocation receives one stress or two, and to this extent both types of collocation are uninterruptable. However, this particular criterion is not as clear-cut as that might suggest. This is because it is possible to find complex words of the form AB such that there is also a complex word of the form ACB. This is not usually taken to contravene the uninterruptability criterion as long as the element C forms a unit either with A or with B.[1] For this criterion to be contravened it is usually required that elements should be inserted between parts of the basic form "more or less freely" (Lyons, 1968: 204). While both derivatives and single and double stressed noun + noun collocations can be interrupted in this way, as is illustrated in Table 5.1, they cannot be interrupted "more or less freely".

Table 5.1.

	basic form	interrupted form	incorrectly interrupted form
derivative	sensationism	sensationalism	*sensationsism
single stressed	library book	library comic-book	*library boring book
double stressed	city office	city insurance office	*city big office

The third criterion of "wordness" is internal stability. Here again the point is not absolutely clear-cut. In its strongest form, this criterion says that it should be impossible to reorder elements within a word. In fact there are examples where elements within a word can be reordered, and the result is still a word. The crucial point is, though, that in such cases the result is not the same word: there is a change in meaning. This is illustrated in Table 5.2, where once again it can be seen that single and double stressed noun + noun collocations operate in the same way. As far as the form *Biblistic* in the table is concerned, I must admit that I cannot find it in dictionaries, but it is formed according to productive rules, and its nonce status does not affect the point being made here.

---

[1] For a discussion of this point with reference to inflection, see Matthews (1972: 98 fn. 2) and the works referred to there.

Table 5.2.

	AB	BA
derivative	Biblicist	Biblistic
single stressed	armchair	chair-arm
double stressed	garden city	city garden

Some scholars have also suggested that there might be a semantic difference between the single and double stressed noun + noun collocations. For instance, it has been claimed that one reason for single stress rather than double stress is implicit contrast (Kingdon, 1958: 151; Marchand, 1969: §2.1.21): thus Kingdon suggests that 'day time receives single stress because of implicit contrast with 'bed time, 'night time, etc. If this were the case, all compounds might be expected to have single stress (rather than merely the majority): 'globe 'artichoke, for example, requires a modifying element only because it contrasts with Je'rusalem 'artichoke; 'cherry 'brandy is implicitly contrasted with 'apricot 'brandy, 'peach 'brandy and 'grape 'brandy despite its double stress. Another suggestion is that single stress is bound up with "a permanent lexical relation" whereas double stress is connected with "a mere syntactic relation" (Marchand, 1969: §2.1.26). While it seems to be true that there is a tendency for lexicalized compounds to assume single stress (see Kingdon, 1958: 150), this distinction cannot account for the difference between 'Regent Street and 'Regent 'Terrace or between 'literature book and 'literature 'textbook, and nor can it explain why 'world 'war (which is presumably a "permanent lexical relation") should take double stress.

It is examples like these last ones which lead Lees (1960: 120) to suggest that the stress in English noun + noun groups is lexically conditioned by the second of the two nouns. He points out, for example, that in his dialect (and the same seems to be true in most – though not all – English dialects) all collocations in -Street and -cake receive single stress, while all those in -Avenue and -pie receive double stress. This accounts for series like the one below:

'literature book	'literature 'textbook
'physics book	'physics 'textbook
lin'guistics book	lin'guistics 'textbook
'law book	'law 'textbook

To generate such series it is only necessary to note in the lexical entry for BOOK that compounds where *book* is the second element take a single stress, whereas the entry for TEXTBOOK will include the information that when it occurs as the second element of a compound, the compound takes double stress. There are, however, a number of examples which seem to contradict this proposal:

'wine glass	'plate 'glass
'town house	'country 'house
'troop leader	'world 'leader

It is suggested in Bauer (1977) that where such pairs exist it is always the case that at least one of them is lexicalized, and that Lees's proposal in fact holds as far as productive series of compounds are concerned.

This is not quite true in every case. Occasionally there is a semantic pattern which demands a specific stress pattern, independent of the lexemes involved in the compound. Thus if, in a noun + noun compound of the form AB, A denotes the material of which the whole is made, the compound will have double stress, as in 'cherry 'brandy, 'chocolate 'frog, ma'hogany 'table, 'olive 'oil, 'plastic 'toy[2] (Bauer, 1977: 334; Kingdon, 1958: 150). This rule can over-rule the lexical conditioning, so that even though STREET and BOOK normally involve single stressing, 'concrete 'street and 'cardboard 'book receive double stress.

Unfortunately, however accurate Lees's proposal is (and with the provisos that have been made and under the assumption of consistency of stress-patterning I have no reason to believe it to be inaccurate), it is not particularly helpful. This is because there are, relatively speaking, so few lexemes in the same class as AVENUE, PIE or TEXTBOOK. Other lexemes which appear to be in the same class are ADMINISTRATION (*the 'Carter admini'stration,*

---

[2] Marchand (1969: §2.2.12.6.1) lists a few counter-examples, e.g. 'snowball and 'soap flakes. These must be assumed to be lexicalized. Sampson (1980) points out that the generalization 'material of which the whole is made' is in fact not specific enough. In the light of examples like 'water droplet, 'oil slick he suggests a gloss like 'made as an artefact out of N', but then he points out that his own rule will not account for 'sandstone 'ridge. It seems that some refinement is needed here, though it is not yet obvious whether the generalization will have to be discarded as untenable.

uni'versity admini'stration), PRAYER (*'morning 'prayer*, *'school 'prayer*) and WALL (*'city 'wall*, *'cell 'wall*), but such lexemes are very much in the minority. In fact, lexemes that cause this kind of patterning are so rare that it is probably true to say that the majority of double stressed compounds in English arise not through lexical conditioning of this kind, but through a semantic (or possibly syntactic) over-ruling of lexical conditioning of the kind illustrated above. There are also instances which appear to be lexicalized with double stress, despite the tendency for the drift to be in the other direction. An example is *re'turn 'ticket*, whose stress pattern I cannot explain in view of the fact that the regular pattern appears to be for single stress: *'theatre ticket*, *'season ticket*, *'flight ticket*, and even an unlikely nonce formation like *uni'versity ticket*.

It has been argued here that according to the criteria which are generally provided for deciding on whether (or to what extent) an item is a word, single and double stressed noun + noun collocations cannot be distinguished from each other. It has also been argued that generally speaking the difference between single and double stress does not correlate with a semantic difference, but that the stress patterns in productive noun + noun collocations can be seen as being lexically conditioned. All this suggests that the difference between single and double stressed collocations is not a distinction between two very different syntactic structures, but an accidental surface structure division in a unitary group of compounds, and that it makes more sense to talk of single and double stressed compounds than of compounds as opposed to noun + noun syntactic phrases.

The generative phonological approach to the generation of stress in compounds and phrases, as will be shown in the next section, depends crucially on there being a syntactic difference between single and double stressed compounds. It has been argued here that there is no such syntactic difference. It can thus be concluded that the generative phonological approach is defective. To show this more clearly, the approach to the generation of compounds taken in Chomsky & Halle (1968) will first be explained.

5.2.3 *The generative approach*

Stress assignment in compounds and in phrases is used by Chomsky & Halle as primary evidence for the cycle in phonology. They point out that in compounds in English, the general rule seems to be to give primary stress to the leftmost element, whereas in phrases the primary stress is assigned to the rightmost element. However, if that were all there was to it, then *blackboard eraser* 'an eraser for blackboards' and *black board eraser* 'an eraser of black boards' would be stressed identically, because at surface level they are both compounds. This is not what happens. Chomsky & Halle assign the following stress contours to these two interpretations of the same string of morphemes (where '1' represents the strongest degree of stress):

$$\begin{array}{ccc} 1 & 3 & 2 \end{array}$$
blackboard eraser

$$\begin{array}{ccc} 3 & 1 & 2 \end{array}$$
black board eraser

They suggest that the only way to arrive at this answer is to start by assigning stress to the innermost brackets in the bracketed structure, then to delete those brackets, and assign stress to the new innermost brackets, and so on until stress has been assigned to the whole structure. They add a convention that the confirmation or addition of a '1' stress level in any cycle of the stress rules reduces every other marked level of stress by one (adds one to every marked integer). Thus, for the two appropriate readings of the string, the pattern in Figure 5.1 emerges, where the compound stress assignment rule confirms a leftmost primary stress, and the phrase stress assignment rule confirms a rightmost primary stress within the constituent in question.

If the stress difference between '*literature book* and '*literature* '*textbook* is to be predicted by this model, '*literature book* will have to be generated under an N node, and '*literature* '*textbook* will have to be generated under an NP node. But it has been argued above that the difference in stress pattern between these two depends on the lexeme that occurs in second place. This implies that a specific lexical item generated in a tree should be able to influence the node under which it was generated, i.e. "choose" whether it should be generated under an N node or an NP node. This could only be done by some kind of global constraint in a standard transformational grammar, and this would increase the power of the grammar so much that it is undesirable if an alternative can be found. The

Initial bracketing	$[[[\text{black}]_A$	$[\text{board}]_N]_N$	$[\text{eraser}]_N]_N$	$[[[\text{black}]_A$	$[\text{board}]_N]_{NP}$	$[\text{eraser}]_N]_N$
Stress assignment to lexemes	1	1	1	1	1	1
New bracketing	[[black	$\text{board}]_N$	$\text{eraser}]_N$	[[black	$\text{board}]_{NP}$	$\text{eraser}]_N$
Cycle 1						
Compound stress assignment	1	2	—	—	—	—
Phrase stress assignment	—	—	—	2	1	—
New bracketing	[black	board	$\text{eraser}]_N$	[black	board	$\text{eraser}]_N$
Cycle 2						
Compound stress assignment	1	3	2	3	1	2
Phrase stress assignment	—	—	—	—	—	—
Final bracketing	black	board	eraser	black	board	eraser

Figure 5.1

alternative that has been suggested here – lexical conditioning with the possibility of a semantic override – does not fit easily into the framework of generative phonology, where semantic information is taken to be irrelevant for the phonological component.

5.3 Derivatives and stress
5.3.1 *A first approximation*
      The assignment of stress to English derivatives is an area in which there is currently a lot of disagreement. The disagreement is not about the data, since in the majority of cases adult native speakers of English do not seem to be in doubt as to how to stress familiar lexemes, but about the degree to which stress in derivatives can be predicted by general rule, and how such rules are best expressed.

      The data below will provide a starting point for the discussion.

(1a)	'perish	'perishable
	de'tach	de'tachable
(b)	'person	'personhood
	un'likely	un'likelihood
(c)	com'pact	com'pactness
	'nervous	'nervousness
(2a)	'tonsil	tonsil'litis
	'thyroid	thyroi'ditis
(b)	'picture	pictu'resque
	Ja'pan	Japa'nesque
(c)	'journal	journa'lese
	of'ficial	officia'lese
(3a)	'symbol	sym'bolic
	sur'realist	surrea'listic
(b)	ab'surd	ab'surdity
	'modern	mo'dernity
(c)	'Mongol	Mon'golian
	e'piscopal	episco'palian

    Three affixes are illustrated under (1), and in each case the stress of the derivative is on the same syllable of the base as it is when the base is pronounced in isolation. English has a lot of suffixes which do not affect the stress patterns of the base. Others are -*ish* (*'yellow* > *'yellowish*; *No'vember* > *No'vemberish*), -*like* (*'lady* > *'lady-like*), -*ment* (*'argue* > *'argument*; *a'chieve* > *a'chievement*).

    The three suffixes illustrated in (2) all bear the major stress of the derivative. The stress in derivatives like these is thus independent of the stress of the base, and determined solely by the suffix. Other suffixes which act in the same way are *-ee* (*ex'amine > exami'nee*), *-ette* (*'purser > purse'rette*, *'kitchen > kitche'nette*), and *-iana* (though this suffix may in addition, preserve the stress of the base: *'Shakespeare > 'Shakespeari'ana*).

Finally, the suffixes illustrated in (3) all take the stress on the syllable preceding the suffix in the derivative. This frequently causes variations in vowel quality, as in the examples in (3c): /'mɒŋgəl/ > /mɒŋ'gəʊlɪən/; /ɪ'pɪskəpəl/ > /ɪpɪskə'peɪlɪən/. Again, the stress of the derivative is determined by the suffix rather than by the base. Other suffixes which have the same effect are *-ia(c)* (*i'nert > i'nertia*, *'regal > re'galia*; *'demon > de'moniac*) and *-ial* (*'industry > in'dustrial*, *'circumstance > circum'stantial*).

Where a derivative contains more than one suffix, it is the last of these three types of suffix to be applied to the base which determines the main stress of the new lexeme, even if others have applied previously. Thus *'national* (which is itself the output of the suffixation of *-al* to *nation*) can act as the base to a formation in *-ist*. This suffix belongs to group (1) and does not affect the stress of the base, so that the output is *'nationalist. Nationalist* in turn can provide the base for suffixation in *-ic*. This suffix belongs to group (3) and thus causes the stress to fall immediately before it, so that the output is *nationa'listic*. If suffixation in *-ity* were possible on the base *nationa'listic*, the stress would change again. Similarly, *discover* can act as the base in *-able* suffixation. One of the suffixes listed in group (1), *-able* does not affect the stress of the base, so the output is *dis'coverable*. Any form in *-able* can act as the base to suffixation in *-ity*. This was mentioned in group (3) as a suffix which changes stress, and the output is *discovera'bility*.

The examples given above have all been chosen with care to illustrate general principles, but unfortunately the complete picture is not as simple as this outline would seem to imply. In what follows a number of points will be discussed which obscure the general pattern which has been set out above.

5.3.2 *Distinguishing a suffix*

Patterns of the type given above apply only when the final part of the word is a genuine suffix. That is, while such patterns can be used to predict the stress in words like *'perishable* and *de'tachable*, where *-able* is a suffix, they cannot be used to predict the stress in words like *'vegetable* and *'syllable*. In these last two words the same sequence of letters or phonemes (*-able*, /əb(ə)l/) occurs, but this sequence does not constitute a suffix. This point may seem totally self-evident, but can become very important when the linguist as analyst attempts to discover regularities in stress patterns from lists of lexemes (see Kingdon, 1958, where this confusion occurs).

While it is clear from the form class of *vegetable* and *syllable* that they do not contain the suffix which produces adjectives from verbs, there are many cases where it is far less clear whether a suffix is involved or not. Consider, for example, the suffix *-ic*. This suffix, as was mentioned above, usually takes the stress on the syllable preceding the suffix. This rule is still productive, as can be seen by the stress patterns on neologisms in *-ic*, e.g. the following listed in Barnhart *et al.* (1973): *alea'toric, allo'steric, bi'onic*. There are, however, a number of exceptions, of which the clearest is *'Arab·ic*. Since *Arabic* goes against the productive rule, it is a fairly clear case of a phonologically lexicalized form. The question is what other forms are also lexicalized because they break the same rule. To answer this question it is first necessary to know which of the candidates actually contain the suffix *-ic*.

Hill (1974: 8) lists twenty words ending in the letters *-ic* which are either normally pronounced with stress on the antepenultimate syllable rather than the penultimate, or have a common variant pronunciation with such a stress pattern. His list is reproduced here: *agaric, Arabic, arithmetic, arsenic, cadaveric, catholic, chivalric, choleric, climacteric, dominic, extuberic, heretic, lunatic, niccolic, nickelic, oghamic, phylacteric, politic, rhetoric, theoric*. However, as was shown with *-able* above, the fact that the final letters of a word are the same as those which form a suffix is no guarantee that the same suffix is present. Criteria must therefore be provided for separating the sheep that have nothing to do with the *-ic* suffix stress rule from the goats which break the rule.

The first possible criterion is that *-ic* is an adjective-forming suffix, and only adjectives should be covered by the rule. Hill clearly feels that there is no reason to separate the *-ic* which forms adjectives from the *-ic* which forms nouns like *lunatic* (that is, he takes them to be the same suffix), since several of the words can function in both ways, e.g. *catholic* (Hill, 1974: 9).

The second possible criterion is that there should be a base which is a potential stem. This would allow *Arabic*, *cadaveric*, *choleric*, *nickelic*, *oghamic*, *rhetoric* but disallow all the others. On the other hand, this is clearly too restrictive, since this criterion strictly applied would not show that *nomin·ee* is derived regularly from *nominate* with the *-ate* deleted (Aronoff, 1976: 88; below, §8.2.1). This process, which Aronoff terms **truncation**, is relatively common, and should not be excluded from regular word-formation. If truncation of the base is permitted, then at least *chivalric*, *phylacteric* and *theoric* can be included, and it should be noted that the same element *-y* has been truncated from each of these. *Heretic*, *lunatic* and *politic* provide an extra problem here, because although a *-y* has been deleted, there has also been a consonant change of /s/ to /t/. It seems likely that this criterion should be relaxed sufficiently to allow these three forms to be included, but perhaps only because the alternation between /s/ and /t/ is fairly regular in English before *-y* (*clement/clemency*, etc.).

Although the truncation of the base must be permitted in making decisions of this kind, the existence of extra phonemes between the base and the putative suffix must be treated with extreme caution, otherwise *bishopric* would have to be included as a possible exception to the rule, despite the presence of the /r/. Note that the unpronounceability of **bishopr* is no clue, since *metric* is regularly derived from *metre* despite the unpronounceability of **metr*.

The biggest problem, however, in deciding whether or not the suffix is present is where, even when truncation is allowed for, the base is not a potential stem. In English this arises particularly frequently when the base is a root from a foreign – usually classical – lexeme. An example with *-ic* (although not a relevant example in terms of the exceptions to the stress rule) is *ludic*. There are no clear examples of this type in the list given earlier, since in the examples given there the *-ic* was always part of the classical stem. Hill (1974: 10) suggests that such forms should be accepted as suffixed forms in those cases where the word-form without the putative suffix is a recurrent formative in a derivational paradigm. He gives the example of *pubic*, where the *pub-* recurs in *pubescent*, *puberty* and *pubis*. The objection to this decision method is that it is not clear that *-escent*, *-erty* and *-is* can be treated as English suffixes in the way that *-ic* can, so that this might not represent a genuine derivational paradigm. Since many of the words in which this is a problem are loans, there is also an etymological reason for not treating the *-ic* in such forms as an English suffix.

Semantic criteria are even less reliable than formal criteria. It might be expected that a single suffix would have a single semantic effect, and that the lack of this semantic effect could be used as evidence for not taking the element under consideration as a suffix. However, it is perfectly possible for the semantic effect to be obscured by lexicalization. Indeed, an etymological suffix could eventually lose its motivation as a result of lexicalization, and a word in which it occurs come to be viewed as simplex. An example is *nimble*, which is probably not felt to contain a suffix, although etymologically it does. It thus seems misleading to use meaning as a decisive criterion, although it may be useful as a supplementary criterion.

The discussion here has outlined the problems rather than provided a solution. It seems likely that the solution adopted by any individual on any one occasion will depend on the weighting given to the various factors mentioned here, and to the usefulness of the result provided by any given set of criteria: in other words, there may not be a simple, eternally valid answer to the problem. The important thing to note is that there can be a problem here, and that the answer is not always as straight-forward as the *vegetable* example which began this section may have suggested.

5.3.3   *General stress rules*

Although there is not general agreement on the form that the rules for English stress take, there does seem to be agreement that the stress in the majority of English words can be generated by very general rules (Chomsky & Halle, 1968; Goyvaerts & Pullum, 1975). These rules interact with the rules of word-formation so that they ignore some affixes, but take others into account. In this section I shall consider briefly some of these general rules.

The first of these is that in words of three or more syllables there is a tendency in English to put the stress on the third syllable from the end, the antepenultimate syllable or the **antepenult**. This can be seen in such words as *a'pology*, *'charlatan*, *cur'riculum*, '*parody*. There are innumerable exceptions to this (hence the use of the word "tendency"), some of which can be accounted for by sub-regularities. Examples of words which do not fit with this tendency are *ab'scissa, chande'lier, kanga'roo, mayon'naise, re'plenish*. With disyllabic suffixes, the antepenult will be the syllable immediately preceding the suffix, and the application of this general tendency can lead to stress patterns like those illustrated in type (3b, c) in §5.3.1 above.

A second tendency in English is for the final tense vowel in a word to be stressed when this comes later than the antepenult. The tense vowels of English are all the diphthongs, /i, ɔ, u/ and, on most analyses, /ɑ, ɜ/. This tendency accounts for the stress on the last syllables of *chande'lier, kanga'roo* and *mayon'naise* listed above, and for the penultimate stress on *barra'cuda, o'asis* and *bam'boozle*. It will be noted that many of the suffixes of English that bear the main stress of the derivative contain a tense vowel, for example *-ee, -ese, -iana, -itis*.

A third tendency is for the penultimate syllable to receive the stress when it is closed by a consonant cluster. Examples are *a'genda, as'bestos* and *ve'randah*.

5.3.4 *Illustration: adjectival '-al'*

To illustrate the way in which stress interacts with word-formation three different suffixes will be considered. The first of these is the *-al* used to form adjectives. In terms of the three groups listed in §5.3.1, *-al* appears to act like a group 1 suffix some of the time and a group 3 suffix at other times. Some examples of each pattern are listed below:

Group 1: stress of the base remains constant

'comic	'comical
'culture	'cultural
di'vision	di'visional
'doctor	'doctoral
'person	'personal
pro'fession	pro'fessional
'ration	'rational
'season	'seasonal
sta'tistic	sta'tistical
'stomach	'stomachal

Group 3: stress on the syllable before the suffix

'adjective	adjec'tival
'ancestor	an'cestral
'anecdote	anec'dotal
'baptism	bap'tismal
'dialect	dia'lectal
'ornament	orna'mental
'parent	pa'rental
'patricide	patri'cidal
'triumph	tri'umphal

However, these examples can be rationalized in terms of the general stress rules discussed in the last section. If the vowel in the penultimate syllable is tense, then it is stressed: *adjectival*,[3] *anecdotal*, *patricidal*. If the penultimate syllable is closed by a consonant cluster, then it is stressed: *ancestral*, *baptismal*, *dialectal*, *ornamental*, *parental*, *triumphal*. Otherwise the stress falls on the antepenult, as in all those listed in group 1 above. These rules apply even in cases which would not be accounted for by either a group 1 or a group 3 classification of *-al*:

'architecture	archi'tectural
'agriculture	agri'cultural
'concubine	con'cubinal
'maniac	ma'niacal (/mə'naɪək(ə)l/)
'medicine	me'dicinal
'origin	o'riginal
'pseudonym	pseu'donymal
'residue	re'sidual

and there are cases where the rules will even account for alternative stress patterns:

'doctrine	'doctrinal (/'dɒktrɪnəl/)
	doc'trinal (/dɒk'traɪnəl/)
in'testine	in'testinal (/ɪn'testɪnəl/)
	intes'tinal (/ɪntes'taɪnəl/)

---

[3] A question has been begged here, since it might equally well be asked how it is known that the penultimate vowel in *adjectival* is tense when the corresponding vowel in *adjective* is lax. In generative phonology this problem would be solved by giving the lexeme ADJECTIVE (or the appropriate formative in that lexeme) an underlying tense vowel which would be made lax in just those cases where *-al* did not follow. That /ɪ/ is the lax vowel which corresponds to tense /aɪ/ is verified from such pairs as *divine/divinity*. Similar problems are raised by an example like *concubine/concubinal* listed below.

The general rule, then, seems to be that the stress rules of English ignore the fact that *-al* is a suffix, and apply to derivatives in *-al* in the same way that they would apply to simplex forms. There are some exceptions to this general rule, but not very many. *Disciplinal* has two possible stress patterns, *dis'ciplinal* which obeys the general rule and *'disciplinal* which does not. The same is true of *gerundival*, where *ge'rundival* is the regular pronunciation and *'gerundival* the irregular one. Finally, *'caricatural* has the stress much further from the end than is normal in English. It is probably not coincidence that the irregular stresses here maintain the original stress of the base lexeme.

The general rule is also applied when truncation occurs. The question of the regularity of the truncation illustrated in the examples below will not be considered here, except to point out that a final /ə/ must be deleted before *-al* to avoid the impossible sequence /əə/:

abo'rigine	abo'rigin(e)al
a'pocrypha	a'pocryph(a)al
la'cuna	la'cun(a)al
'minimum	'minim(um)al
o'blivion	o'blivi(on)al

Finally, the same rules seem to apply – not surprisingly this time – in cases where the affixal status of the *-al* could be called into doubt because of the fact that the base is not a free lexeme: *'criminal, di'agonal, 'lachrymal, 'seminal*.

5.3.5 *Illustration: '-ette'*

Semantically it is possible to distinguish a number of meanings, or possibly a number of distinct suffixes, for the form *-ette*. These include a pure diminutive as in *rangette, sermonette, storiette*, a marker of imitation material, as in *beaverette, flannelette, leatherette*, and a feminine marker as in *farmerette, majorette* and *suffragette*. As far as stress is concerned, however, all these types of *-ette* appear to act in the same way, and they can accordingly be treated together for the purposes of this section.

The suffix *-ette*, like *-ic*, does not allow for the same kind of simple treatment in terms of general stress rules as *-al*. In fact, Chomsky & Halle (1968: 158) list *-ette* as an irregular suffix, since it does not contain a tense vowel and yet is stressed on the suffix. In this it is like *-esque*. Although most words in *-ette* have two syllables before the suffix, the stress remains on the suffix independent of the number of syllables preceding it: *ran'gette*, *roo'mette*; *kitche'nette*, *leade'rette*; *paraso'lette*; *undergradu'ette*. The stress remains on the suffix whether the word is etymologically a loan, as *ciga'rette*, *statu'ette*, or a native formation, as *lectu'rette*, *line'nette*. The stress remains on the suffix when the base is truncated, as in *crinol(ine)'ette*, *jock(ey)'ette*, *pian(o)'ette* and *undergradu(ate)'ette*. There are very few cases where the suffixal status of *-ette* is in question, but even in examples like *cosmo'nette* and *fu'mette* the stress is on the *-ette*. The only possible instances of a break with this pattern that I have found are *'letterette* (stress as marked in the *OED*), which has a variant *lette'rette* (marked in *Webster's*), and *'tablette* which is a variant of *'tablet*.

While stress patterns for words ending in *-al* could be explained by general rules of English stress, the same is not true for the stress patterns of words ending in *-ette*. In this a word-formation-based approach which notes that the suffix always carries stress is a far more satisfactory way of predicting stress in the derivatives.

5.3.6 *Illustration: '-ism'*

With *-ism*, only instances where the suffix is added to a lexeme will be considered, although there are many cases where *-ism* is added to something other than a lexeme, and where the affixal status of the *-ism* might therefore be in doubt: *anachronism*, *feminism*, *hedonism*, etc. The general rule with *-ism* is then that the stress on a derivative ending in the suffix *-ism* is on the same syllable as in the unsuffixed base. This is true with a monosyllabic base (*'cubism*, *'racism*), a disyllabic base (*'magnetism*, *'symbolism*; *ca'reerism*), a trisyllabic base (*'cannibalism*, *'hooliganism*; *con'sumerism*, *fa'naticism*; *absen'teeism*, *suffra'gettism*) and even with longer bases (*ma'terialism*; *dilet'tanteism*; *evan'gelicalism*; *parliamen'tarianism*). The general rule remains true even after truncation: *ca'tastroph(e)ism*, *propa'gand(a)ism*. It makes no difference whether the stress on the base is determined by general stress rules, as in *ca'reerism*, *'hooliganism*, *'symbolism*, or by rules associated with word-formation, as in *di'dacticism*, *suffra'gettism*.

In this case the stress rules appear to ignore word-formation, but not in the same way as they did with *-al*. With *-al* the stress rules applied to the complete derivative, while with *-ism* they apply only to the base, and not to the complete derivative.

There are a number of examples which are lexicalized with respect to this general stress rule. The stress on *me'tabolism* can be predicted from general principles, but not by the general rule with *-ism* if it is assumed that *me'tabolism* is derived from *meta'bolic* with truncation of the *-ic*. In at least two very interesting cases, *a'rabicism* and *ca'tholicism*, the stress on the *-ism* derivative is that which would be predicted if the base had regular stress according to the rule pertaining to *-ic*; what is surprising is that both *'Arabic* and *'catholic* are lexicalized with respect to the *-ic* stress rule (see above, §5.3.2). That means that although the stress pattern appears to be regular here, it must be lexicalized because the stress on the base is lexicalized.

5.3.7 *Summing up suffixes*

At the beginning of this section, suffixes were divided into three groups according to the placement of stress in relation to them. This type of structural approach to the problem of stress in derivatives is basically that taken by, for example, Kingdon (1958), and although it is frequently helpful, it does not show up all the possible generalizations about stress in derivatives.

The examples considered in §§5.3.4–6 have been chosen as representative examples of quite large classes. In particular, *-al* and *-ism* behave in the same ways as large numbers of other suffixes; most of the suffixes that behave like *-ette* contain a tense vowel, and can be treated according to general rules independent of word-formation (see §5.3.3). The suffix *-ic* is unique in its behaviour with respect to stress. Further examples of each type of suffix are listed in Table 5.3. In addition to the derivational suffixes, all inflectional suffixes act like *-ism* as far as stress is concerned. The lists are not exhaustive.

In generative phonology the difference between suffixes like *-al* and suffixes like *-ism* is accounted for by postulating two different boundaries, a formative boundary, marked '+', and a word boundary, marked '#'. Each suffix is associated with a boundary. The formative boundary does not block the application of the general stress rules, so that in a string like:

#season + al#

Table 5.3.

Like -*al*	Like -*ette*	Like -*ism*
-ian	-ee	-age
-ify	-eer	-er
-ity	-ese	-ful
-ous	-esque	-ist
-y (n.)		-ive
		-ize
		-less
		-ness
		-ship
		-y (adj.)

the stress rules apply to everything between the word boundaries. The word boundary, however, is stronger, and blocks the application of general stress rules, so that in a string like:

#cannibal # ism#

the general stress rules apply to the base, but are prevented from taking the suffix into account by the presence of the internal word boundary. Suffixes like -*ette* are treated in the same way as suffixes like -*al*, except for -*ette* itself and -*esque* which, as was pointed out earlier, do not fit the general rules. They have to be marked as irregular, despite the evident regularity in their behaviour. The suffix -*ic* provides a major problem for the generative account. Chomsky & Halle (1968: 88) suggest that it should have the underlying form +*ic* +*al*, and the -*al* should be deleted in an *ad hoc* manner where it is not required, by a rule operating after the general stress rules. This provides difficulty in deciding when the -*al* is and is not required, since there does not seem to be any general way of deciding, and in fact there are even synonymous pairs where one member has just -*ic* and the other has -*ic·al*: e.g. *geometric*/*geometrical*. Also, since Chomsky & Halle have no concept of lexicalization built into their model, it implies that pairs such as *economic*/*economical*, *electric*/*electrical* and *historic*/*historical* are simply free variants and synonymous, which is manifestly not the case.

On the whole, then, it appears that the generative approach to stress in derivatives has considerable advantages over the purely taxonomic approach outlined in §5.3.1, despite a number of disadvantages that are peculiar to the generative formulation. There have been numerous attempts in the years since the generative phonology orthodoxy was first established to improve upon this standard model (see, for example, the very technical papers collected in Goyvaerts & Pullum, 1975), but none has yet been generally accepted, although various aspects of many have met with approval. It is perhaps worth noting that at least one of these alternatives (Fudge, 1975), while accepting many of the benefits accruing from the generative formulation, has returned to something more closely resembling the taxonomic approach with the suggestion that individual affixes should be marked as having one of a small number of possible behaviour characteristics with reference to stress. It is suggested that such a system might be more realistic as a model of what actually goes on inside a speaker's head, since speakers seem to use the information provided by suffixes when stressing words that they have never met before (Fudge, 1975: 287). This kind of approach fits in well with the kind of description that has been presented here.

5.3.8 *Prefixes*

The most general rule that can be given for prefixes is that they do not bear primary stress and do not affect the stress of derivatives, but there are innumerable exceptions to this. There is, however, frequently a subsidiary stress on a prefix, and always one if the prefix consists of more than one syllable.

There is some disagreement in the literature about exactly what should be classed as a prefix. The disagreement concerns the initial syllables of words like *confer*, *defer*, *infer*, *refer*; *admit*, *commit*, *remit*, *submit*. If these are prefixes, then the -*fer* and -*mit* elements must be bound roots. However, no single meaning can be given either for the putative bound root or for the putative prefixes in such series of words (Aronoff, 1976: 11–15). In this way they are unlike normal roots and prefixes, and this leads some authorities (e.g. Marchand, 1969: 137) to conclude that such words are synchronically simplex, though etymologically complex. On the other hand, scholars whose interest is primarily phonological consider such words to be complex. Firstly, unlike other prefixes and unlike simplex words, the first syllables in words of the *refer*, *submit* type can bear neither secondary nor primary stress (Chomsky & Halle, 1968: 94). Furthermore, the putative bound root sometimes acts phonologically in an idiosyncratic way. Thus *-mit* has the allomorph *-miss* before the suffix *-ive* (*admissive*, *omissive*, *permissive*, *remissive*, *submissive*) while other words that just happen to end in *-mit* do not show the same allomorphy, for example, *vomitive* (Aronoff, 1976: 13). The best solution here, and the one that Aronoff adopts, seems to be to admit the elements in these words as formatives, but not to classify them as morphs; this excludes such elements as prefixes (for the terms 'formative' and 'morph' see §2.5).

There are a few genuine prefixes which never take subsidiary or primary stress, but these are in the minority: they are *a-* (as in *ablaze*), *be-* (as in *becalm*) and *en-* (as in *enslave*). These prefixes are all slightly productive. Other prefixes take a certain degree of stress: Marchand (1969: §3.1.6) notes that most sources mark only secondary stress on most prefixes, indicating that a full vowel is used, but not full length or maximal pitch distinction. Under exceptional circumstances, such as contrast or emphasis, these prefixes can take full stress: so that *re'type* would normally have secondary stress on the prefix, but in a sentence like *I know you've already typed this once, but you made so many mistakes that I want you to retype it* the primary stress can fall on the prefix *'retype*.

There are also several sets of circumstances under which a prefix can take primary stress without any emphasis or contrast. The first of these is if the prefix is lexically marked as taking full stress. The clearest example of this type is *step-* as in *'step-father*, which is probably no longer productive, but *counter-* added to nouns seems to be another candidate: *'counter-attraction*, *'counter-move* (Marchand, 1969: §3.1.18 lists some others which do not appear to take full stress regularly).

Prefixes are stressed much more often in nouns than in verbs; there are even pairs of noun and verb with the same prefix where the distinction between the two is a difference of stress (often with consequential vowel changes):

noun	verb
'discharge	dis'charge
'discount	dis'count
'infix	in'fix
'interchange	inter'change
'refill	re'fill

Non-prefixed forms, some of which contain the Latin formatives discussed earlier in this section, also take part in such stress alternations:

'permit	per'mit
'segment	seg'ment

(see Gimson, 1970, 234ff for a more complete list). But even in cases where there is no corresponding verb, the tendency for the noun to be stressed on the prefix seems to persist, so that there are, for example, far more nouns in *sub-* with stress on the first syllable (*'subcommittee*, *'subdivision*, *'substructure*, *'subway*) than there are adjectives (*sub'alpine*, *subcu'taneous*, *sub-'human*) or verbs (*sub'classify*, *sub'edit*, *sub'join*). There are also cases of nouns in *sub-* not being stressed on the prefix: *sub'junction*, *sublieu'tenant*, *sub-ma'chine gun*; it may be the case that one of these series is lexicalized. This tendency to stress the prefix in nouns is particularly strong when the prefix is disyllabic or longer; sometimes the base still retains a primary stress under these conditions: *'antifreeze*, *'antechamber*, *'crypto-(')communist*. It is difficult to know whether such learned prefixes as *crypto-*, *pseudo-*, etc., should be included here, since it will be argued later (see §7.3) that these are not genuine prefixes in English.

On the whole the interaction of prefixes and stress is far less well studied and understood than the interaction of suffixes and stress in English. It seems fairly certain, however, that some of the same factors apply: in some cases lexical marking of affixes seems to be a desirable way of predicting stress (see also Fudge, 1975); in other cases more general rules apply to affixed forms; in other cases the general rules ignore the affixes. It also seems likely that there are many prefixed forms which display lexicalized stress patterns, and this should be taken into account when discussing the ways in which prefixes and stress interact.

5.4 Segmental variation in word-formation

One frequent concomitant of word-formation in English, particularly, but not exclusively, in established forms, is a change in the phonemic make-up of an item. Realizations of a morpheme which, while clearly related to each other, differ in at least one phoneme, are termed **morphophonemic alternants** of that morpheme. Strictly speaking, morphophonemic alternants are allomorphs conditioned by the word-formation process undergone. This will be illustrated below. A list of pairs of words is given, where the members of each pair are related by some process of word-formation, and then the phonemes involved are listed beside each pair. The symbol '∼' is to be read as 'alternates with'.

(1a)	author	authority	ɔ ∼ ə	ə ∼ ɒ
	commerce	commercial	ɒ ∼ ə	
	cremate	crematorium	eɪ ∼ ə	ɪ ∼ e
	particle	particular	ɑ ∼ ə	
	photograph	photography	əʊ ∼ ə	ə ∼ ɒ
	telegraph	telegraphy	e ∼ ə	ɪ ∼ e
(b)	regal	regalia	i ∼ ɪ	ə ∼ eɪ
(c)	tutor	tutorial	u ∼ ʊ	ə ∼ ɔ
(2)	divine	divinity	aɪ ∼ ɪ	
	profane	profanity	eɪ ∼ æ	
	profound	profundity	aʊ ∼ ʌ	
	serene	serenity	i ∼ e	
(3)	broad	breadth	ɔ ∼ e	
	long	length	ɒ ∼ e	
	wide	width	aɪ ∼ ɪ	
(4)	Aberdeen	Aberdonian	i ∼ əʊ	
	appear	apparent	ɪə ∼ æ	
	approve	approbation	u ∼ əʊ	v ∼ b
	compel	compulsory	e ∼ ʌ	
	example	exemplary	ɑ ∼ e	
	glass	glazier	ɑ ∼ eɪ	s ∼ z
	hilarity	hilarious	æ ∼ eə	
	lion	leonine	aɪ ∼ i	
	number	numerous	ʌ ∼ (j)u	
	obey	obedient	eɪ ∼ i	
	peace	pacifist	i ∼ æ	
	school	scholar	u ∼ ɒ	
	Troy	Trojan	ɔɪ ∼ əʊ	ø ∼ dʒ
	war	warrior	ɔ ∼ ɒ	
(5)	advice	advise	s ∼ z	
	belief	believe	f ∼ v	

	sheath	sheathe	θ ~ ð
(6)	convulse	convulsion	s ~ ʃ
	electric	electricity	k ~ s
	fuse	fusion	z ~ ʒ
	part	partial	t ~ ʃ
	persuade	persuasion	d ~ ʒ

Groups (1)–(4) show morphophonemic vowel alternations of various kinds, and groups (5) and (6) show consonantal alternations. Group (1) presents some examples of vowel alternation under varying stress conditions which are the result of word-formation. In (1a) are examples of the alternation of full vowels with /ə/, in (1b) is an example of the alternation of a full vowel with /ɪ/, and in (1c) an example of the alternation of a full vowel with /ʊ/. /ə, ɪ, ʊ/ are the three reduced vowels in the Received Pronunciation of English, and as the examples indicate /ə/ is by far the most common of these. Vowel reduction when an item is not stressed is a very common phenomenon in English, and is not restricted to word-formation. Consider the sentence *I must have the money and an apology from all of them.* If each of the words were to be pronounced in isolation and under stress, a transcription for this sentence would be /'aɪ 'mʌst 'hæv 'ði 'mʌnɪ 'ænd 'æn ə'pɒlədʒɪ 'frɒm 'ɔl 'ɒv 'ðem/. This would not, however, be a normal way of saying this sentence. One possible pronunciation would be /ə 'mʌst əv ðə 'mʌnɪ ənd ən ə'pɒlədʒɪ frəm 'ɔl əv ðəm/, where the vowels in the unstressed words have been reduced to /ə/. Precisely the same kind of thing happens in word-formation, and since vowel reduction is predictable in conjunction with stress, it is just as predictable in word-formation as stress is. This kind of alternation need thus be of no further concern in this section.

Group (2) presents some examples of one particular kind of alternation between stressed vowels: it is the type of alternation that resulted from the Great Vowel Shift in the fifteenth century. Before the Great Vowel Shift, *divine* and *divinity* were pronounced [di'viːn] and [di'viːniti]. Then a sound change took place which shortened all long vowels in antepenultimate syllables (this is something of a simplification, but sufficient for present purposes) so that the forms became [di'viːn] and [di'viniti], and then in the Great Vowel Shift the articulation of long vowels was changed. In the case of [iː], it became [əi] and later [ai], so that the modern pronunciation /dɪ'vaɪn/ and /dɪ'vɪnɪtɪ/ arose. Equivalent changes took place in all the other pairs in group (2) to give the morphophonemic alternants that are found today. These variants now correlate with established derivational processes.

The stressed vowel alternants in group (3) can also be explained in historical terms, though the changes involved took place much earlier, and were established by Old English.

The vowel alternants in group (4) are a miscellaneous group, and have arisen for a number of reasons historically. One reason, which comes out in, for example, *approbation*, *leonine* and *pacifist*, is that the non-affixed form came into English through Old French, while the affixed form was a late borrowing direct from Latin, so that the sound changes which differentiated Latin from Old French have taken place in one member of the pair, but not in the other.

The consonantal alternants in group (5) all arose because of the sound pattern of Old English. In Old English, [f] and [v], [θ] and [ð], [s] and [z], were allophones of the same phoneme, and not individual phonemes. In each case the voiced member of the pair occurred intervocalically. In each of the cases illustrated, the fricative occurred intervocalically in the verb, because the final *e* was pronounced in Old English. When the final *e* ceased to be pronounced, the pairs of words were kept apart by the voicing in the fricatives, and so the fricatives provided two different series of phonemes: /f/ vs. /v/, /θ/ vs. /ð/ and /s/ vs. /z/.

The alternations in group (6) occurred because of rules which are still productive (except possibly for the /k/~/s/ alternation, whose productivity is disputed; see below, p. 138). Most of them show coalescent assimilation, whereby /s, z, t, d/ were palatalized to /ʃ, ʒ/ before /i/ or /j/. This process can be seen to be productive in instances like *issue*, pronounced /'ɪsju/ or /'ɪʃu/, or *this year* pronounced /ðɪʃ'jʒ/.

These examples are merely symptomatic of a phenomenon which is extremely widespread in English. If the alternants in strong verbs and irregular plurals are included, it can be shown that somewhere in the English language most vowels alternate with most other vowels. Consonant alternation is more restricted, but is also wider than the examples given illustrate. The question now to be answered is: what role does this variation play in the phonology? As far as the structuralist phonemicists were concerned, the answer was 'none'. In structural terms it is important that /aɪ/ and /ɪ/ are separate phonemes (as is evidenced by minimal pairs such as *dine/din*), and that /aɪ/ and /ɪ/ have different distributions (/aɪ/ can occur word-finally in a monosyllabic word, /ɪ/ has to be followed by a consonant, so /daɪ/ is an existing word, but */dɪ/ is not even a possible word of English), but it was not important that they alternated in different realizations of the same morpheme.

Even those structuralists who were interested in morphophonemics did not show a great deal of interest in such alternants. They were mostly concerned with morphophonemic alternants that showed up in inflectional paradigms. Thus the /f/~/v/ alternation in *knife* as opposed to *knives* was of interest, but the/f/~/v/ alternation in *a calf* as opposed to *to calve* was not given the same amount of attention.

It was left to the generative phonologists to make a major issue of morphophonemic alternation. Generative phonology takes as its input the output of the syntactic component in a transformational generative grammar. This means that the input to the phonological component is a labelled and bracketed (but not semantically interpreted) string of morphemes. Each morpheme has to be listed in the lexicon, so that its meaning can be discovered. To list the morpheme with the same information about its meaning in every form in which it occurs would obviously be uneconomical, and so it is seen as desirable that each morpheme should be listed only once. This is seen to imply that each morpheme should, ideally, be listed with only one form, and that form should be changed, by a number of general rules, each dependent upon the phonological, morphological or lexical environment, to provide the full range of morpheme variants found in English. This means that, to account for data like that in (2) above, the phonological component has to have a rule which shortens vowels in the antepenultimate syllable of words (Chomsky & Halle's rule of "trisyllabic laxing") and another rule, or set of rules, which recreates the effects of the Great Vowel Shift. That is, many of the rules of generative phonology as expounded in Chomsky & Halle (1968) recapitulate historical developments in English, and (not surprisingly when it is considered that English spelling represents the phonemics of an earlier stage of the development of English) there is frequently a close resemblance between the traditional orthography and the underlying phonological representations with which Chomsky & Halle operate.

There is no doubt that a phonology of this type can be made to work, in the sense that it is possible to create underlying representations and a set of rules which will produce the correct surface forms. There are always a few exceptions to the rules, but they can be handled by marking particular morphemes as exceptions to specific rules. Thus the pair *obese/obesity* show that the morpheme {obese} does not undergo the trisyllabic laxing rule, since if it did, the result would be /əʊbesɪtɪ/ (note *serene/serenity*). {Obese} must thus be marked in the lexicon as [− Rule x], where x is the number of the trisyllabic laxing rule. Despite the fact that this standard model of generative phonology works, it has been criticized from a number of points of view.

Firstly, there does not appear to be any principled way to decide under what conditions two surface phonetic strings should be derived from the same underlying morpheme, that is, when the rules of the phonology should predict a given alternation, and when they should not, and consequently, when words should be considered as being linked by a process of word-formation. Consider the following pairs:

orange	orange juice
love	lover
medicine	medicinal
Johnson	Johnsonian
malign	malignant
doubt	dubious
young	youth
holy	holiday
acre	agriculture
moon	menstrual
duke	seduce
dear	dearth
rule	regular
gonads	germ
doff	hacienda

Everyone would probably agree that the first pair should be related, although the delight of one small girl when she discovered that *orange* had something to do with *orange juice* has already been mentioned (§3.1). There would also be general agreement that *love*

and *lover* should be related, even though there are two separate
lexemes here, and not a repetition of the same lexeme. *Medicine*
and *medicinal* have a change of stress, but are still close enough for
people to feel that they are related. *Johnson* and *Johnsonian* have a
change of stress and a vowel change, but are still felt as related. In
the next pair, there is a vowel shift, and a difference in the
consonants, and yet *malign* /mə'laɪn/ and *malignant* /mə'lɪgnənt/
are still felt as related, and presumably it would be expected that a
generative phonology should show this. The orthography might be
one factor involved in the recognition of a relation here. In *doubt*
and *dubious* things might be starting to become slightly less
clearcut. The vowel is different, the /t/ is replaced by /b/, but still
the meaning relates the pair. *Young* and *youth* are connected by
meaning, and possibly by spelling, though phonemically speaking
they have no more in common than *yes* and *yawl*. *Holy* and *holiday*
I would probably not associate if I hadn't had the etymology of
holiday pointed out to me in school: in the modern world holidays
are frequently pagan. In the next pairs, *acre* and *agriculture* and
moon and *menstrual*, the forms are diverging more, and the
meanings are also further apart, but with a little thought they can
be connected. To link *duke* and *seduce* requires a knowledge of
Latin, and they may be too far apart for the native speaker of
English to think of them as being connected. *Dear* and *dearth* have
the spelling in common, but semantically have so little to do with
each other that most people would probably not think of them as
linked, even though they are etymologically related in the same way
as the other adjectives and nouns in group (3) at the head of this
section. *Rule* and *regular* have a certain amount in common
semantically, but not a great deal formally, and the phrase "a
regular rule" is common enough to suggest that many people don't
see any semantic relation between the two. *Gonads* and *germs* seem a
very long way from each other, both formally and semantically,
although it is possible to work out a vague semantic link, and they
are both derived by different routes from an Indo-European
element **-gn-*, to do with begetting, and are also etymologically
related to *cognate*, *generate*, *genital*, *kin* and *pregnant*. *Doff* and
hacienda seem to have nothing whatsoever to do with each other
although they are both derived ultimately from a common source,
hacienda deriving from Latin *facere* 'to do'.

If the intuitions of the native speaker are to be taken as the yardstick whereby the relatedness of lexemes is judged, then (assuming the above list to reflect a hierarchy of relatedness) the cut-off point is likely to be somewhere around *holiday*. Unfortunately, native speakers' intuitions are also capable of linking forms which are etymologically unrelated, such as *limb* and *limber*, for example. There is also a problem in that the cut-off point is likely to be in different places for different people. Some phonologists claim that since the phonological component has to provide a phonology for the ideal speaker-listener who has a perfect knowledge of his language, it is unfair to look at the reported knowledge of a few individuals. The question then must be what to use in the place of intuition. Since the generative phonology so often recapitulates the etymology, should the etymology be used as a criterion in those cases when it is known? By that criterion all the pairs in the above list (including *doff* and *hacienda*) would be related by word-formation, and should thus be derived from an underlying morpheme of constant form. (See Lightner, 1975, for a proposal along these lines. Some of the examples in the above list were taken from his article.) In many ways the etymology seems an even less reliable guide than intuitions. Not only do ordinary speakers of a language (i.e. those who have not made a special study of etymology or linguistics) not have any knowledge of the history of words, but there seems to be no reason to expect the ideal speaker-listener to know the history of his own and a number of related or culturally important languages either. Quite apart from anything else, it implies that although the linguist can work out what the competence of the ideal speaker-listener of English should be like, since the history of English is known back to Proto-Indo-European, it is impossible for the linguist to work out what the competence of the ideal speaker-listener of any language whose history is not known should be like.

One of the reasons that it is possible to make such proposals within the framework of generative phonology is that there are no restrictions on how abstract an underlying representation may be. There have recently been a number of proposals made in the literature for restrictions on abstractness of this type, but so far none of them have won general acceptance. For example, one such proposal was that the underlying form of a morpheme should always be identical to one of the forms in which that morpheme appeared on the surface. The idea is that if such a restriction is held to, it will prove impossible to provide general rules to derive extreme forms from it: if the underlying form were taken as *doff* it would not be possible to motivate general rules with a wide application to give *hacienda*, or vice versa. Unfortunately, however, it turns out that this restriction is unsuitable. This can be seen from the pair *telegraph* and *telegraphy*. Although an /e/ appears in the first syllable of *telegraph* and the second of *telegraphy* there is no form containing the formative *tele* which has an /e/ in both syllables: there is always a reduced vowel in one syllable or the other. Now, it was stated above that it is possible to predict a reduced vowel from the full vowel and a knowledge of the stress pattern. It is not possible, however, to predict a full vowel from a reduced vowel, since the majority of vowels reduce to /ə/. To predict the vowel qualities here, therefore, an underlying /e/ must be present in both syllables, even though the formative never appears on the surface in this form. The proposed restriction can thus be seen to be unsuitable.

This is just one example of the type of proposal that has been made in an attempt to deal with the abstractness problem. A useful summary of a number of others can be found in Jensen (1974), but these need not be of concern here. Two proposals at the most concrete end of the scale are worth considering in greater detail: the proposals put forward in natural generative phonology, and those put forward under the title of "upside-down" phonology.

Both these proposals contest the claim that it is necessarily more economical for a single morpheme to have only one underlying representation, and in both it has been suggested that words should be entered as basic forms. "Upside-down" phonology (Leben & Robinson, 1977) uses the same kinds of rules as standard generative phonology, but applies them in reverse order: instead of starting with the morphemes and changing the form of the morphemes to provide surface phonetic forms, "upside-down" phonology starts with the surface forms and uses the rules to change them until it becomes clear whether or not two morphemes are related. Thus rather than applying a process of word-formation to a base, "upside-down" phonology starts with a derivative and shows it to be related to its base. Consider the example of *divine/divinity*. In standard generative phonology, as has been said, the underlying form of the morpheme {divine} is something like [divi:n], and when this appears before the suffix -*ity* the rule of trisyllabic laxing applies, while where the vowel remains stressed and long the vowel shift rule applies to give /dɪvaɪn/ and /dɪvɪnɪtɪ/. In "upside-down" phonology, the forms /dɪvaɪn/ and /dɪvɪnɪtɪ/ form the starting point. In a stressed long vowel like /aɪ/ the vowel shift rule works in reverse, to give [i:], and in the antepenultimate syllable the trisyllabic laxing rule works in reverse to change the second /ɪ/ to [i:]. It is then possible to compare the two forms, and say that they are identical, and so that the same morpheme is present in both *divine* and *divinity*. There is a convention that rules which would make forms less like each other should not apply, so that in the case of *obese*/*obesity* any rule will make the two occurrences of /əu'bis/ less like each other: no rules apply, and it can be seen that the two are the same morpheme. This means that exceptions are more easily dealt with in "upside-down" phonology than in standard generative phonology.

There are, however, a number of problems with this approach. Consider examples like *cute*/*cutaneous*, *pie*/*pious* and *sail*/*unassailable*. The sequences /kjut/, /paɪ/ and /seɪl/ in each of these pairs are not related semantically or etymologically, and yet the rules of "upside-down" phonology will relate them, since the application of any rules will make the sequence less like each other. *Pious* would thus be analysed as the result of -*ous* suffixation to the base *pie*, for example. Even if it is assumed that speakers only test "suspicious" pairs, pairs that they think may be related, there is no way of preventing them from linking *sail* and *unassailable*, which are not related, while allowing them to link *arrive* and *rival*, which, etymologically speaking, are related.

Secondly, this approach still does not give any principled way of deciding whether certain pairs should be linked by the grammar or not. It is still not clear that there should be rules associating *holy* and *holiday*, but not associating *doff* and *hacienda*.

Thirdly, and perhaps most importantly, this approach does not allow the productivity of morphological processes to be accounted for. Leben & Robinson (1977: 2) assume that "the function of the morphological and phonological rules is simply to parse the lexicon", but this is to take the lexicon as something fixed, finite, and given, whereas it has been shown (chapter 4) that this is far from being the case.

The version of natural generative phonology put forward by Vennemann (1974) is open to the same criticism, but to an even greater degree. Vennemann suggests that the basic elements in the lexicon should be not morphemes, as suggested by Chomsky & Halle, nor even lexemes, but word-forms. That is, Vennemann does not expect his phonological component to provide an account of even the (relatively) full productivity of inflectional processes. Indeed, as far as Vennemann is concerned, the function of the phonological component is not to state whether lexemes, morphemes or word-forms are related to each other morphophonemically, but simply to account for those phonetic processes which occur when word-forms are put side by side in an utterance: phenomena such as assimilation and tone sandhi, for example.

Other versions of natural generative phonology do not go as far as Vennemann's. Hooper (1976a) seems to adopt a proposal put forward by Hudson (1974) which does allow for the productiveness of phonological and morphological processes. Hudson suggests that morphophonemic alternants should be listed in the lexical entry for each morpheme in those cases where the rule(s) giving rise to the variants are not productive. The lexical entry would also specify the conditions under which the non-productive variant should be used. For example, using the notation of Hudson (1974: 219), the *divine/divinity* pair would receive a lexical entry something like the following:

$$[\text{div}{<}\text{a}{>}\text{in}] \rightarrow \begin{bmatrix} [\text{divin}]/ \text{---} \begin{Bmatrix} \text{ation}^4 \\ \text{atory} \\ \text{ity} \\ \text{ize} \end{Bmatrix} \\ [\text{divain}] \quad \text{elsewhere} \end{bmatrix}$$

(Note that depending on one's view of the suffixes, it might be possible to conflate the first two environments for the non-

---

[4] This assumes that DIVINE 'godlike' and DIVINE 'prophesy' come from the same morpheme, as etymologically they do. However, it would be possible to argue that synchronically these should be treated as different morphemes, in which case the fact that the two *divine* morphemes share common variants is a coincidence which this theory does not account for.

productive form.)[5] This type of proposal captures the fact that the forms with /dɪvɪn/ are lexicalized phonologically since it is the phonological form which is specifically listed, and, given that this is a non-productive variant, it must be possible to give an exhaustive list of the environments in which this variant occurs; it is hypothesized that it is not possible to give an exhaustive list of the environments in which the productive form occurs, and this is captured by the "elsewhere" marking. The fact that /dɪvaɪn/ and /dɪvɪn/ are related is captured not by rule but by their co-occurrence in the lexical entry for a single morpheme. The standard generative phonological objection to this solution to the problem would be that it misses a generalization, namely that not only *divine* and *divinity* are related, but that in the same context /ɒbsin/ and /ɒbsen/, /prəufeɪn/ and /prəufæn/ and other pairs are also related, and that these differ in ways which are parallel to the difference between /dɪvaɪn/ and /dɪvɪn/.

Generalizations of this type have to be captured in this model in a different way. This is done by rules which have gained the rather inappropriate name of **via-rules** (Hooper, 1976a; Vennemann, 1972). Via-rules express lexical relations (Hooper, 1976a: 47) – that is they state that forms are related by word-formation – but between the sets rather than between the individual items. They are to natural generative phonology what non-productive phonological rules are to standard generative phonology, except that they do not show a step in a synchronic derivation, but merely note that a relationship exists. It is not at all clear from the examples in the literature whether the whole of the vowel shift rule in English is to be shown by a single via-rule or not: since examples given by Hooper (1976a) are given in terms of segments, it seems likely that it is not. The vowel shift would thus be expressed in natural generative phonology by a number of via-rules of the following type:

$$aɪ \leftrightarrow ɪ$$
$$eɪ \leftrightarrow æ$$
$$i \leftrightarrow e$$

---

[5] The question of whether *-ation* and *-atory* should be seen as made up of one or two morphemes is a vexed one. For some discussion and opposing points of view see Aronoff (1976: 99ff) (monomorphemic analysis) and Strauss (1980: 97ff) (bimorphemic analysis).

In the lexical entries for *divinity* and *malignity* it is stated that these are related to *divine* and *malign* respectively by the first of these via-rules, and *vice versa* (hence the two-headed arrow).

Although the vowel shift is a particularly complex example and it may thus not be possible to capture the full "generalization" of the vowel shift in a single via-rule, in the majority of cases via-rules will be adequate for capturing generalizations like this. If features are allowed in via-rules, they become even more adequate. The trisyllabic laxing rule for example could be expressed by a via-rule of the following type:

$$[+\text{ tense}] \leftrightarrow [-\text{ tense}]$$

The problem is that lexical entries of the type Hudson proposes, and via-rules, appear to reduplicate information, and are thus uneconomical. Morphemes are related in the lexical entries, lexemes are related by via-rules, and it would seem that both morphemes and established lexemes (at least) have to be listed in the lexicon. Despite this, Hooper (1976a: 157ff, 163) apparently uses both mechanisms in her phonology.

Whether both mechanisms are required in a phonological component, or whether there are grounds for preferring one over the other, it is interesting to note that in effect both function with some notion of lexicalization. Hooper (1976a: §4.2) even uses the term. Productive rules are stated in a different way from non-productive rules whichever mechanism is used. In Hudson's lexical entries, the productive form is shown by the "elsewhere" marking, and all via-rules are non-productive, while the productive rules in natural generative phonology are of a different type, and are termed 'phonological rules'.

"Upside-down" phonology might also make more sense if it were restricted to lexicalized forms, and a standard generative phonology used for the productive phonological processes. The difficulty would be that productive and non-productive phonological rules may both be involved in the derivation of a lexicalized form, and if the derivations of lexicalized and non-lexicalized forms were kept strictly separate, a lot of productive rules would have to be repeated in two places.

Standard generative phonology avoids the problem by putting all rules, productive or non-productive, in a single list. It is for that reason that many generative phonological derivations recapitulate historical derivations. For example, in standard generative phonology there would be no difference in principle between the rules giving rise to the /t/ ~ /ʒ/ alternation in *equate/equation* and those giving rise to the /t/ ~ /ʃ/ alternation in *vibrate/vibration*, even though the /t/ ~ /ʒ/ alternation is exceptional and the /t/ ~ /ʃ/ alternation is still productive: any verb in *-ate* /eɪt/ can form a nominalization in *-ation* /eɪʃən/. This gives rise to a number of problems. For example, consider the fate of loan words. *Divine* was a loan word into Old English from Old French. Since it was borrowed before the Great Vowel Shift, the original /iː/ has changed to /aɪ/. *Fedayeen* is a recent loan into English from Arabic. But because it was borrowed after the Great Vowel Shift it has not become */fedæˈjaɪn/. If the Great Vowel Shift is still a current rule of phonology, on a par with, say, the variation in the form of the plural morpheme {s} after sibilants, voiced and voiceless sounds, then either it should apply to new loan words, or those loan words should have pre-Great-Vowel-Shift underlying representations, for which there is no independent motivation.

There has recently been a lot of experimentation in phonology to discover whether the constructs that are proposed by generative phonology have any psychological reality. It has been found that when asked to apply word-formation rules to bases which do not normally undergo them, naive native speakers do not apply the Great Vowel Shift, do not alternate between /k/ and /s/ before /ɪtɪ/, and so on. Thus if people are asked what *obtain + atory* would be, they tend to say /ɒbˈteɪnətərɪ/ and not /ɒbˈtænətərɪ/ (cp. *profane*, *profanatory*). If they are asked what *metric + ity* would be, they tend to say /meˈtrɪkɪtɪ/ and not /meˈtrɪsɪtɪ/ (cp. *electric*, *electricity*) (Ohala, 1974; Steinberg & Krohn, 1975). Examples of this type seem to show that, however the ideal speaker-listener would react if such a being existed, real speakers do distinguish between productive and non-productive phonological processes, and that a linguistic theory that fails to do this will be failing to account for an important part of human linguistic behaviour.

What has been said about segmental variation in word-formation can be summarized as follows. It is only with the advent of generative phonology that morphophonemic alternation has been seen as something which the phonology should provide an account of. While it seems to be possible to construct a phonological component that will account for all such alternation in a language like English (which is rich in morphophonemic alternation), such a component creates problems connected with abstractness and psychological reality. Notions of productiveness and lexicalization are only just beginning to be incorporated into phonological theory, mainly in the school of natural generative phonology. When these notions are fully exploited, it ought to be possible to give a far more satisfactory account of morphophonemic alternation.

6

Syntactic and semantic issues in word-formation

> It is with semantics and syntax that we should really begin if our study is to
> have results more interesting than lists of patterns.
>
> (Adams, 1973: 215)

6.1 Introduction

6.1.1 *Semantics*

It has become generally recognized over the past few
years that syntax and semantics are inextricably linked. Indeed, the
reason for the growth of the Generative Semantics school of
linguistic thought was that many scholars felt that the two could not
be distinguished at all. The fact that syntax and semantics are being
dealt with here in the same chapter is meant to reflect the fact that it
is frequently impossible in the study of word-formation to say
whether one rather than the other is at issue. Syntax and semantics
are distinguished in this introductory section purely for expository
reasons, and even here the distinction is not absolutely clear.

In discussing current approaches to syntax it is possible to
distinguish major approaches quite succinctly because although
they diverge in many ways, they also have much in common: in
particular, they all share theoretical assumptions about the general
form of syntactic rules, and about the use of transformations. When
semantics is considered, however, there is much less consensus
about what a semantic component (if such a thing exists) should do
and how. Indeed, there are even distinct schools of semantics
dealing with what might be called word-semantics as distinct from
sentence-semantics, and in the area of sentence-semantics there are
many different approaches to meaning.

There have been two main approaches to the problem of
word-semantics. The first is illustrated by ordinary dictionaries of
English, where word-meaning is specified in a number of ways
including the listing of near synonyms, the listing of superordinates

or hyponyms, and the specification of function. The second is componential analysis in some form or other (see e.g. Leech, 1974; Lyons, 1968; 1977). It is clear that the specification of word-meaning in these ways is crucial for the way in which lexemes are used in sentences – indeed, it was originally hoped that the synthesis of word-meanings would be sufficient to specify sentence meaning (Katz & Fodor, 1963), although this approach has now been discarded. However, it can be seen from examples like *Mao*, *Maoist*, *Maoize* that this is not sufficient in a discussion of word-formation processes: either of these approaches would define *Mao* as a name, *Maoist* as a person who is a supporter of the policies of the late Mao Tse Tung, and *Maoize* as a verb meaning 'to bring under the influence of the policies supported by the Maoists' (*Maoist* can, of course, also be an adjective, but this usage will be ignored here for simplicity's sake); but while this says something about the meaning of each of these words, it does not say anything about the way in which these lexemes come to mean these things, which is the domain of word-formation. For the study of word-formation it is more important to know how and why *Maoist* is a human noun than it is to know that it acts as such in a sentence. While such approaches are no doubt useful in the consideration of the meanings of lexicalized forms, they are not strictly speaking concerned with the semantics of word-formation.

Approaches to sentence-semantics demand answers to two main queries. The first concerns the influence of word-meaning in sentence-meaning. While I do not wish to underestimate the importance of this element, it seems it is largely equivalent to the consideration of word-meaning, which I have just argued is not relevant for the study of word-formation. The second concerns the way in which syntax combines the meanings of words to give the meanings of larger units – phrases and sentences. This is only relevant to word-formation if the types of syntactic process that collocate elements in word-formation are comparable with those that collocate elements in sentence formation or in phrase formation. It will be argued in this chapter that word-formation is syntactically and semantically distinct from sentence formation in important ways. As far as phrase formation is concerned, however, some scholars (notably Marchand, 1969) see certain types of word-formation (especially compounding and derivation) as being the collocation of a head ('determinatum') and modifying element ('determinant') in the same way as a phrase such as *clever linguists* can be analysed as a collocation of a head (*linguists*) and a modifier (*clever*). This implies that there may be a parallel between word-formation and phrase formation in the way that syntactic collocation determines meaning. There are, however, important differences here, too. In word-formation, but not in phrase formation (except in isolated idiomatic instances), modification can give rise to a change in form class (see §2.13). In word-formation, because constructions with bound formatives are often involved (see §§2.5, 2.6), syntactic paraphrases are often impossible. And, perhaps most vitally, it is frequently the case in word-formation, though rarely so in phrase formation, that it is not possible out of context to deduce what the denotatum of a newly coined collocation must be from the material in the collocation (see §3.2.1, and the discussion there of the example *world-sky*. See also Bauer, 1979a.)

Some scholars take this inherent vagueness in word-formation as evidence that it is not possible to construct a semantic theory to account for productive word-formation. This seems to me, however, to be an over-reaction. Rather it points to a crucial distinction between word-formation and other syntactic processes: sentences and phrases describe, while lexemes – some of which are produced by word-formation – name (see Downing, 1977: 823). Mathesius (1975) even uses the term 'naming unit' for lexeme. The difference between descriptions and names is that while descriptions have to be coherent or compositional, names merely have to be associated with an appropriate denotatum.

If the production of new lexemes is seen as the production of new names, it might be thought that the most economical way of going about it would be to produce random strings of phonemes which have not previously been assigned a meaning and which accord with phonotactic constraints for the language in question. This type of word-manufacture is, however, relatively uncommon outside the fields of science and trade names. It is much more common in natural language to produce motivated new lexemes than to produce unmotivated ones. The reason for this is almost certainly that motivated lexemes act as better mnemonic devices than unmotivated ones.

Once complex lexemes are seen as motivated mnemonics the

paucity of semantic information in them makes sense. Their job is not to provide a comprehensive description, but to recall, in as concise a manner as possible, some salient feature of the deno-tatum. That is why the use of word-formation requires hypostatiza-tion (see §4.5.1.1) and has an effect of "clarity, brevity, concentra-tion" (Johannisson, 1958: 22).

Returning to the question of a semantics of word-formation in the light of this discussion, it can be seen that there is no reason to suppose that the same kind of semantic rule will be required to account for word-formation and phrase formation. This does not mean, though, that no generalizations can be made about the kinds of semantic information that are inevitably present in word-forma-tion and the kinds that are likely to be avoided. A specification of these two kinds of information might be expected to be part of a full theory of word-formation. The most hopeful area for progress in this kind of project at the moment seems to lie in the specification of the semantic relationships that can or must hold between the elements involved in a process of word-formation: the relationships holding between the elements of compounds, between affixes and bases, and so on. This is the kind of semantic information that will be dealt with most in this chapter. It may not be coincidence that it is semantic information of this type which it is frequently most difficult to separate from the study of syntax, and it is for that reason that I have chosen in this chapter not to impose an arbitrary division between syntactic and semantic matters as they are related to word-formation.

In concluding this section, let me stress that although the heading to this chapter mentions "semantic issues" this is far from being the only place in the book where semantic topics are treated: semantic notions have been important throughout the discussion in earlier chapters, and will continue to be so in later chapters.

6.1.2 *Syntax*

This chapter will be concerned, among other things, with the applicability of certain syntactic categories and features to the processes of word-formation. As elsewhere in this book, the system of syntax proposed in Chomsky (1965) will be assumed in this chapter, but other models of syntax will also receive mention. These are case grammar, $\overline{\text{X}}$ syntax (read as "X-bar syntax"), and

Generative Semantics, and a brief outline of the important features of each of these follows.

The case grammar that will be used in discussions here is basically that of Fillmore (1968). Case grammar differs from the type of grammar used by Chomsky (1965) in two main ways. Firstly, in Chomsky (1965), most morphemes that have linear order in the surface structure are given an appropriate linear position in the deep structure, so that, for example, tense is always generated in close connection with auxiliary verbs. A few markers such as those of the interrogative, imperative and negative are generated at the beginning of the sentence, and are given their appropriate surface realizations by transformational rules. Fillmore, on the other hand, distinguishes sharply between the propositional content of a sentence, and the elements which modify this propositional content. In a sentence like *John may not finish this book*, the propositional section of the sentence would be *John finish this book* and the rest would be present tense, *may* and negation. Consequently the first division under the Sentence node in Fillmore's grammar is between Proposition on the one hand and the Modality on the other.

The second big difference between Chomsky and Fillmore is that while Chomsky sees the sentence as made up of a noun phrase and a predicate, and the predicate in turn as being made up of optional adverbials and a verb phrase which may include further noun phrases, for Fillmore the Proposition is made up of a verb and a number of arguments of that verb. Each argument is a noun phrase which bears a particular semantic relationship to the verb, a relationship such as being the agent of the verb, or marking the location of the action of the verb. These relationships are the deep structure cases, and the verb is chosen in terms of the array of deep structure cases with which it can co-occur. The surface realizations of the deep cases are frequently surface case markers in inflecting languages, but in English prepositions fulfil the same role. In certain positions in the sentence (e.g. subject position) the preposition is transformationally deleted, while in other positions it is maintained. Thus the difference between *Edward kissed Felicity* and *Felicity was kissed by Edward* is, for Fillmore, a matter of which of the arguments (or case phrases) has been chosen as the subject. The agent is marked by the preposition *by* in the passive, but the preposition is deleted if the agent is the subject of the sentence.

To illustrate this difference, consider the way in which the sentence *George cannot put the car in the garage* would be generated in the two types of grammar. The appropriate deep structure trees are given in Figures 6.1 (Chomskyan deep structure) and 6.2 (Fillmorean deep structure).

Obviously, there is a lot more to case grammar than has been stated here. Nothing has been said here about the reasons for preferring one type of grammar to the other, about the number and nature of the cases and so on. While these are all interesting questions, they are beyond the scope of what is required here, and the important factor for the understanding of the present discussion will be the different types of configuration illustrated.

$\bar{\text{X}}$ syntax differs from Chomsky (1965) in a very different way. It is Chomsky's own development of the model in Chomsky (1965), and was first expounded in Chomsky (1970). $\bar{\text{X}}$ syntax provides a limitation on the phrase structure rules that are permitted in a grammar. The limitation works in the following way: for every category X (e.g. noun, verb, adjective, etc.) there is a category

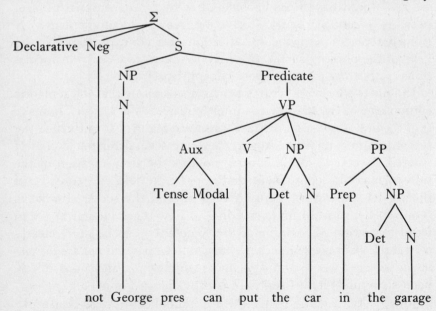

Figure 6.1

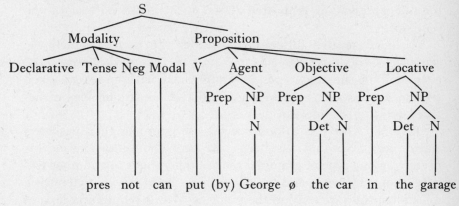

Figure 6.2

node Complement of X, such that the Category $\overline{X}$ is rewritten as X (+ Complement of X). There is also a category node Specifier of $\overline{X}$, such that every category $\overline{\overline{X}}$ is re-written as (Specifier of $\overline{X}$ +) X. This means that in any phrase, the category which replaces X in the general formulation will be the head of the phrase. Consider, for example, a noun phrase like *the old man of the sea*. Previously, *of the sea* would have been considered to be a prepositional phrase, possibly introduced by transformation. Now it is Complement of N (which replaces X in the specification of a noun phrase). N, the head of the phrase, is *man*. *Old* may still be introduced transformationally, but *the* is, in the new system, Specifier of $\overline{N}$.

Linguists who work with $\overline{X}$ syntax also assume that the semantic component of the grammar is interpretative, as it was in Chomsky (1965), but allow some surface structure features to influence the semantic interpretation. Again, there are several further points of interest involved with $\overline{X}$ syntax, notably the simplification of the transformational component that appears to be a consequence of the model. However, these are also beyond the scope of what is required here for an understanding of how these models apply to word-formation. The value of the $\overline{X}$-notation can be more clearly seen if the example sentence is changed to *George cannot see the car in the garage* (where *in the garage* qualifies *car*), and a possible $\overline{X}$ deep structure for this sentence is provided in Figure 6.3.

Finally, Generative Semantics is a school of thought that broke away from Chomsky's (1965) model because it was felt that the

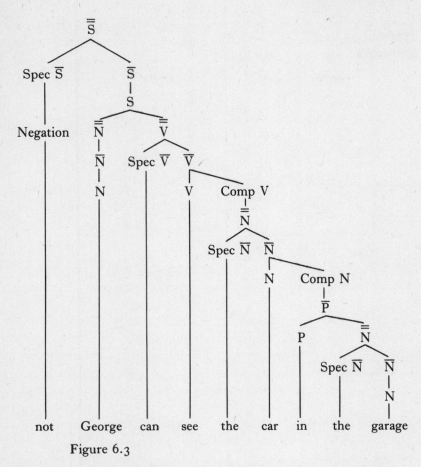

Figure 6.3

arguments that had been presented by Chomsky up to that point would motivate far more abstract syntactic analyses than Chomsky himself was willing to condone. In particular, categories such as tense, negation and modality were analysed in Generative Semantics as higher predicates, and lexical items, even if morphologically simplex, were seen as being derived from an underlying complex semantic tree structure. In Generative Semantics, underlying structure is semantic as well as syntactic, and there is no single level of deep structure as this was defined in Chomsky (1965). It is not possible to give a definitive idea of what the underlying structure of a sentence would look like in a Generative Semantics framework, but the tree in Figure 6.4 can be seen as showing at least some of the principles involved. The sentence illustrated is again *George cannot*

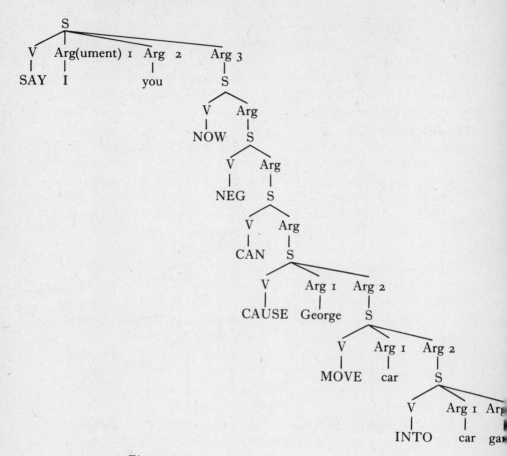

Figure 6.4

put the car in the garage. As previously, the arguments for this kind of structure are omitted here, since it is the type of configuration envisaged which will be of interest in the further discussion, rather than the finer points of the reasoning leading to the postulation of the various deep structure verbs.

6.2 On the "sentential source" analysis in word-formation[1]

The question is frequently raised of whether instances of word-formation can be derived from the same strings as underlie

---

[1] This section recapitulates and expands arguments first put forward in Bauer (1978d: §§4.1.2–4).

sentences by the application of the appropriate rules, or whether a clearly different set of input strings is required. The former hypothesis, which may be rather loosely termed the "sentential source hypothesis", was the one adopted in early transformational accounts of word-formation (e.g. Lees, 1960; Rohrer, 1967). A non-sentential source hypothesis for the origin of compounds at least (though not of derivatives, as far as I know) is implicitly adopted by those scholars (e.g. Hatcher, 1960; Žepić, 1970) who derive compounds from prepositional or deep-case relationships. Rohrer (1974: 114), who addresses this problem specifically, is obviously worried that the adoption of a non-sentential source hypothesis will lead to the creation of a "special component for wordformation". But this is not a necessary consequence. If it can be shown, for instance, that just those items which appear in Fillmore's Modality component do not occur in word-formation (as is argued by Brekle, 1970: 58; Teleman, 1970: 38, and others) then word-formation can be seen as the result of embedding a Proposition rather than a Sentence. Or again, in the case of compounds, if these can be accounted for in terms of an underlying Noun + Prepositional Phrase, a configuration which will have to be generated in the syntax to account for sentences like *A bird in the hand is worth two in the bush*, then no special component for word-formation is being created. Thus Rohrer's worries here seem to be rather exaggerated. On the other hand, Rohrer is doubtless right when he says (1974: 113) that "if compounds are derived from sentences [i.e. from the strings underlying sentences, LB] then they should contain explicitly or implicitly all the elements of actualized sentences". In this connection it is particularly the elements which Fillmore (1968: 23) puts in the Modality component (i.e. negation, tense, mood and aspect) which are of interest. Rohrer claims that all of these play a role in word-formation. They will be dealt with individually below.

There is one point, however, which must be made first, since it seems to have given rise to a certain amount of confusion in discussions on this subject (Brekle, 1975; Rohrer, 1973, 1974). This can be illustrated in relation to (1) and (2):

(1)   Our house-boat has been turned into a cafeteria
(2)   When I grow up I want to be a teacher

Following Bach (1968), it can be claimed that *house-boat* and *teacher* in (1) and (2) respectively are tensed: that *house-boat* must be seen as being something which *was* a houseboat, and *teacher* as someone who *will be* (or *might be*) a teacher. This can be termed the external application of tense; it is not relevant to the process of word-formation as such. Internally, the relationship between *house* and *boat*, between *teach* and *-er*, is not subject to tensing. A *house-boat* is a boat which is used and is meant to be used as a house, a *teacher* is an agent who teaches professionally. In what follows only the internal application of the categories under consideration will be taken as relevant.

6.3   The Modality component

In this section the various parts of Fillmore's Modality component will be considered in turn, with a view to deciding whether or not they have a role to play in word-formation.

6.3.1   *Negation*

Rohrer (1974: 114), discussing the role of negation in word-formation, argues purely from such French examples as:

(3)   Votre raisonnement n'est pas logique 'your reasoning is not logical'

(4)   Votre raisonnement est illogique 'your reasoning is illogical'

which he claims are synonymous. In fact, the synonymy of these seems to be an idiosyncratic feature of the pairs that Rohrer cites, rather than a general rule. Consider, for example:

(5)   Le chef n'est pas content   'the boss is not content'
(6)   Le chef est mécontent   'the boss is discontented'
(7)   The director is not capable
(8)   The director is incapable

That these pairs are not synonymous can be seen by applying Quine's biconditional test (see Lyons, 1977: 202), where the results (9) and (10) are not analytic:

(9)   Le chef n'est pas content si et seulement si il est mécontent
(10)   The director is not capable if and only if he is incapable

For example, if someone had done something that the boss did not approve of, but which he was willing to put up with, it might be true to say (5), but false to say (6), because (6) implies a greater degree of dissatisfaction, probably with visible physical signs of emotion. CAPABLE implies more than average ability or efficiency (Hanks, 1971), so that if the director was of average ability it might be true to say (7), though untrue to say (8), which implies far less than average ability. (Note that (5) if (6) and (7) if (8) are true, but not (5) only if (6) and (7) only if (8) so that there seems to be some kind of hyponymy rather than synonymy here.) In both these cases, and in others like them, the derived form seems to be in some sense stronger than the negation of the base form. This lack of synonymy does not invalidate Rohrer's argument, but it does indicate that the relationship between the derived form and the postulated underlying string is not a direct one; there must be more information in the underlying strings for (6) and (8) than in those for (5) and (7).

Brekle (1975: 31) agrees with Rohrer that negative elements are present in such derived forms, but adds that he personally has "not claimed that negation does not play a role in the whole field of word-formation – i.e. including derivation – but confined [him]self to the field of nominal compounding" (my translation, LB). It is not at all clear how Brekle can accept the presence of a negative element in *illogique* but not in French *non-sens* 'no sense' = 'nonsense', German *Nichtkämpfer* 'not fighter' = 'noncombatant', Danish *intetkøn* 'no gender' = 'neuter' or in *no-go-area*, which must presumably be classified as compounds. But in these cases it is much clearer than in (3)–(8) that the negation cannot stem from an underlying sentence negation. If this were the case, then the (a) and (b) sentences in (11)–(15) would have to be synonymous, which they clearly are not:

(11a) Ce n'est pas un sens   'that is not a sense'
  (b) C'est un non-sens   'that is nonsense'
(12a) Hans ist kein Kämpfer   'Hans is no fighter'
  (b) Hans ist ein Nichtkämpfer   'Hans is a noncombatant'
(13a) *Barn* er ikke noget køn   '*Barn* is no gender'
  (b) *Barn* er intetkøn   '*Barn* is neuter'
(14a) *This part of Belfast is not a go-area
  (b) This part of Belfast is a no-go-area
(15a) Peter didn't see a smoker
  (b) Peter saw a non-smoker

Thus it is clear that a string underlying a negative sentence cannot form the input to a transformation – or set of transformations – which gives rise to a derived word including a negative particle. This does not deny the presence of some kind of negation, note, but it does circumscribe the possible sources of this negation.

The fact that the string underlying a negative sentence cannot form the input to the derivation of these forms containing a negative also means that these forms cannot be derived from embedded sentences, since these give exactly the same problems, but at a slightly deeper grammatical level. For instance, it might be claimed that the paradox implicit in (15) could be solved by providing the following deep structure strings:

(16a)   Peter neg. see one [one smoke]
 (b)   Peter see one [one neg. smoke]

But this kind of solution would not solve the problem in all cases since it would imply that (11b) contained (11a) as an embedded sentence in its deep structure, so that no better result is provided, and it would not allow (13) and (14) to be accounted for.

Furthermore, the negation contained in derived forms does not really express any internal relationship within the form. Thus, although *non-smoker*, for example, can be glossed as 'one who does not smoke' (and might usefully be glossed this way in a language teaching situation), linguistically it is not a negation of the predicate 'to smoke' as applied to the entity 'someone unspecified'. What it is, rather, is a classificatory device, used to classify people by excluding them from the set of 'smokers'.

All that is required for the generation of derived forms containing a negation is (a) the base and (b) the negating element. Anything further that is generated in the deep structure is redundant. The question still is, however, where the negative element comes from. I should like to suggest, following traditional grammar, that this negative element is a deep structure adverb, and is thus probably a case phrase, like most other adverbials. In forms like *illogique*, *incapable* this adverb modifies the adjectives *logique* and *capable*, and in the formation of compounds it acts just like any other adverb of the appropriate classes (cf. German *Jetztzeit* 'now time' = 'present', Danish *efterår* 'after year' = 'autumn', *away game*, French *entre-temps* 'between time' = 'meanwhile'). Whether this, or any other, adverb is lexically decomposed at a deeper level of grammar will depend on the form of the grammar as a whole. If it is decomposed, then it might prove necessary to generate a

Modality node at the level of that decomposition to account for the negative meaning of the element.[2] But at the level at which the word-formation takes place no negation from the Modality is involved. Thus it is quite possible to generate cases of word-formation from a Propositional structure (which may, of course, include embedded sentences), and still have negative elements in word-formation.[3]

6.3.2 *Tense*
Rohrer (1973, 1974) claims that:

(17)   I knew the owner of that house

has two readings:

(a)   I knew the person who owns that house
(b)   I knew the person who owned that house

In the earlier version of the paper, he then concludes that "these examples show that there are elements of the lexicon that contain tenses" whereas in the later version his conclusion is just the opposite: "We have found no compounds or derivatives that contain tenses."

The view that forms like *owner* are tensed in such sentences goes back to Bach (1968). However, as was pointed out above, the tense in these cases is external to the derived form, not an internal, integral part of the derivational process. As Rohrer himself points out (1974: 116) it is the whole NP which should be viewed as tensed, not simply the derivative. In any case, it seems to be factors from the linguistic or even from the non-linguistic context which specify which reading is required, so that it would seem reasonable to leave the tense interpretation of such nominals to a pragmatic component rather than to write it into the process of word-formation as such. In examples like Rohrer's borderline cases *ex-president*, *ex-champion* the *ex-* can be generated as an adverb, in exactly the same way as was suggested for the negative elements above.

Note that an analysis in which tense is not involved in the process

---

[2] In a Generative Semantics model, the negation would be generated as a predicate rather than in a Modality component, but a Fillmorean model is being assumed here for the sake of the argument.

[3] For some apparent counter-examples, see Downing (1977: fns. 10, 11). See also her argumentation there on why the counter-examples are only apparent.

of word-formation makes good sense intuitively. A *fire engine* is not an engine which is dealing with a fire at the moment of speaking and/or one which has dealt with a fire a short (long) time before the moment of speaking and/or one which will deal with a fire a short (long) time after the moment of speaking, but rather one which has a habitual or inherent connection with fires of a particular kind. Similarly, *owner*, in isolation, merely denotes one who owns, without any reference to the time of the owning, and something which is *implausible* is not being viewed as something that is implausible now but once was, or soon will be, plausible. Lexicographers show the lack of relevance of time in word-formation by using participial constructions instead of tensed forms wherever this is practicable.

6.3.3 *Mood*

It is not clear exactly what Fillmore (1968: 23) means by 'mood', since he does not expand this category, but it does not seem likely that the term has its traditional meaning of indicative/subjunctive, as these categories are surface structure verbal inflections. It seems more likely that 'mood' is to be understood as being made up of two sub-categories: modal verbs and declarative/interrogative/imperative. Fillmore has not published any treatment of these categories within a case grammar framework, and it might well be that he would prefer to deal with them in the same way as the Generative Semantics school, i.e. by putting them in higher predications (but see Lyons, 1977: §16.5 for arguments against the higher performative analysis). Nonetheless, in the interests of comprehensiveness they will be dealt with here.

It is difficult to find objective arguments to show that modal verbs cannot apply internally in the process of word-formation, although it seems fairly clear intuitively that this is the case. A *longbow* is not a bow which may/might/must/can/could be long, nor is *un argument illogique* an argument which ought not/should not/will not/must not/may not be logical: a *longbow* is long according to specified norms and in a specific way, and something which is *illogique* is not logical.

An apparent counter-example is the suffix *-able* (*-ible*) or its equivalent in other languages. Where this occurs productively a paraphrase of the type 'able to be Ved' is usually possible

(Marchand, 1969: §4.2), where 'able to' could be replaced by 'can'. Here again I should like to suggest that the suffix should be treated as an unanalysable whole at the level of the word-formation processes, although it might be lexically decomposed at deeper levels. There is, however, no hard evidence for this point of view, only a suggestive parallelism with other parts of the grammar of word-formation. If it turns out that none of the other components of the modality needs to be generated in instances of word-formation, then this is a very important generalization, and it should not be lost completely because of the existence of a single suffix. More persuasive, perhaps, is the fact that of all the modals only *can* might be said to play a role in word-formation; it might be expected that if the modals were freely part of the process of word-formation there would also be suffixes indicating obligatoriness and moral obligation, but these do not seem to exist. Thus if the suffix *-able* is to be accounted for by the generation of a Modality node in the deep structure, an extra rule will be required at some point to specify that if an instance of word-formation is being generated Modality must be empty or specified as *can*. Such a process seems much more complicated than simply marking *-able* in the lexicon as having a modal meaning.

As far as the categories of declarative/interrogative/imperative are concerned, it is again intuitively obvious that *mécontent, teacher, blackbird* are not used to ask whether the happiness is negative, the person teaches or the bird is black,[4] nor to order the happiness to be negative, the person to teach or the bird to be black. Only the category statement is thus left to consider.

Rohrer (1974: 119ff) claims that the category Assertion does play a role in word-formation. But his argument is based on two crucial assumptions: (a) that assertion can be defined as a relation between sentences, a relation which can be specified in logical terms, and (b) that compounds are derived from embedded sentences. If (a) is

---

[4] This is certainly true when these lexemes occur as word-forms in an utterance with unmarked intonation. With a high-rise on *black*, it might, however, look as if the blackness of the bird IS being questioned. In fact, though, it would seem to be more accurate to say that it is the assigning of an entity to the category of blackbird that is being queried, or alternatively the suitability of the label (rather than the category) in a given case. Compare the usage of a high-rise on a simplex lexeme like *sparrow*, or in a non-compound like *little brother*.

true, it is only true because Rohrer chooses, idiosyncratically, to define assertion in this way. The more normal interpretation of assertion is that it is an illocutionary act (see Brekle, 1976: XI; Lyons, 1977: 177, 769). As far as (b) is concerned, this is the point that Rohrer is trying to prove, and to use it as an assumption in his argument is thus to make his argument totally circular. Rohrer's claim for the relevance of Assertion in word-formation thus does not really hold water.

If it were true that a form like *blackbird* contained an assertion, it might be expected that the assertion could not be queried or contradicted within the same utterance. It is, however, perfectly possible to ask *Is a blackbird black?* or to state *That blackbird is brown.* Furthermore, if such a form did contain an assertion, it would have to be explained how and why the process of lexicalization deleted the assertion marker: in the transparent form *alba spina* 'white thorn', there is room for an assertion ('the thorn is white'), but in its etymological descendant in French, *aubépine* 'hawthorn', there cannot be an assertion because the form is opaque and unanalysable. Note also that sentences like *That blackbird is brown* do not presuppose that the bird is black, either, although an embedded sentence would, as in *That bird, which is black, is (not) brown.* This is a further argument against a sentential source analysis.

In fact, even Rohrer, in his conclusion (1974: 122), goes on to state that "sentences which are specified for tense and mood cannot be transformed into compounds", and he later includes all cases of word-formation under this generalization. Thus it might seem that he contradicts himself here, and in any case, even though he is trying to show that the elements of the Modality component appear in word-formation, he does not believe that mood does appear.

6.3.4 *Aspect*

Rohrer's (1974: 116) entire section on aspect in word-formation reads as follows: "Aspect plays a role in word-formation in several European languages. The cases that are best known are Greek and Russian derivatives. Relevant examples may be found in all standard grammars." Taking Ward (1965: ch. 5) as a "standard grammar" of Russian (although it is rather more comprehensive than most standard grammars on the subject of word-formation) it appears, however, that this is not true. While there are affixes which productively change an imperfective verb into a perfective verb or *vice versa* (Ward, 1965: 134), this only affects the external aspect of the newly formed item (i.e. its aspect as it functions in the sentence) and has no internal application to the actual process of word-formation. Similarly, there are some de-verbal nominal forms which are formed on the basis of imperfective verbs (e.g. *zažigalka* 'cigarette lighter' from *zažigat'* 'to light' (impf.)) and others which are formed on the basis of perfective verbs (e.g. *srabotannost'* 'the welding into a team by working together' from *srabotat's'a* (pf.): examples from Ward), but the aspect of the verb from which the nominal is derived has nothing to do with the relationship between the stem and the affixes; it is only of importance to the extent that a difference in aspect implies a semantic difference (e.g. 'instantaneous' vs. 'iterative'). That is, as far as the word-formation process is involved, these differences are purely lexical differences, not differences of aspect in the generation of the various forms: the aspects of the verbs involved are of no more relevance than is the semantic make-up of the modifier in the compound *future time* to the claim that tense plays no role in word-formation.

There is, however, a sense in which aspect can be said to play a role in word-formation, and that is connected to the discussion of tense above. Tense is usually defined as relating to the time of an action, event or state, while aspect is not relative to the time of the action, event or state, but to the internal temporal make-up of the action, event or state (see Lyons, 1968: 305, 315). If tense is not considered (if an action is regarded as tenseless), the time of the action ceases to be important, but, by that very fact, the internal temporal make-up of the action comes to be of importance – namely that the action considered is true independent of time, or throughout time. Thus it may be argued that tenselessness is itself a type of aspect. If this argument is followed, then the decision taken earlier to see tense as irrelevant in word-formation might mean that aspect automatically must be taken into account. The tenselessness of a compound like *madman* can be seen in the non-analytic result of the application of Quine's biconditional test to (18) and (19) which differ in that (18) has a tensed predicate in the relative clause, whereas (19) has the compound:

(18)   John is a man who is mad
(19)   John is a madman

The biconditional is (20):

(20)   John is a man who is mad if and only if John is a madman

(Note that, as was the case with negation, (18) if (19) is true, but not (18) only if (19), so that there thus would seem to be some kind of hyponymy here.) Brekle (1970: 31), discussing this same example, talks of the difference between *madman* and *mad man* (the latter presumably derived from a reduced relative) in rather different terms: "For example, in the type *madman*, as compared with the syntactic group *mad man*, the feature 'habitual' is regularly predicated of the underlying modifying element." (My translation, LB.) Brekle also points out that this is not limited to compounds of this type, but occurs in several other kinds of compounds, and in fact it seems to be true of all kinds of word-formation, not just compounds: consider, notably, agentives like *teacher*, *lover*. However, the main point here is the use of the term 'habitual' which sounds very much as if it should be an aspectual marker. Bauer (1978d: §3.2) uses the term HIP (= habitual/inherent/permanent) or 'inherent' for this feature. Again the terms sound aspectual.

It has been claimed by several authors (see e.g. Winther, 1975: 57 on French; Lipka, 1977: 158 on English) that agentives like those mentioned above are only strictly habitual when they mark professions, and that they can also be punctual:

(21)   Dites donc, les chanteurs, ça suffit! 'Hey, that's enough, you singers!'
(22)   The writer of this letter is ill

Downing (1977: fn. 24) also points to some examples where a compound is formed on the basis of a single, non-habitual event, and Bauer (1978d: §3.2.3) points out that a thief can be so termed even after stealing only once. The point here seems to be, as Downing remarks, that such formations show the speaker reacting as though the activity were habitual: the speaker abstracts from the single event, and sees it as something typical or habitual for the entity denoted. Sentences of type (22) may be an exception to this rule, depending on how they are generated, but one possibility is to see the 'here and now' reading as being a pragmatic inference from the context in which the lexeme is used, while the lexeme itself has no such interpretation.

Part of the difficulty in deciding whether genuine aspect is in question here is that it is not clear whether this HIP feature is identical with the failure to specify the tense, or whether it is something separate in its own right, and thus whether a failure to generate a Tense node is sufficient to specify something as HIP, or whether it has to be specifically generated under an Aspect node. It is argued in Bauer (1978d) that it is sufficient to fail to generate a Tense node. The argument runs as follows: (i) the copula in English has two readings depending on context, one [+HIP] as in *He is tall* and one [−HIP] as in *He is on his way*, corresponding to the two copulas of Spanish and other languages; (ii) this distinction is, in the terms of Lakoff (1970b), vague rather than ambiguous; (iii) since it is not ambiguous, there should only be one deep structure form, not two; (iv) but to use HIP as a rewrite of Aspect would be to provide two deep structure forms which could be used to distinguish the two readings of the copula, and this would lead to a contradiction.

It seems, therefore, that the only aspectual feature which might be necessary for the generation of complex words can be seen as the natural result of the failure to specify any Tense node, or, since it has now been argued that none of the elements in Fillmore's Modality is required in word-formation, as the natural result of the failure to specify any Modality component. Word-formation can then be seen as the result of the embedding of a Proposition, and contrasting with clause formation in that the latter arises from the embedding of a whole sentence (including a Modality).

6.4 The underlying verb in compounds

Lees (1960) derives noun + noun compounds like *wind-mill* and *flour mill* from underlying NP + VP strings like 'wind powers the mill' and 'the mill grinds flour' respectively. This means that an indefinite number of verbs, a number which is potentially unlimited, can be deleted on the way to the surface in the grammar of any language which has compounds of this form – and that seems to be most, if not all languages. To do this, however, is to go against one of the basic tenets of Transformational Generative grammar, since it leads to a non-decidable system, and it is generally agreed that there should not be any deletion which cannot be recovered in a grammar (see Chomsky, 1965: 138 *et passim*; Fiengo & Lasnik, 1972).

The deletion involved in moving from the deep to the surface structure in compounds like those mentioned above is non-recoverable if they are generated in this fashion, not only because any verb may have been deleted, but also because there may be a number of verbs which could have been deleted from any given compound. For example, should *police-dog* be derived from an underlying 'the dog serves the police', 'the police use the dog', 'the dog works with the police', 'the police work with the dog' or from some other structure entirely? There does not seem to be a non-arbitrary answer to such a question. It should also be noted that this is as much of a problem in a case-grammar framework as it is in the type of grammar expounded in Chomsky (1965) since the case roles of the two nominals vary in the sentences provided as glosses above, as well as the immediate constituent structures of the sentences.

This point seems first to have been raised by Rohrer (1966), and since then a number of possible solutions have been suggested. Lees (1970) suggests that it may be possible to reconstruct the meaning of a compound from the meaning of the head noun and the speaker's knowledge of the real world. To a certain extent this view is justified (see also Bauer, 1978d: §3.5, 1979a: 46). Lees cites examples like *plane pilot* and *ashtray*, where it is clear that the pilot must fly the plane, and the tray hold the ash. This point of view is similar to that of Vendler (1968: 92) who claims that the co-occurrence of the two nouns involved specifies a very limited set of possible verbs. But the point is that it is still a SET of verbs, and not one verb unambiguously. Vendler quotes *milkman* as 'man sells/delivers/handles/etc. milk'. In examples like this, it can be seen that Lees's stronger version of the hypothesis does not hold, and that Vendler's weaker version still gives rise to a theoretically non-recoverable deep structure.

Motsch (1970) provides three possible solutions. His first is that it might be only a very small number of verbs that is involved in the formation of compounds. It might be, for example, that only semantic primitives (always assuming that these could be isolated) could be accepted as deep structure verbs in the generation of compounds. This is basically the approach adopted by Levi (1978). This, however, would still lead to a non-recoverable deep structure, since there would be no way to discover which of the semantic primitives had been deleted. In any case, Lees (1960: 143) is sceptical about the possibility of treating such a large productive class as his 'subject–object' compounds in terms of a limited number of verbs.

Motsch's second hypothesis is that a complex symbol should be generated under the V node, but that the verb defined by this complex symbol should not be assigned a phonological matrix; that is, the verb should have semantico-syntactic content, but no phonological content (i.e. never occur as a surface form). At first sight, this seems more appealing, but the difficulties are still just as great because of the nature of the complex symbol. Since this contains information on strict subcategorization and selection features corresponding to a specific verb, the deep structure can still not be recovered from the surface structure. And if the complex symbol is not fully specified, then the proposal is substantially modified, and corresponds to Motsch's third hypothesis.

According to this, Motsch's preferred solution, verb classes rather than individual verbs are specified by the content of the complex symbol; that is, the complex symbol represents the neutralization of a number of individual verbs. Motsch (1970: 219) suggests that lexicalization could then be seen as the specification of further features in the complex symbol, so that the verb comes to correspond to an individual verb. This assumes, of course, that a lexicalized example (or an institutionalized one, it is not quite clear what Motsch means by the term) can be defined by a single verb; the *police-dog* example suggests that this is not so. What is not clear from Motsch's exposition, however, is what degree of neutralization the complex symbol is supposed to represent. If only small groups of individual verbs are neutralized in any given complex symbol, then presumably this proposal does not differ essentially from Vendler's proposal mentioned above. If the complex symbol is supposed to represent a neutralization of all the verbs that can possibly appear in a fully specified deep structure of a compound, then it is difficult to see, given the range of meanings that compounds can cover, how the complex symbol can contain any specification other than [+V].

It is only in the case where the complex symbol is minimally specified in this way that the problem of non-recoverable deletion is solved, and in this case it seems rather misleading to speak of neutralization rather than the creation of a completely new unit, a pro-verb. This is the solution proposed by Bauer (1978d: §4.2). Such an element would have to be interpreted semantically as meaning that one item stands in a specific but non-specified relationship to another item, and that this relationship has to be inferred from lexical meaning and contextual information. This fits in well with Adams's (1973: 88) comment that "in many cases the first element functions as a sort of mnemonic device, a reminder of the nature and associations of the object or notion that the whole refers to." (See also above, §6.1.1.) Furthermore, if it is true, as Lees (1960: 144) suggests, that there are compounds of this type where it is not possible to find an appropriate verb in the language to fill the semantic space (*milk tooth* might be an example), then an analysis with a pro-verb will still allow the compound to be generated, while an analysis which demands a particular verb – or possibly even a neutralization of a small number of verbs – will block the generation of the particular example. The greatest advantage of an analysis using a pro-verb, however, is that it allows an appreciable reduction in the number of deep structures under-lying compounds, since the pro-verb can represent a semantic content which would normally be conveyed by means of a preposi-tion or of a verb + preposition. Thus while Lees (1960) works with eight basic types of compound which are subclassified to give 49 types, and Brekle (1970) operates with 25 Propositional types to give over 100 types of compound, Bauer (1978d) operates with a maximum of two types of compound. This represents a vast simplification, and a much more powerful generalization.

Given that it was argued above (§6.3) that it is not necessary to generate a Modality component for instances of word-formation which can be seen as the result of embedding a Proposition rather than a Sentence, it might seem redundant to generate a pro-verb in the underlying structure of a noun + noun compound when all this pro-verb has to do is reiterate that the process being dealt with is a process of (a particular kind of) word-formation. The semantic gloss given for the pro-verb could just as easily be specified by some kind of redundancy rule which operates in just those cases where a Proposition was embedded and the V node was not filled.

While this would be possible if only the semantics of the process were at stake, the syntax must also be taken into consideration, and this militates against such a solution. A verb is an obligatory element in any Proposition, and one of its functions is to be marked for the case nodes that can co-occur with it. If it were true that the case nodes which can occur in compounds had no limitations on them, then it might be possible to ignore this function of the verb. However, Bauer (1978d: §4.5.3) shows that there are in fact severe restrictions on the case nodes that can co-occur in a compound, and for these restrictions to be built into the grammar a verb marked with the appropriate case frames must be generated.

6.5 Syntactic limitations proposed in recent literature

Roeper & Siegel (1978) summarize some of the properties of rules of word-formation (WFRs) that have been proposed in recent transformational literature. They give six such properties:

(a)	WFRs involve no phrasal categories
(b)	WFRs shift syntactic category
(c)	WFRs involve no medial variables
(d)	WFRs have no extrinsic ordering
(e)	WFRs involve semantic compositionality
(f)	WFRs permit statement of idiosyncratic information

These properties suggest quite strict limitations on the syntax and semantics of word-formation, and are accordingly worth considering in some detail, even though it will be necessary to criticize most of them quite severely. Roeper & Siegel's paper is an important one, particularly since it summarizes some widely-accepted proposals, proposals which have not been critically considered from the point of view of word-formation, as opposed to the syntactic point of view.

6.5.1 *Phrasal categories*

The fact that WFRs involve no phrasal categories predicts the non-existence of words like *washslowlyable*, where *-able* attaches to an entire verb phrase *wash slowly*. Notice the meaning would be perfectly comprehensible.
(Roeper & Siegel, 1978: 202)

While it does seem to be the case that **washslowlyable* is not an acceptable form, it does not seem to be correct that this can be ruled out by the restriction that Roeper & Siegel state. The fact of the matter is that there are cases of word-formation on phrasal bases. Admittedly, these seem to be most common in those compounds which Roeper & Siegel (1978: 206) term **root compounds**, i.e. those which do not have a verb base in the head element, nor suffixes such as *-ed*, *-ing* and agentive *-er*. Examples of root compounds formed on phrasal bases abound; a few examples are: *a don't-tell-me-what-to-do-look*, French *son côté m'as-tu-vu* 'his have-you-seen-me side', Swedish *kom·och·tag·mig·om·du·kan·min·en* 'come and get me if you can look-the' (all cited in Bauer, 1978d: §5.3.5), *an oh-what-a-wicked-world-this-is-and-how-I-wish-I-could-do-something-to-make-it-better-and-nobler expression*,[5] *a pain-in-stomach gesture*,[6] and *a blended historical-political-only-ninety-miles-from-our-shores approach to language* (Williams, 1965: 279). However, phrases also act as the bases in other types of word-formation. Consider, for example, *stick-to-it-iveness*[7] and *cut-down-ness*.[8] There are also those cases where phrases are converted into lexemes, e.g. *love-lies-bleeding*, *jack-in-the-box* (see Marchand, 1969: §§2.50, 2.53.2). In a set of experiments designed to test Roeper & Siegel's claim about phrasal categories in compounds, Carroll (1979) discovered that native speakers generally find examples like *a home-for-the-aged inspector* acceptable. As far as derivatives on phrasal bases are concerned, very few of them seem to become established, though *get-at-able* and *come-uppance* would seem to fall into this category, and consider also *with-itness*, *up-to-dateness* (Barnhart *et al.*, 1973) and *one-up-manship*.

Not only do WFRs involve phrasal categories, it seems that in rare cases they can involve sequences which are not even immediate constituents. Bauer (1978d: §5.3.5) cites the Danish example of *kulturen-ud-til-folket-idealister*, and there seems no reason to suppose that an English equivalent *culture-to-the-people-idealists* would not also be acceptable, even though on most analyses *culture*

---

5 J. K. Jerome. 1889. *Three Men in a Boat*. Penguin edn, 1957, p. 21.

6 P. Mann. 1978. *Steal Big*. London, etc: Granada Publishing, p. 134.

7 Paul Gallico. 1960. *Mrs Harris Goes to New York*. London: Michael Joseph, p. 8.

8 C. Harrison. 1975. *How to be a Pom*. Palmerston North: Dunmore Press, p. 57.

to the people would not be a single constituent. WFRs seem to be much more complex than Roeper & Siegel allow for here.

In later discussion of this restriction, Roeper & Siegel (1978: 213) point out that it accounts for the fact that "an *old church-goer* must refer to an aged or frequent worshipper, and not someone who goes to an old church. The adjective *old* applies to the whole compound: it is not an expansion of an incorporated NP." If this is the case, then Roeper & Siegel have to account for the fact that cases are found where the adjective in such structures does refer just to the first part of the compound. While this may not be common in English, lines like the following (cited in Bauer, 1978d: §5.1) do exist, and must be accounted for:

> I said, "Mr Purple People Eater, what's your line?"
> He said, "Eating Purple People and it sure is fine"

This is another argument against this proposed restriction on WFRs.

6.5.2 *Syntactic category shift*

Shifts in syntactic category occur when one adds an affix: *bake* ⇒ *baker*. There are no syntactic operations that shift category. This is therefore a distinctive feature of lexical rules.
(Roeper & Siegel, 1978: 202)

A more accurate statement of this restriction would be "shifts in syntactic category MAY occur when one adds a derivational SUFFIX": typically, in the Indo-European languages at least, adding a prefix does not cause a change in syntactic category, and it was pointed out earlier (§2.13) that there is some suffixation which only changes syntactic category on a fine analysis of syntactic category. However, the general point being made by Roeper & Siegel here remains valid as long as there are no cases where syntactic operations cause shifts in syntactic categories.

It is not clear that this can be consistently maintained. In the case of word-formation, there are instances such as *teacher*, a noun, derived from a verb *teach* and the suffix *-er*. This could be written as

$$N \rightarrow V + \textit{-er}$$

In the case of syntax, there are instances such as *teach Latin*, a verb phrase, derived from a verb *teach* and a noun *Latin*. This could be written as

$$VP \rightarrow V + N$$

Roeper & Siegel are apparently claiming that the first of these involves a shift in syntactic category, but not the second. Yet VP is a different syntactic category from V, just as N is, and it is not clear that this claim can be substantiated.

It might be objected that in the syntactic case cited above lexical items are combined, whereas in the word-formation case cited a lexical item was combined with a bound morph, and that it is this which differentiates the two examples. But this objection is also untenable. Firstly, lexical items are combined in compounds (instances of word-formation) in ways that may or may not involve a change of form class: for example, *windmill* is a noun made of two nouns, so there is no shift of syntactic category, while to *brownbag* is a verb made up of an adjective and a noun, where there is a shift in syntactic category. To account for this it is necessary to claim either that the rules forming compounds are syntactic rules which may involve category shift or that they are lexical rules involving the combination of lexical items. If the latter, then the crucial difference between examples like *teacher* and *teach Latin* cannot be that only syntactic rules combine lexical categories. In either case the argument goes against Roeper & Siegel's position. The converse situation is illustrated by the *'s* formative in *Harry's dictionary* which makes a determiner of the proper noun *Harry*. In this case a bound morph is combined with a lexical item in a syntactic rule with a resultant shift in category. Again Roeper & Siegel's position is contradicted.

In the transformational literature there are also innumerable examples of items in one syntactic category being derived from elements of another syntactic category. For example, in Generative Semantics it is frequently argued that the category of tense should be derived from a deep structure predicate (i.e. verb), that the negative adverbial *not* is derived from a deep structure predicate, and that auxiliary verbs are derived from the same syntactic category as main verbs, although the two are clearly distinct at the surface level. Roeper & Siegel might fairly object to this that such abstract derivations typify the Generative Semantic approach to syntax, and not the Interpretative Semantic $\overline{X}$ syntax that they, and the scholars they quote, are using, and that if this distinction between rules and WFRs can be upheld in $\overline{X}$ syntax it may well be a point in favour of their kind of syntactic component. The question must be whether this restriction is supposed to say something about word-formation or about the syntactic component. As far as Roeper & Siegel are concerned, they clearly hope it will do both (despite the risk of being circular, inherent in this approach). In the context of a more general study of word-formation, it seems dangerous to make such definite assumptions about syntax, given how little agreement there is on the form of the syntactic component in present-day linguistics.

6.5.3 *Medial variables*

The absence of medial variables means that WFRs attach an affix to a specific contiguous environment.
(Roeper & Siegel, 1978: 202)

There are no lexical items, compound or otherwise, that involve discontinuous elements.
(Ibid.: 214)

This proposal depends so crucially on the type of underlying syntax that is proposed that it scarcely makes sense to discuss it in a theoretical vacuum. For example, Lees (1960: 146) has a section on compounds which are formed from the subject and the object of an underlying sentence, such as *windmill* and *car thief*. At the deepest level of underlying structure in Lees's model, these are separated by a verb, which is a variable, even if the transformation which actually forms the compound operates by deleting that extra variable so that the two elements of the compound come to be together without anything intervening (see the derivation provided by Lees, 1960: 144–5). In the type of grammar provided by Bauer (1978d), on the other hand, the two elements of *windmill* or *car thief* would be contiguous at the deepest level of underlying structure, and so the restriction would be valid. Moreover, such a claim would be totally vacuous if the base was held to be unordered (as many linguists now believe), unless it did not apply until after such transformations as impose order on a series of randomly generated items. Thus it seems that such a restriction is as much a restriction on the form of grammars as it is on the form of WFRs, and as such is virtually circular. Certainly some specification is required as to the level at which this constraint is supposed to hold in the syntax, and this in turn presupposes some statement about the level of syntax at which WFRs operate. Until such clarification is forthcoming, this limitation can not really be given serious consideration.

Even if, at some stage in the future, this claim could be shown to be of interest for English, it cannot be a universal claim. This is because of the existence of discontinuous morphs in some languages. Consider, for example, the following data from Egyptian Arabic (derived from Mitchell, 1956, 1962):

*ktb	write	'kaatib	clerk
*rkb	ride	'raakib	rider
*skn	inhabit	'saakin	inhabitant
*nʃr	publish	'naaʃir	publisher
*ktb	write	'maktab	office
*ṭbx	cook	'maṭbax	kitchen
*xzn	store	'maxzan	store
*dxl	enter	'madxal	foyer
*ktb	write	ki'taab	book

In such cases the consonants are variables in the specification of each process of word-formation, and the WFR must make reference to the vowels, stress pattern and the positional relation of these to the consonantal variables. For example, the agentive rule for the class illustrated here must be something like:

$$\text{Agentive} \rightarrow \text{'}C_1aaC_2iC_3$$

where C_1, C_2 and C_3 are the variable consonants of the root.

6.5.4 *No extrinsic ordering*

Extrinsic ordering is impossible: it would rule out the pair *industrialize* and *organizational*, since *-ize* and *-al* appear in opposite orders.
(Roeper & Siegel, 1978: 202)

The point needs to be made that the pair of forms quoted is not sufficient evidence to exclude the extrinsic ordering of WFRs. The different orderings of suffixes would be compatible with the extrinsic ordering of WFRs in either of the following cases: (a) if the WFRs applied cyclically; (b) if WFRs allowed affixes to be inserted into already generated strings. The second of these is ruled out if the word-based morphology hypothesis is adhered to (see below, §6.5.8), but it will be shown that there are grounds for believing that this hypothesis is too restrictive anyway. Thus the case against extrinsic ordering is not particularly good.

In any case, the status of extrinsic rule ordering in linguistics is not clear: many linguists now believe that, at least in phonology, rules are never extrinsically ordered, but that such ordering of rules as there is should be determined by universal principles. If this is true, then it may be the case that syntactic rules are not ordered either, and the proposed distinction between syntactic rules and WFRs would become vacuous.

In either case, it can be seen that the distinction between syntactic rules and WFRs is not as clear-cut on the subject of ordering as Roeper & Siegel claim.

6.5.5 *Semantic compositionality*

Semantic compositionality is always present where morphological rules are productive. This is because we can understand new derived words only by systematically decomposing them.
(Roeper & Siegel, 1978: 202)

I have made this assumption throughout this book, and in general it seems to be a basic assumption in work on word-formation. The only point that ought to be made here is that in some cases the meanings into which the lexemes can be decomposed may be grammatical rather than, or as well as, strictly semantic (see below, §6.7); that is, 'nominalization of V' might be a "meaning", just as much as 'capable of being Ved'.

6.5.6 *Idiosyncratic information*

Linguistic idiosyncrasies can be defined as knowledge that departs from rules . . . If words have idiosyncratic meanings, there must be a lexicon in memory in which to represent those idiosyncrasies.
(Roeper & Siegel, 1978: 215)

It has been part of the general thesis of this book that complex words tend to become idiosyncratic with time. I can, therefore, only applaud this statement. However, it is not clear to me that agreement with this statement implies agreement with the statement that "WFRs permit statement of idiosyncratic information" (Roeper & Siegel, 1978: 202). In fact, it seems that the contrary must be the case, since "idiosyncrasies can be defined as knowledge that departs from rules" and WFRs are precisely rules. The proposal that has been put forward here has therefore been that the rules describe the regularities, and that irregularities are listed in the lexicon and not described by the rules.

Roeper & Siegel also state (1978: 216) that "It is . . . an idiosyncratic property of each [lexical item] that it either exists or does not exist." This may be true, but the implication is that because this is an idiosyncrasy it should be listed in the lexicon, and that each new word produced by the WFRs should be marked as [occurrent] in the way suggested by Halle (1973).[9] Such a suggestion seems rather more doubtful, particularly in the light of the theory of lexicalization propounded above. Firstly, it is far from clear that it is theoretically possible to say what lexemes are occurrent, and secondly it is not clear that there is any difference in principle between a lexeme which clearly is occurrent and regular, and one which is regular but, as far as can be seen, is non-occurrent in the lexicon of the speaker-listener involved with it. The problem is not made easier by reference to an ideal speaker-listener, since the competence of such a being would have to include a list of all the words which could ever possibly be formed. Since new affixes and principles of word-formation can be introduced at any synchronic stage of development of a language this is clearly impossible. This is the difficulty with the "full entry theory" (Aronoff, 1976; Halle, 1973; Jackendoff, 1975; Roeper & Siegel, 1978: 200) of the lexicon in general, the theory that the output of the WFRs is stored in the lexicon immediately.

6.5.7 *The First Sister Principle*

Roeper & Siegel (1978: 208) introduce their own restriction on the syntax of verbal compounds, a restriction which they call the **First Sister Principle**. This states that "All verbal compounds are formed by incorporation of a word in first sister position of the verb." They point out that given a sentence like *She makes peace quickly* the first sister of the verb, *peace*, can be incorporated with the verb to form *peace-maker*, but that other elements cannot be incorporated, and notably, independent of the acceptability of items after the first sister, further elements cannot

---

[9] For severe criticism of this paper, both on these and other grounds, see Beard (1977), Boas (1974) and Lipka (1975).

be incorporated in this way: *quick(ly)-maker*. This principle is specifically stated to hold only for verbal compounds and not for root compounds.

The first point to be noted about this claim is that it presupposes an analysis of the underlying strings which is close to the surface structure of the sentences which those strings could be developed into. Either this would seem to rule out very abstract syntactic analyses, or some specification is required as to the level of deep syntax at which the principle is supposed to apply.

The second point to note is that Roeper & Siegel are talking in terms of derivation of compounds from strings which also underlie sentences. It has been argued above that the same strings should not underlie sentences and instances of word-formation. This is not a crucial objection to Roeper & Siegel's proposal provided that their grammar can be made capable of generating underlying strings which are not marked for tense, aspect, mood, etc., as discussed above. In $\overline{\mathrm{X}}$ syntax, this might be done by generating strings that do not contain Spec $\overline{\mathrm{V}}$ (i.e. Aux, in traditional terminology), or any of the elements dominated by the $\overline{\mathrm{X}}$-equivalent of Σ, but not by the $\overline{\mathrm{X}}$-equivalent of S. It is pointed out by Bauer (1978d: §4.1.4) that this is not a particularly satisfactory solution, since it allows the generation of far too many deep structures that will have to be filtered out because there is no Aux in the top sentence; but it is a possibility.

A more serious objection to this proposal is also an objection to all models which propose to derive instances of word-formation from the strings underlying sentences (e.g. Lees, 1960; Rohrer, 1967), namely that most of the string is irrelevant for the WFR. *She makes peace quickly*, if it is related to a sentence including a verbal compound, is related to *She is a quick peace-maker* rather than just *peace-maker*. The question must be whether the relationship between these two sentences is a syntactic one, or just a semantic one. Now, if a Generative Semantic approach is assumed, the two are, of course, identical. But it was pointed out above that Roeper & Siegel's conclusions depend crucially in other instances on their approach not being a Generative Semantic one. Given an Inter-pretative Semantic approach to the semantic component, there would seem to be no objection to deriving *She makes peace quickly* and *She is a quick peace-maker* from separate syntactic configurations, and discovering their near synonymity from interpretative semantic rules, which will point out that the semantic effect of an adverb modifying a verb is similar to that of an adjective modifying a noun. In fact, there are sound reasons for supposing that this is not only possible, but actually preferable to a solution which sees a common source for the two sentences. *She makes peace quickly* is ambiguous between a reading on which this is a habitual and characteristic fact about 'her' and one where it is a stage direction or a commentary on an on-going situation. *She is a quick peace-maker* only has the first of these two readings. This would be predicted by the approach that is espoused in this book, but would have to be specifically explained by an approach which tried to give the two sentences the same underlying string.

Once it is assumed that the two sentences above come from different underlying structures, further assumptions can be made. For example, it would seem reasonable to assume that only those morphemes that are actually necessary in the derivation of the instance of word-formation should be generated in the Proposition from which the instance of word-formation is to be derived. Consider again *She makes peace quickly*. Apart from the information that is present in the modality, this sentence contains two pieces of information that are not present in the compound *peace-maker*: firstly that the agent is female, and secondly that the action is carried out swiftly. Neither of these facts is relevant for the generation of *peace-maker*. If they were, it would not be possible to find sentences containing the compound *peace-maker* which correspond semantically to the sentences *He makes peace quickly*, *All the people who work in the Kremlin make peace slowly* and so on. Furthermore, an assumption of this kind would solve the problem of what happens to determiners in word-formation. Roeper & Siegel's transformation as it is formulated will derive *clothes drier*, for example, from any one of:

> it dries clothes
> it dries some clothes
> (s)he dries clothes
> it dries the clothes [that I was talking about]
> it dries my clothes
> it dries his clothes

and so on (see their example *cave dweller* where, if it is to be grammatical, the underlying string must have some determiner for *cave*). Yet *clothes drier* is not as many ways ambiguous as there are possible determiners in the language. Somehow, then, the grammar must prevent determiners from being generated with any noun that is going to become part of a complex lexeme. Talking in terms of embedded Propositions (as was suggested above) allows a simple way of stating the environment in which all nouns must (often atypically) be determinerless.

To return now to the example *She makes peace quickly* and *She is a quick peace-maker* in the light of these proposals, it can be seen that the two sentences could be derived from different syntactic configurations independent of the particular syntactic theory espoused. Figures 6.5 and 6.6, while not formulated according to any particular syntactic theory, show the kind of way in which this

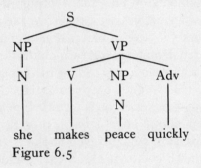

Figure 6.5

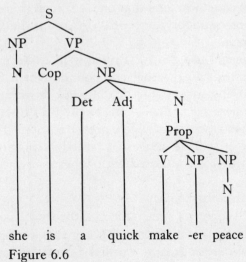

Figure 6.6

might be done. Trees of this general type were proposed in Bauer (1978d). The principles implicit in these trees can presumably be extended to all types of word-formation. But if this proposal is accepted, it has quite serious effects for the FS Principle. Since only relevant morphemes are generated in the Proposition from which complex words derive, all the complex words which have a structure made up of two parts will contain only two morphemes on the tree which will automatically be first sisters. Now, as far as compounds are concerned, it has been commented on fairly frequently in the literature that they are basically made up of two parts at each level of analysis. Even very long compounds can almost invariably be divided into two, even if each of the two parts is complex and made up of elements which are further analysable into two parts. The exceptions to this are dvandva compounds, which may have several elements on an equal footing (see Bauer, 1978d: §4.2.2.3). As far as derivatives are concerned the matter is not so clear, but even there it seems likely that a majority of derivatives will be generated from structures including only two elements, even if some of those elements can be further analysed. Under these conditions the FS Principle becomes a statement of the obvious, rather than a strong restriction on a specific type of WFR. With a further assumption about an abstract pro-verb in compounds (see above, §6.4) the FS Principle even applies to precisely the set of compounds from which Roeper & Siegel exclude it. In fact, given the other assumptions that one is forced to make about the syntactic structures underlying word-formation, the FS Principle is totally vacuous.

Yet Roeper & Siegel use the FS Principle to make predictions about the grammaticality of verbal compounds which are by no means vacuous. For instance, they rule out *quick-owner*, *fool-looker* and *boy-looker*. If these are not ruled out by the FS Principle, there must be some other restriction which prevents them from being generated. In §6.6 it will be suggested, still following Roeper & Siegel (1978), that this is connected with subcategorization.

6.5.8 *Word-based morphology*

Aronoff (1976: 21) introduces a theory of word-based morphology in the following terms: "all regular word-formation processes are word-based. A new word is formed by applying a regular rule to a single already existing word" where "word" is to be taken in the sense of 'lexeme'. This is a very attractive theory, and one which is implicit in many treatments of word-formation (e.g. Lyons, 1968: 195). The theory is so attractive because it applies in the vast majority of cases (at least as far as English is concerned) and in the most obvious cases, and also because it provides a principled limitation on possible bases for word-formation. Unfortunately, such a limitation is too strong.[10]

It can be shown to be too strong in a number of ways. Firstly, all the examples that were quoted in §6.5.1 of words coined from a phrasal base are counter-examples, because they show that words can be formed by applying a rule to a unit which is larger than the word. The problem is in fact more serious than might appear in §6.5.1, because, as is shown in Bauer (1979d) the agentive *-er* formative is regularly added to noun phrases – as in *hot mooner* 'person who believes there is thermal activity in the moon's core'. Twelve per cent of the formations in the corpus for that work were formed on the basis of a noun phrase, and a further 3 per cent on other phrasal bases as illustrated by *far-outer* 'one who is far-out' (i.e. nonconformist). While it is true that such phrases are typically idiomatic, this is not the same as saying that they are one lexeme. That the phrases involved are not necessarily idiomatic is shown by an example like *I feel particularly sit-around-and-do-nothing-ish today* (attested in conversation).

Secondly, it is shown in Bauer (1979c) that new lexemes can be formed by applying rules to units which are smaller than the word. These are the elements of neo-classical word-formation which do not really fit definitions of 'prefix', 'suffix' or 'root', although they do fit the definition of 'affix'. The examples quoted in Bauer (1979c) are *Anglo-*, *bio-*, *electro-*, *Euro-*, *Franco-*, *homo-*, *-crat*, *-phile* and possibly also *-phobe* and *-naut*. The natural sciences provide plenty of other examples. Lexemes such as *Eurocrat*, *Francophile*, *Anglophile*, *biocrat*, *homophile* and so on, which are formed according to productive processes (there are several listed in Barnhart *et al.* (1973), a dictionary of neologisms) cannot be formed on the basis of existing lexemes.

The third argument against the word-based hypothesis depends

---

[10] The arguments in this section appear in greater detail in Bauer (1980b).

upon the interpretation of Aronoff's terms. It concerns the base involved in back-formation. For back-formation to be possible, there has to be a form which can be interpreted as containing an affix but no corresponding form without that affix. In the classic example of *pedlar* > *peddle*, it is the interpretation which is at fault, and there is no etymological *-er* suffix. In the cases which are important here, though, there is a genuine affix present. Consider as an example the word *unflappable*. If the word-based hypothesis held, this would have to be formed by the prefixation of *un-* to an already existing *flappable*. Yet *flappable* is listed in Barnhart *et al.* (1973) as a back-formation from *unflappable*, so it is clear that it cannot have been the base for *unflappable*. If Aronoff's claim that word-formation rules apply to "a single already existing word" means that the base must be a possible word, one which the speaker feels could exist, then such examples prove nothing. But if, as seems more likely, "already existing" is to be interpreted as 'established', then the bases involved in such back-formations provide further counter-evidence to the word-based hypothesis.

Finally, though far less crucially, there are quite a lot of words which appear to have been formed not on lexemes but on clipped forms of lexemes. For example, the neologism *commitology*[11] is the study of *committees*, with the *tee* syllable deleted. A more systematic example is provided by the regular truncation of verbal *-ate* in certain formations (Aronoff, 1976). As far as I know, no study of this kind of deletion has been made, and I would not even like to guess how regular or irregular it is. If it turns out to be totally regular, then it can be treated as a kind of sandhi phenomenon in word-formation (this is approximately how it is treated by Aronoff); if it is irregular it threatens more than just the word-based theory.

6.5.9 *Summary*

In this section the restrictions on WFRs proposed in recent transformational literature and (except for the word-based hypothesis) summarized by Roeper & Siegel (1978) have been considered. Of the six of these, only one, "semantic compositionality", has been accepted, and Roeper & Siegel's own First Sister

[11] *American Speech* 46 (1971), 292.

Principle has been criticized. In particular, these restrictions have been found failing because they seem to be proposals for restrictions on the syntactic component as much as, or more than, restrictions on WFRs *per se*.

In the next section another proposal from Roeper & Siegel's paper will be considered more favourably, and it will be suggested that it can be extended to cover the generalizations Roeper & Siegel tried to gain by the First Sister Principle.

6.6 Subcategorization
6.6.1 *Patterns of subcategorization frames*

Roeper & Siegel (1978: 202–3) point out that derivatives can differ from the words which form their bases (in cases of derivation from established lexemes) in the ways in which they are grammatically subcategorized. They see lexemes as occurring in a syntactic or semantic environment of the type that is specified in Chomsky (1965) by selectional and strict subcategorization rules. For example, KILL appears in environments which can be specified as [NP — NP] and [— +Animate]. Each of these Roeper & Siegel term a 'subcategorization frame'. Processes of forming derivatives from bases may cause alterations to the frames, and Roeper & Siegel claim that word-formation processes can be classified according to whether frames are inherited, deleted or added in such processes.

6.6.1.1 Inherited frames

This is what is found in cases where the nominalizations of transitive verbs allow prepositional phrases with *of* in the same semantic relationship to the derivatives as the direct object held to the base lexeme, or where prepositional marking is the same for a verb and its nominalization. Thus:

> He criticized this book
> His criticism *of* this book
> He qualified *for* the new job
> His qualification *for* the new job

This type of inheritance was discussed above (§4.3) in relation to the discussion in Chomsky (1970).

Subcategorization frames are frequently inherited by complex words from their bases in this way. For instance, non-idiomatic endocentric noun + noun compounds will have the same marking for categories such as countability, gender,[12] animacy, concreteness and so on, as the head noun in the compound, and a derivative like LIONESS includes all the semantic features in the base LION (in its literal sense), but adds a specification for sex. These are straightforward cases. In others the frame is inherited, but applies in a slightly different way. Roeper & Siegel (1978: 204–5) cite a paper by Vergnaud as having pointed out that the selectional restrictions on the subject of a deverbal *-able* derivative are identical to those on the object of the verb base. (For a similar point in a different field see Ljung, 1970: 24.)

> John ate the meat
> The meat was eatable
> *John ate the love
> *The love was eatable

In cases where this does not hold, it would seem to be the result of lexicalization, because the generalization seems to be true in productive cases. Consider the following, which may be a case where the generalization does not hold:

> John kissed her
> She was kissable
> John kissed her hand
> ?Her hand was kissable
> He kissed the rod
> *The rod was kissable

The non-acceptability of *The rod was kissable* may be related to the idiomatic nature of the expression *kiss the rod*, but the same is not true for *Her hand was kissable*. If my intuition about the non-acceptability of this is correct, then it may have to be noted in the lexicon, since it is an exception to the general rule of inherited frames with the suffix *-able*. Consider, also:

---

[12] There are lexicalized instances where the grammatical gender of a compound is not that of a head element, for example German *der Mut* 'spirit' (masc.) but *die Grossmut* 'great spirit' = 'generosity' (fem.) and *die Wehmut* 'woe spirit' = 'melancholy' (fem.), or Danish *en tid* 'time' (common gender) but *et måltid* 'meal time' (neut.). There are also cases where a specific pattern of compounding appears to demand a particular grammatical gender. Thus in French, compounds made up of a verb stem + a noun which could act as the direct object of that verb are productively masculine: *un tire-bouchon* 'a (masc.) pull-cork' = 'cork-screw', *un pèse-lettre* 'a (masc.) weigh letter' = 'letter scales', *un lèche-culture* 'a (masc.) lick culture' = 'cultural toady'.

He kissed the bishop's ring
?The bishop's ring was kissable

which might suggest that only people (and lips) can be kissable, in which case the restriction is easily stated.

6.6.1.2 Deleted frames

Roeper & Siegel point out that in some cases a verbal lexeme can have either a nominal or a sentential object when it is used alone, but cannot have a sentential object when prefixed by *re-*. Thus they predict the following pattern of acceptability:

I told her the story
I retold her the story
I told her that Lucy was coming
*I retold her that Lucy was coming

This pattern is, however, not repeated with all lexemes, so that the rule cannot be a general one. Consider, for example:

The president affirmed his love for her
The president reaffirmed his love for her
The president affirmed that he would stand for re-election
The president reaffirmed that he would stand for re-election

Roeper & Siegel (1978: 254) also cite the example of EAT as prefixed by *over-*:

I ate
I ate the potato
I overate
*I overate the potato

Such cases, where they are regular, are taken by Roeper & Siegel to be instances of a frame being deleted by a word-formation process. In general they comment that affixation deletes syntactic frames in this way, though there are isolated exceptions. If this deletion of syntactic frames is a regular concomitant of a particular word-formation process it can be noted as part of the rule governing that process. If, on the other hand, the deletion of syntactic frames is sporadic and unpredictable it would seem that such deletion must be equated with syntactic lexicalization.

6.6.1.3 Added frames

Any suffix which changes the syntactic class of a derivative must also change the syntactic classification of the derivative to fit in with the syntactic patterns ascribed to the new form class. Thus while DEPEND takes a subject and an optional phrase introduced by *on*, DEPENDABLE can modify a noun or be used in predicative position after a copula verb, and so on.

There are also cases which are the converse of the *retell* and *overeat* examples in §6.6.1.2, where the derived form allows a wider range of arguments than the non-derived form. Consider, for example:

> He grew
> *He outgrew
> *He grew his electric train set
> He outgrew his electric train set

Another example is:

> *He supposed the answer
> He supposed that the answer would not come in time
> He presupposed the answer
> He presupposed that the answer would not come in time

Again, such addition of frames is equatable with lexicalization unless it is a regular feature of a particular word-formation process.

6.6.2   *Subcategorization and the First Sister Principle*

In §6.5.7 the proposed First Sister Principle limiting certain kinds of WFR was discussed, and it was suggested that such a principle might be vacuous once a more complete grammar for word-formation had been elaborated. In this section an attempt will be made to show how the generalizations which the First Sister Principle was meant to capture can be made by using subcategorization frames instead.

According to the First Sister Principle, the first sister to the right of the verb is moved to the left of the verb by transformation and an affix is added on the right of the verb when verbal compounds are generated. If the verb is a transitive verb with an obligatory object, then the first sister on the right of the verb will always be the direct object of the verb. This accounts for the fact that so many N + V + *er* compounds have the direct object of the verb in the N slot (see the comments in Kingdon, 1958: 152, and the institutionalized examples listed there). But there is no need to see this as depending on the position of the node relative to the verb in the shallow structure. It could equally well be related to the fact that these verbs are marked as being transitive with a nominal object. Note that transitive verbs with sentential objects cannot take part in this transformation, even though such objects are first sisters:

> I want to see him
> *A see-wanter
> *A to-see-him-wanter
> I helped wash up
> *A wash-up-helper

Transitive verbs which have an absolute usage (i.e. a usage without an object, as in *Smith drinks, Do you smoke?*) and intransitive verbs will allow an adverbial in first sister position. Roeper & Siegel (1978: 244ff) point out that transitive verbs used absolutely do not allow compound formation with an adverbial, so that **clearly-hearer* is not a possible verbal compound. They see this as an argument that the transitive verb used absolutely has a zero marker for its direct object in the deep structure, but it could equally well mean that all transitive verbs are treated the same way, and can only form verbal compounds with items which could be their direct objects. There are, in any case, counter-examples where the adverbial is not an adverb but a prepositional phrase. Thus a *vacuum cleaner* does not clean vacuums, nor does a *town crier* cry towns, nor does a *breech-loader* load breeches, and in British English (though not in American English) a *school-teacher* does not teach school but *in* a school. These examples are all established and I do not know whether such patterns are productive or not, but the short list given by Kingdon (1958: 152) suggests that they might not be, even though that list is not necessarily definitive. If they are not productive, then on the approach taken here they are listed in the lexicon and do not present any problem, though Roeper & Siegel still have to account for them under their approach. If they are productive, then the true generalization seems to be not that the first sister on the right can be compounded with these verbs but that a noun can be used in the formation of a verbal compound of this kind containing a transitive verb. Also, if the transitive verb does not allow an absolute usage, then the noun in the compound has to be the direct object of the verb, but if the transitive verb does allow an absolute usage, then the noun is not constrained in this way.

Intransitive verbs do not have a position for a direct object, and so the first sister must be an adverbial of some kind. Roeper & Siegel give examples of compounds formed from intransitive verbs where the adverbial is a non-*ly* adverb (1978: 222) (*slow burner, late bloomer*) and where the adverbial is a noun (ibid.: 243) (*church-goer, city-dweller*). Where the adverbial is an -*ly* adverb, Roeper & Siegel (ibid.: 222) show that the derivation of a compound is blocked, and an adjective + noun phrase is generated in its place: they cite examples such as *beautiful dancer* and *smart dresser*. Such examples are exceptions under any approach, but there is again no reason why the possibility of including other adverbials in such compounds should not be made an automatic result of the intransitive marking for the verb concerned. To judge from Roeper & Siegel's examples, it seems that the adverbial in such compounds is always a locative (either spatial or temporal). The same appears to be true of the adverbial that occurs with transitive verbs used absolutely, though in these compounds the locative node must always dominate a surface noun. With a transitive verb which does not allow an absolute usage, on the other hand, the noun that is made part of the compound is always in the objective case. Thus verbs whose direct objects are not in the objective case are not used to form such compounds: *She reached London* but **London-reacher*; *She inhabits the city* but **city-inhabiter*; and a *dog-fetcher* could only be a person who fetches dogs for someone, and not a person who, for example, fetches a dog a bone. Roeper & Siegel's First Sister Principle fails to account for such phenomena, while the proposal being made here has other advantages as well: it uses grammatical categories which have to be marked in the lexicon in any case, and since it could be reformulated so as to avoid the notion of deep case, it is less theory-specific. It is therefore suggested that, by extending the use of subcategorization which Roeper & Siegel advocate, a preferable alternative to their First Sister Principle can be elaborated.

6.7 The specification of meanings in word-formation

A recurrent problem in studies on word-formation is how closely the rules of word-formation should specify the meaning of a complex lexeme. This can be illustrated with reference to the suffix -*ish* in English, as discussed by Neuhaus (1977). Neuhaus points out that the precise meaning of the suffix has to be seen in relation to the adjective base to which it is added. In *oldish* it can only mean 'younger than the adjective base', while in *youngish* it can only mean 'older than the adjective base'. These two can, however, be reconciled if the generalization is made that when *-ish* is added to a base which is one member of a pair of gradable antonyms (see Lyons, 1968: 463ff) the *-ish* derivative always means 'further from the end point of the scale than would be denoted by the adjective base alone, but closer to the end denoted by the adjective base than to the opposing end'. This suggests that the lexical meaning attached to the suffix *-ish* should be considerably less specific than dictionary-type definitions of examples like *oldish* and *youngish* would seem to imply. The problem with *-ish* is even more complex than this, though. It can also be added to another set of adjectives, as in *fortyish*. Here, as Neuhaus points out, it appears to mean 'on either side of forty' and not just on one side of it. The 'further from the end point' kind of reading does not work with such adjectives. One solution to this problem might be to set up a second, completely separate, meaning for the suffix *-ish*, but in this case such a solution would in fact lose a generalization. *Forty* denotes a point on a scale of age which stretches from before forty to after forty, thus:

Young and *old*, on the other hand, denote the ends of a parallel scale, thus:

It is not possible to be younger than *young* or older than *old* (though, of course, neither indicates a precise point, and each can be further modified: *very young, fairly old*, etc.). The result of this is that a gloss of *fortyish* as 'close to forty on the appropriate scale' will mean, in real terms, either more or less than forty, whereas, 'close to young on the appropriate scale' for *youngish* can only mean 'not as young as *young*' and similarly, 'close to old on the appropriate scale' for *oldish* can only mean 'not as old as *old*'. Thus if the meaning of *-ish* is given as 'close to the adjective base on the appropriate scale', the meanings shown in *fortyish*, *oldish* and *youngish* can all be accounted for by a single lexical entry. The meaning specified in that lexical entry, it should be noted, is far less precise than the first approximations suggested by Neuhaus, and might even be considered to be of a different order of abstractness, since it is not even paraphrasable once and for all in terms of specific semantic features, but makes mention of 'an appropriate scale' which can change depending on the base used.

A further example is provided by compound nouns of the form noun + noun. According to most analyses of such compounds there is a large number (and according to some an infinite number) of different deep structures – and hence different meanings – associated with this surface structure pattern. The number of deep structures postulated usually depends on the number of predicators which are held to be found in such compounds.[13] If, however, the approach outlined in §6.4 above is adopted, all nominal compounds of this form have a single meaning connected with this surface pattern. The single meaning is, of course, very much less specific than those usually given in the literature, and also makes reference to pragmatic factors so that it cannot be specified in terms of a fixed set of semantic features. Nevertheless, the point is made that it is possible to specify the meanings of word-formation processes in very general terms, and that this kind of approach, while reducing the precision with which it is possible to paraphrase complex lexemes without any knowledge of the entities, actions or properties denoted, can bring about a vast simplification in the semantic specification of a rule of word-formation.

The matter of the precision needed in the semantic specification of word-formation processes becomes particularly important in the discussion of word-formation processes which are class-changing. This can be illustrated with two processes: adjectivalization and nominalization. Levi (1973, 1978) argues that the denominal adjectives in constructions like *traumatic event*, *musical comedy*, *national resources*, *salivary glands*, *floral wreath*, *marine life*,

---

[13] Consider, for example, the number of possible deleted elements underlying compounds in the following studies, all of which concentrate on compounds to a large degree: Adams (1973); Brekle (1970) (over 100); Hatcher (1960) (4); Kürschner (1974); Lees (1960) (an infinity); Levi (1978) (9); Rohrer (1967); Warren (1978) (12); Žepić (1970). For a review of some other works with similar principles see Bauer (1978d: §2.4).

industrial equipment, etc. (the examples are taken at random from Levi, 1978: 28off) are derived from the corresponding nouns (*trauma, music, nation* and so on) by a transformation of morphological adjectivalization, and that a previous stage in the derivation of these complex nominals is the appropriate noun + noun compound (*trauma event, music comedy*, and so on). The important point for this discussion is that the transformation of adjectivalization influences the form class of the lexeme but, it is argued, does not affect the meaning. That is, the rule of morphological adjectivalization is a syntactic rule which may have stylistic value (Levi, 1978: §6.1), but which is totally meaning-preserving.

Compare this with the situation of nominalization as discussed in the literature. First of all, standard dictionaries provide a large number of glosses for nominalizations, and a single form is frequently ambiguous (or vague) between two or more of these readings. To illustrate something of the range of these glosses, consider the following non-exhaustive list, which is derived from a small sample of nominalizations in *-ation* listed in a few dictionaries:

(i)   Act of Ving: *His* CLASSIFICATION *of the material took years*

(ii)   State of being Ved: CIVILIZATION *is a recent stage in the history of mankind*

(iii)   Process of being Ved: *The* COAGULATION *of the blood was well advanced*

(iv)   Place where one is Ved: *His* ACCOMMODATION *was a luxurious flat in the city*

(v)   The uncountable result of (i): *The* CONDENSATION *on the inside of the windows impaired my view*

(vi)   The countable result of (i): *There have been several* CONFRONTATIONS *between students and the Minister of Education*

(vii)   Something used in carrying out (i): *I received ample* COMPENSATION *for the trouble I had been put to*

(viii) System for carrying out (i): *This library uses the Dewey decimal* CLASSIFICATION *for books*

(ix)   Means of Ving: COMMUNICATIONS *with the capital have been restored*

(x)   Object which Vs someone or something: *This monument is a* COMMEMORATION *of the signing of the peace treaty*

(xi)   Something Ved: *I have received a brief* COMMUNICATION *from her*

(xii)   Measure of the degree to which something is Ved: *What is the* CONCENTRATION *of salt in this solution?*

None of these glosses is unique to the particular nominalization in question, although it is clearly the case that the first three are the most common. If each of these glosses represents a distinct meaning for the nominalization, then there will have to be at least twelve distinct deep structures to account for the range of meanings found in nominalizations. Nothing like this range of deep structures is discussed in the linguistic literature, although this may be purely accidental. Indeed, the number of types of nominalization discussed in the literature (apart from the so-called "agentive nominalization" e.g. *killer*, *lover*, which is of a rather different type) is remarkably small: 'Act' and 'Fact' nominalizations are those most frequently discussed (see Fraser, 1970; Lakoff, 1970a; Lees, 1960; Newmeyer, 1970, 1971), although other types are mentioned, for example 'Product' and 'State' nominalizations (Levi, 1978), 'Manner' nominalizations (Newmeyer, 1971). The exact details of the configurations from which these nominalizations are derived differ from authority to authority, but in general terms look something like that in Figure 6.7. The nodes X and Y differ in the various accounts: X is NP in Fraser (1970), but N in Levi (1978); Y is S in Fraser (1970), but V in Levi (1978). The notation ". . . V . . ." is intended to show that V is an obligatory part of this structure, whether or not anything else is included.

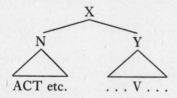

Figure 6.7

This type of notation is designed to capture the differences between the nominalizations in sentences like those in (23):

(23a)   His condemnation of the government lasted for hours (Act)
  (b)   His condemnation was a bitter blow for the government (Fact)
  (c)   His condemnation of the government was verbose (Manner)
  (d)   His behaviour was sufficient condemnation (Reason)

However, it should be noted that if this approach is taken, a similar diversity of deep structures will be needed underlying simplex nouns as well. Consider (24) and (25):

(24a) His joy caused others great heartache (Fact)
  (b) The joy of being Prime Minister is overestimated (State)
  (c) His children are a great joy to him (Reason)
(25a) The sudden noise made him jump (Act)
  (b) The noise is causing people to move away from the airport (Fact)
  (c) There's so much noise in here I can hardly hear myself think (State)
  (d) The noise near the airport is horrifyingly loud (Manner)

This conclusion, however, would seem to be totally undesirable, since it would lead to a much more complex deep structure for every noun phrase than seems warranted by other evidence. In particular it seems that the reading of the noun in the sentences in (24) and (25) is a feature of the sentence in which the noun appears rather than a genuine ambiguity in the noun itself. That is, the nouns are vague rather than ambiguous.

The classic test for ambiguity is the non-existence of so-called "crossed" readings under deletion based on identity (Lakoff, 1970b). Thus:

(26) George likes questioning linguists

is (intuitively) ambiguous between the reading in which George questions the linguists and the reading where the linguists do the questioning. Sentences like:

(27) George likes questioning linguists and so does Jim

or:

(28) George and Jim like questioning linguists

from an underlying structure corresponding to:

(29) George likes questioning linguists and Jim likes questioning linguists

have only two readings: one where George and Jim both question, and one where neither of them does. The crossed readings where George likes to question linguists and Jim likes linguists who question (or *vice versa*) are not possible, and thus (26) is proved to be ambiguous rather than vague (or, better, "unspecified", see Zwicky & Sadock, 1975). By contrast, with sentences which are not genuinely ambiguous but only unspecified it is possible to create sentences parallel to (27) and (28) where the crossed readings are acceptable. Consider:

(30)   Ian went to Rome

which might be recent past or remote past. In sentences like:

(31)   Ian went to Rome and Ken to Salzburg

or:

(32)   Ian and Ken went to Rome

readings where Ian went in the recent past and Ken went in the remote past (or *vice versa*) are possible, and so (30) is seen to be unspecified rather than ambiguous.

In the light of this, consider again the sentences in (23)–(25):

(33)   The noise near the airport is horrifyingly loud and is causing people to move away

is a perfectly acceptable sentence as far as I am concerned, and it demands a crossed reading whereby *noise* is Manner in the first conjunct, but Fact in the second. Therefore *noise* must be unspecified rather than ambiguous. Similarly,

(34)   His condemnation of the government was verbose and lasted for hours

demands a crossed reading, and therefore cannot be ambiguous. If such nominalizations are not ambiguous, they should not have different deep structures corresponding to the Act, Fact, State, etc., readings, but a single deep structure. The meaning of the nominalizations has to be interpreted as so much less specific as a result.

Precisely what the meaning of a nominalization is does not appear to be a question with an easily testable answer. I should like here to put forward a proposal which is consistent with the arguments that have been presented in this section, but which is not necessarily the only possible solution to the problem. I should like to propose that the basic meaning of a nominalization is inherent in the term 'nominalization' itself: a change of form class from a verb to a noun. Nominalization suffixes are formal markers of this changed status. The range of interpretations possible for any given nominalization – just like the range possible for any other noun – should be seen not as a matter of grammar, but as a pragmatic matter, dependent on the linguistic and non-linguistic context in which the nominalization occurs. Nominalizations can then be seen as being derived from the kind of configuration shown in Figure 6.8, in which the node NML (= nominalization) is realized as an appropriate suffix depending on a number of factors including lexical

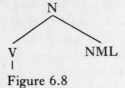

Figure 6.8

marking. Note that this structure, while not identical to the structure suggested in §4.3.3, is compatible with the arguments provided there, and also compatible with the general approach to word-formation advocated by Beard (1977, 1981) in which suffixation and derivation are seen as completely separate processes. Note also that a solution of this type implies that there is no difference in meaning between the various nominalization suffixes. I believe this to be the case. If, however, it could be shown that certain nominalization suffixes invariably excluded or demanded a specific subset of the set of possible readings for nominalizations, this type of approach would have to be substantially revised.

It seems to me to be a very useful approach in the study of word-formation to distinguish between what might be termed the 'grammatical' meaning of a word-formation process and the 'lexical' meaning (the terms are to be found in Hanks, 1979, and the general approach is implicit in Aronoff, 1976: 50, 71). Some processes, like adjectivalization and nominalization discussed here, have purely grammatical meaning, others, like the prefixation of *un-*, have only lexical meaning. Probably the majority have both types of meaning. Thus, for example, nominalizations in *-er* have a grammatical meaning in that the lexemes they produce are nouns, and also a lexical meaning which might be glossed loosely as 'person or object which is typically the subject of the verb used as the base'. It is for that reason that it was claimed earlier that the so-called 'agentive' nominalization is of a rather different type to the straight-forward nominalizations in *-ation*, *-ance*, *-ment* and so on. The consideration of grammatical as well as lexical meaning frequently makes the postulation of a single semantic effect for a word-formation process a far more credible and useful analytical tool, and often helps to explain an apparent variety in the meanings of an affix.

6.8 Lexical entries

6.8.1 *The lexicon*

The **lexicon** (or dictionary) provides a list of the lexemes of a language with information about each lexeme. Whereas a standard dictionary orders lexemes in alphabetical order of the citation form of the lexeme, the entries in a linguist's lexicon are in principle unordered (Chomsky, 1965: 84): when there is no orthography to use as a criterion, there is no obvious principle by which to order lexical entries anyway. The information about each lexeme that is listed in the lexicon is that information which is idiosyncratic, i.e. which cannot be predicted by general rule (Bloomfield, 1935: 274; Chomsky, 1965: 87). Perhaps the most idiosyncratic thing about lexemes is the relationship between the pronunciation and the meaning, which, with a few onomatopoeic exceptions, is arbitrary: there is no reason other than the chance of etymology why 'book' should be called /bʊk/ in English rather than /bɔʔu/ (Danish), /kirja/ (Finnish), /livrə/ (French), /bux/ (German), /libro/ (Italian), /kniga/ (Russian) or even /blɪk/. Lexemes also have other idiosyncratic information of various kinds associated with them. In inflecting languages, it may be unpredictable what declension a noun or adjective belongs to, or what conjugation a verb is. Where this is not predictable by general rule (based, for example, on the phonological form of the lexeme) this morphological information will have to be listed in the lexicon. In English, adjectives like *former* and *afraid* differ from adjectives like *red* and *cold* in that while *red* and *cold* and others like them can be used either attributively or predicatively, *former* can only be used attributively and *afraid* can only be used predicatively:

> The red house is on the hill
> The house on the hill is red
> The former president is in the audience
> *The president in the audience is former
> *The afraid man is at the bar
> The man at the bar is afraid

This syntactic information will also have to be listed in the lexicon.

6.8.2 *The lexical entry for a simplex lexeme*

For any simplex lexeme, the lexicon will have to list at least the pronunciation and the meaning. In standard Transformational Generative Grammar both of these are given in terms of feature matrices. The specification of the phonological form is not at issue here, and need be of no further concern; where a phonological specification is required a phonemic transcription will be used for the sake of simplicity. The specification of meaning, however, is rather more relevant.

While some form of componential analysis is very common in discussions of the meanings of lexemes, it has a number of drawbacks. There are theoretical drawbacks associated with the theoretical acceptability of binarism and the nature of the semantic features (see, for example, the discussion in Lyons, 1977: §9.9), but there are also more specific practical problems. One of these is that componential analysis appears to be better suited to the description of some semantic fields than to others. Thus it works relatively well in the description of animal names such as BOAR, SOW, PIGLET, HORSE, STALLION, MARE, FOAL, GELD-ING, etc., but works very badly in, say, the description of citrus fruits, such as CITRON, CLEMENTINE, GRAPEFRUIT, LEMON, MANDARINE, ORANGE, SATSUMA, TANGELO, etc. The differences between such fruits can be described in ordinary language (as witness dictionary definitions) but it is difficult to find any general features to distinguish between them. Another problem, related to this one, is that it is doubtful whether features are sufficient to give a complete specification of the meaning of a lexeme. Katz & Fodor (1963) use semantic markers such as 'one having the academic degree conferred for completing the first four years of college' for one of the meanings of BACHELOR. While it may be possible to reduce some part of these markers to more general features, it seems likely that, at least for some words, there will always be something left over.

For these reasons, it seems to me to be more satisfactory, at least until such time as a more unified semantic theory becomes available, to gloss the meanings of words in everyday English, i.e. using ordinary lexemes rather than metalinguistic features. This allows a more precise specification of a meaning than a feature notation alone would allow, and at the same time a more homogeneous type of definition. It should be noted, however, that this decision is motivated entirely on practical grounds, not theoretical ones: it is easiest to express meaning in this way, but it is not being claimed that the meaning of a lexeme is best expressed, from a theoretical point of view, in terms of other lexemes. While such a viewpoint does not seem to me to be untenable, a discussion of it would go far beyond what is required here. Note, however, that any adequate semantic theory will have to be able to account for the meaning of sentences and phrases which are made up of lexemes, and will therefore have to be able to interpret glosses of this kind. My decision not to take a theoretical stance on the representation of meanings does not imply any lack of discussion in the literature of what kind of semantic information is relevant and what kind of representation of that information might be employed. For some coverage of these issues, see Leech (1974) and Miller & Johnson-Laird (1976), who tackle the problem from very different points of view. The precise formulation of semantic information will not be theoretically relevant in what follows.

As far as the pronunciation is concerned, not only the segmental form will have to be listed, but also the suprasegmental form. In tone languages this will involve the tones; in English it involves only stress. To what extent stress in English is predictable by general rule is something that phonologists are not completely in agreement about. This was discussed in §§5.2 and 5.3. It seems likely that, given the right input, English stress is largely predictable, although the rules governing it are complex. That being the case, only unpredictable (irregular, idiosyncratic) stress on lexemes will have to be listed in the lexicon for English, though there must be a space in the lexical entry for suprasegmental information.

Finally, idiosyncratic morphological information must be listed. This will include information on declension, conjugation, gender (where it is unpredictable from the meaning or the phonological form), irregular plurals and so on.

Lyons (1977: 517) provides the schematic representation of a **lexical entry** reproduced in Figure 6.9. A similar, independent, proposal can be found in Miller (1978: 62). Most discussion of the lexicon in the literature is more concerned with the contents of one of the boxes in this figure than with the overall appearance of the lexical entry, which is largely what I shall be concerned with here. Box (i) contains the phonological (segmental and suprasegmental) specifications, box (ii) contains all information on inflection, and

| (i) stem(s) |
| (ii) inflectional class |
| (iii) syntactic properties |
| (iv) semantic specification(s) |

Figure 6.9

the parenthesized -*(s)* in box (iv) is to allow for the possibility of polysemy.

6.8.3 *The lexical entry for an affix*

In general, the sections of the lexical entry for an affix will have to be the same as those for a lexeme. The form or forms of the affix will have to be specified, the morphological class of the derivative formed by affixation of the particular affix will have to be specified (and this will include its form class), the syntactic behaviour of the derivative noted if it is not that of all other members of the form class, and the meaning of the affix noted. There are, however, a few modifications that must be made. The first of these concerns the semantic specification. If the suggestion made in §6.7 is adopted, and some affixes are taken to have a meaning which is pragmatically determined, then box (iv) might remain empty for those affixes, the "grammatical meaning" being specified by the form class shift noted in box (ii). Secondly, information on the limitations an affix places on the bases that it can co-occur with will be necessary. This information is probably best put in a separate box, though it might be seen as part of box (ii).

And finally, as will be seen in chapter 8, some affixes are stylistically marked and can be used to provide stylistic effects which would not be present if the base were used alone or with another, near-synonymous affix. This information will also be required in the lexicon, and almost certainly will have to be in a different box. This box might also be added to the lexical entry given above, though, because some simplex lexemes also have a marked stylistic effect: compare BIRD and GIRL(FRIEND), TWINKLE and SCINTILLATE, or PISS, PIDDLE and MIC-

TURATE. It is beyond the scope of this section to suggest what stylistic labels might be required, how many there might be, or how they are to be distinguished, but it seems fairly clear that some kind of marking is necessary. Suggested stylistic markings used later in this book are merely impressionistic labels.

6.8.4 *The lexical entry for a lexicalized complex form*

A complex form which is generated according to productive rules should not require a special lexical entry. The rules themselves, in combination with the lexical entries for the base and the affix (or stems in the case of compounds), should be sufficient to specify the meaning and behaviour of the new form. Lexicalized complex forms, on the other hand, do require specific lexical marking.

There are two possible ways to go about this. The first is to list each new complex lexeme separately; the second is to list the irregularities in the lexical entries for the bases or affixes. For example, consider the lexicalized complex word AWFUL, which is semantically lexicalized since it is now a near synonym of TERRIBLE, and does not mean 'full of awe'. Under the first approach AWFUL would be listed separately, and in the meaning box it would be specified that it meant 'terrible'. Under the second approach, *awful* would be generated when required from AWE + *-ful*, but it would be specified under AWE that it lost its meaning when used as a base for *-ful* suffixation, and that the whole could then mean 'terrible, very bad'. Either of these could be made to work.

The advantage of the first method is that each lexical item has its own entry, and that if phonological or semantic changes affect it to such an extent that it is no longer obviously related to its etymological base, there is no need to run through the whole etymology of a word to discover its present meaning. For example, French *aubépine* 'hawthorn' would not be generated from AUBE 'dawn' (< Latin ALBA 'white') and ÉPINE 'thorn', but would have its own entry. The advantage of the second method is that related lexemes can be seen to be related. For example, CLASSIFY will be known to exist from the entry for CLASS, despite being (in British English at least) phonologically lexicalized, in that the first vowel is /æ/ and not /ɑ/ (contrast *classy*).

But whereas the advantage of the first method cannot be captured using the second method, it is possible, if the first method is used, to have one's cake and eat it. All that is required then is that there should be an extra box in the lexical entry stating what other lexemes are related to the lexeme under consideration. For example, under CLASS there will be a note that it is related to CLASSIFY, and under CLASSIFY a note that it is related to CLASS. This can be done, as is suggested by Lyons (1977: 516), by furnishing each lexeme with an **address** which allows it to be located. Lyons suggests that an integer assigned to each lexeme at random might serve this purpose. Then CLASS might, for example, be lexeme number 792, and associated with lexeme 533, which would be CLASSIFY.

If this method is adopted there must be a separate lexical entry for every lexicalized form. However, not all the information that can be given in a lexical entry will necessarily be idiosyncratic in a lexicalized form – as indeed was implicit when it was stated earlier (§3.2.3) that it was possible to talk of a form being "phonologically lexicalized" or "semantically lexicalized". Thus in the entry for AWFUL, for example, it will be necessary to specify the appropriate semantic information, but the phonological and morphological information about AWFUL may be sufficiently well specified by the information that it is composed of AWE + *-ful*, just as the morphological and semantic information about CLASSIFY might be sufficiently well specified by the information that it is made up of CLASS + *-ify*. It must thus be possible to leave some parts of the lexical entry blank apart from the morphological information about the make-up of the stem of the lexeme.

There must also be space in the lexical entry to specify all the possible kinds of lexicalization discussed in §3.3. This means room to specify irregular segmental form, suprasegmental form, linking elements, morphological factors, etc., for every stem.

With this information a more detailed picture of a lexical entry can now be given, using the same kind of schematic representation as was shown above. In a lexical entry of this kind any box may be empty or minimally specified. Box (vii) in Figure 6.10 is used only for affixes. When the entry is for an affix, the information in box (ii) will concern the complex form containing the affix. Not all of the entries in box (ii) will be relevant in all languages, and others

(i) Phonological specification		
stem no.	segmental form	suprasegmental form
I		
. . .		
n		

(ii) Morphological properties					
stem no.	form class	declension/ conjugation	plural/ past	gender	link element
I					
. . .					
n					

(iii) Syntactic properties
(iv) Semantic specification(s)
(v) Stylistic specification(s)
(vi) Related lexeme(s)
(vii) Limitations on base

Figure 6.10

may be relevant in other languages: for example, the classifier a noun takes may be a relevant category for some languages which have classifiers.

6.8.5 *Some examples*

It will not be necessary to give complete examples of lexical entries for specific lexemes – it is probably not even possible – but some examples of how they will be filled in for complex lexemes may be helpful at this stage. Three examples will be discussed here: EDIBLE, KNOWLEDGEABLE and DES-TRUCTION. The treatment of EDIBLE will be close to that in Lyons (1977: 533); the treatment of KNOWLEDGEABLE differs slightly from that of Lyons (1977: 534); and the treatment of DESTRUCTION can be contrasted with the treatment in Chomsky (1970) and other writings.

For most speakers of English, the meaning of EDIBLE seems to be regular, and to be 'which can be eaten'. EDIBLE is thus synonymous with EATABLE. Those speakers who have a contrast in meaning between these two must have slightly different lexical entries, and they will not be dealt with here. For speakers with the regular meaning, it will be sufficient to mark in box (iv) 'EAT + -*able*', or following Lyons (1977: 531), '259 + 651', where 259 is the address for the lexeme EAT, and 651 is the address for the suffix -*able*. Since all the morphological and syntactic information about EDIBLE is also derivable from this information, this will also be sufficient information for boxes (ii) and (iii). It is, however, not sufficient information for box (i) where '259 + 651' would give the form *eatable*, which also exists. Thus in the box for the segmental form of the stem there must be an entry /edɪbəl/. The suprasegmental form, the stress pattern, is predictable from this and from '259 + 651'. Since the use of a word with a Latin root is slightly more formal than the use of a word with an English root, this information will be put in box (v). Box (vi) will include a reference to 259 (unless this is specified by a redundancy rule, since it appears elsewhere in the lexical entry), but probably not to any other lexeme. Box (vii) is irrelevant, and is left empty.

KNOWLEDGEABLE is rather like the reverse of EDIBLE. Here the form is predictable from its being composed of KNOW-LEDGE (lexeme number 176, say) and -*able*, so that '176 + 651' is a sufficient entry for box (i), but this is not sufficient information for box (iv) since noun + -*able* is not a productive pattern. Box (iv) will thus have to contain the meaning, perhaps something like 'having specialized knowledge'. Note that by marking in box (vi) that KNOWLEDGEABLE is related to KNOWLEDGE, it will automatically be related to KNOW, since KNOW and KNOW-LEDGE will be marked as related lexemes under KNOWLEDGE.

Finally, consider DESTRUCTION. In box (vi) it will be marked that it is related to DESTROY, as well as to DESTRUC-TIVE, DESTRUCTIBLE and, because of a recent back-formation, to the verb DESTRUCT (note especially *self-destruct*). The segmental form /dɪstrʌkʃən/ is unpredictable, but the stress is predictable from the morphological specification of the suffix as *-ion*. However, this raises a problem which is relevant for the entries in boxes (ii), (iii) and (iv). It is not clear that the suffix *-ion* is productive. The only places where there must be a corresponding *-ion* nominalization for a verb are where the verb ends in *-ify* or *-ize*. The corresponding nominalization then ends in *-ification* or *-ization* respectively. Thus the nominalization suffix looks like *-ation* rather than *-ion*. Nonetheless, *-ion* can be analysed as a nominalization ending in a number of words, e.g. *construction*, *evasion*, *infusion*, *inspection*. The question is thus whether *-ion* can be given a separate lexical entry, and the entry under DESTRUCTION can say 'DESTROY' + *-ion*', or whether it must be treated as unanalysable every time it occurs. The standard Transformational Generative answer would be to give *-ion* its own entry, and thus capture a generalization: the information concerning *-ion* will only have to be specified once, and not for every nominalization that uses the suffix. The notion of lexicalization that was provided in chapter 3, however, demands that non-productive forms should have their own lexical entry, and, moreover, that it should be clear that a form like DESTRUCTION is lexicalized because the affix used in it is no longer productive. Thus the problem can be rephrased as a question of whether the irregular entry in the segmental part of box (i) is sufficient for this purpose, or whether some special entry is needed elsewhere as well.

It seems to me that either approach could be justified here, depending on what particular factors are considered the most important. There is, however, at least one solution which falls between the two extremes, and which should also be considered. It is that in boxes (ii)–(iv) the specific suffix should not be mentioned, but it should be noted that the form is a nominalization. The entry would then be 'DESTROY + nominalization'. Certainly as far as box (iv) (the semantic specification) is concerned, it is probably irrelevant in English which particular nominalization suffix or process is used – the meaning will not be altered by the use of one suffix or process rather than another except where a contrasting suffix is employed specifically to provide a new meaning, in which case rather more specification will probably be required in box (iv) anyway.

6.8.6   *Institutionalized words*

The final problem for a theory of lexical entries concerns institutionalized words. The problem will be sketched here, but no solution will be offered. It can be illustrated with the lexeme CLASSIFY.

It was pointed out above that CLASSIFY is phonologically lexicalized (in British English), but nothing was said about the meaning. The meaning, however, is also specialized. CLASSIFY can be glossed as 'put into classes'; this can be seen as one facet of the regular meaning of the suffix *-ify*, which Marchand (1969: §4.46.2) glosses as 'make, convert into, bring into the state of —'. However, if a new intake of children in a school was being put into several classes, they could not be said to be classified. That is, the meaning of the base CLASS is restricted in the word *classify*. It was stated above (§3.2.2) that this ignoring of the potential ambiguity of a complex word was typical of institutionalization. Thus from the semantic point of view, CLASSIFY is probably institutionalized rather than lexicalized.

As far as the lexeme CLASSIFY is concerned, the question is simply whether an entry in box (iv) 'CLASS + *-ify*' is sufficient or not. In other cases, where a word cannot be said to be lexicalized, it is a question of whether a word needs a separate lexical entry or not: should TELEPHONE BOX, for instance, be listed in the lexicon or is it predictable from TELEPHONE, BOX, and the rules of compounding? With CLASSIFY the problem might be avoided by treating CLASS as a number of homonymous lexemes, each with its own address in the lexicon. Then CLASSIFY might be 792 + 91, while CLASS 'division in a school' was 522, say. This solution is possible in the case of CLASSIFY, though it seems to me undesirable, since my feeling is that CLASS is polysemous rather than two homonymous lexemes; in the case of TELEPHONE BOX, however, this solution is simply not available.

If institutionalized forms as well as lexicalized forms are listed in the lexicon, then the lexicon will be much larger than if only lexicalized forms are listed. It seems likely that the list of compounds, in particular, will be dramatically increased. It is possible that on the one hand this will mean a decrease in generality, but on the other, an increase in the psychological reality of the theory. If there are no solid arguments one way or the other, a choice will have to be made here in terms of the priorities of the linguist.

7
An outline of English word-formation

Behind a superficial appearance of simplicity there is concealed a perfect hornet's nest of bizarre and arbitrary usages.

(Sapir, 1949: 114)

7.1 Introduction

The purpose of this chapter is not to provide an exhaustive survey of English word-formation, as this has already been done by, among others, Adams (1973), Koziol (1937) and, especially, Marchand (1969). Rather the intention is to provide an outline of types of word-formation in English, both productive and non-productive, to illustrate the range of patterns that exists in English. As a result, both lexicalized and non-lexicalized examples will be cited in this chapter, and in many cases there will be only brief comments on degrees of productivity. However, where the processes illustrated are still productive, recent examples showing the productive use will be included. Unless a specific source is listed for such recent examples, they are taken from Barnhart *et al.* (1973). This chapter is primarily taxonomic, and aims at presenting and illustrating a range of types of word-formation. However, a certain amount of theoretical discussion is also included, particularly where the discussion in the major sources about English word-formation is unsatisfactory (sometimes even totally lacking). Some theoretical comments will also be made, from time to time, on the implications of the taxonomy for a generative theory of word-formation, especially in cases where the boundaries of the categories are hard to define or where the transformational source of the complex words is not clear.

7.2 Compounding

As intimated in §2.15 the normal way of classifying compounds is by the function they play in the sentence as nouns, verbs, adjectives, etc. The subclassification of compounds is done in many different ways: by the form classes of the items that make up the compound (Marchand, 1969), by semantic classes (Hatcher, 1960; Warren, 1978), by presumed underlying operators linking the two elements (Žepić, 1970), by presumed underlying syntactic function (Lees, 1960) and so on. Many scholars use a mixture of two or more of these methods of classification (Adams, 1973; Jespersen, 1942). With any of these methods, it is possible to subclassify with a greater or lesser degree of delicacy, so that whereas both Brekle (1970) and Hatcher (1960) use semantic classifications for compound nouns, Hatcher has only four categories, while Brekle has about one hundred. As a result, any method of subclassification is bound to be controversial, and none can hope to win unqualified support. The system of classification used here is one in terms of the form classes of the elements of the compound, and is not particularly delicate. This system is used because it seems to me that it is often valuable in the discussion of semantic relationships between elements to concentrate, in the first instance, on semantic relationships within each of the categories provided here. The major disadvantage of this system of classification is that because of the amount of conversion in English it is not always clear what form class a particular element belongs to. This is particularly true when deciding between nouns and verbs. In a compound like *rattlesnake*, for example, *rattle* might be a verb (*the snake rattles*) or a noun (*the snake has a rattle*).

The vast majority of compounds in English are nouns. My impression is that this is even truer of items containing more than two elements (which are usually nonce formations) than of items containing only two elements, with which this chapter will be mainly concerned. It seems that most longer compounds can be analysed as combinations of two elements, each of which may in turn be compound (see Bauer, 1978d: 129), so that no generalizations are lost by looking mainly at two-item compounds; as far as I know, no extended empirical study of longer compounds has been made to check that this is the case.

7.2.1 Compound nouns
7.2.1.1 Noun + noun

This is the largest subgrouping of compounds, and many types of semantic relationship can be isolated within this grouping, as well as different syntactic patterns. The majority of compounds in this class are endocentric. While it would be possible to classify these compounds in terms of, for example, their countability or animacy, such classifications do not appear to be particularly helpful to the student of word-formation. A more helpful classification uses the basic semantic relationships discussed in §2.12 and morpho-syntactic criteria.

The first group in this taxonomy is made up of exocentric compounds. The pattern of noun + noun exocentric compounds is very restricted in productivity, but a few examples are found: two recent ones are *hatchback* and *skinhead*. The second group is made up of appositional compounds. In a large proportion of established appositional compounds the first element marks the sex of a person: *boy-friend*, *manservant*, *woman doctor*, and so on. This function is still productive, but possibly most obviously so with pronominal sex markers used for animals: *she-goat*, *he-cheetah*. Other patterns are also productive, though, and recent examples are *jazz-rock* and *owner-occupier*. Dvandva compounds, which make up the third group, have never been very common in English. However, occasional ones are still coined. I have only found one clear recent example of this type using common nouns, and that is *panty-hose*, but business mergers continue to provide examples of this structure: *Cadbury-Schweppes*, *Rank-Hovis-McDougal*, *Rowntree-Mackintosh*, and so on.

All the other groups to be discussed are endocentric. Within this category, the next group consists of compounds made up of gerund + noun. Since a gerund has both nominal and verbal characteristics, this pattern could be treated as either noun + noun or verb + noun. Unlike other compounds containing a verbal element, however, the elements in these compounds all end in *-ing*, and the semantic relationships between the two elements seem more like those which hold in noun + noun compounds than those which hold in verb + noun compounds. For example, a *fishing rod* is a 'rod for fishing' just as a *bath towel* is 'a towel for the bath', a *shooting match* is 'a match in which there is shooting' just as a *goods train* is 'a train in which there are goods' and *sleeping sickness* is 'sickness which causes sleeping' just as a *death blow* is 'a blow which causes death'. There does not appear to be such a range of semantic parallels with verb + noun compounds like *goggle-box*. Recent examples of gerund + noun compounds are *holding pattern, parking orbit, queuing theory*.

The next group is that where the first element of the compound is a proper noun. While some compounds of this type, particularly those containing place names, show the same semantic relationships between the elements as compounds with two common nouns, this is not so with proper nouns which are people's names. Thus while *Wellington airport* shows a locative relationship parallel to, say, *city museum*, the same kind of relationship cannot hold between the elements in *Chomsky adjunction* or *David Hume Tower*, simply because the process or entity is being named after a person. This process is extremely productive in modern English, and some recent examples are *Duchenne dystrophy, Eaton agent, Lie algebra, Mao flu, Markov chain, Moog synthesizer* and *Utah effect*.

The final group consists of those compounds made up of two common nouns. This is by far the most productive type of compound, and hundreds of examples can be found in any newspaper, magazine or dictionary. The examples provided here are all recent and illustrate something of the range of the semantic relationships that can hold between elements, but no attempt is made to provide a classification of these, nor to be exhaustive: *acid rock, adventure playground, aversion therapy, bang zone, battered baby syndrome, body jewel, brain death, bullet train, cable television, credibility gap, domino theory, family planning, goulash communism, granny glasses, latchkey child, language laboratory, meter-maid, sanitation man, spaghetti western, suicide seat*. It should be noted just how difficult it is to specify the precise meaning relationship linking the elements of the compound in many cases, and how involved the specifications tend to become, unless a theory like that outlined in §6.4 is adopted. This is particularly true of examples like *domino theory* and *spaghetti western*.

7.2.1.2 Verb + noun

Gerund + noun compounds were discussed in the last section, so there are only verb stem + noun compounds to discuss here. There are, however, two distinct patterns of these, distinguishable on functional criteria.

The first of these is where the noun is the direct object of the verb. These compounds are all exocentric (see the discussion in Bauer, 1980a with regard to French, which is also applicable to English). This type used to be common for denoting people: examples are *cut-throat*, *kill-joy*, *pickpocket*, *spoil-sport*; and, not denoting people, *breakfast* and *dreadnought*. If this pattern is still productive, it is only marginally so, and its productivity seems to be limited to non-human denotata now, as in the trade name *Xpel-air*.

The second pattern is where the noun is not the direct object of the verb. These compounds are all endocentric, and the pattern is definitely productive. It is here that the difficulty in deciding whether the first element is a noun or a verb is most sharply felt, but some recent examples which seem clearly to contain a verb are *dangle-dolly*, *drownproofing*, *goggle-box*. Other recent examples where the first element may be (but is not necessarily) a verb are *crashpad*, *giggle-smoke*, *hovercraft*, *jump jet*, *play pit*.

7.2.1.3   Noun + verb

Again in this group there is the problem of knowing whether the second element is a noun or a verb, but established examples which seem to fit this pattern are *nosebleed* and *sunshine*. The pattern does not appear to be productive, but this may be because the second element is usually interpreted as being a noun, as in *birth control* and *nosedive*.

7.2.1.4   Verb + verb

This pattern is extremely rare, and probably not productive. An established example is *make-believe*, which is also used as an adjective and a verb.

7.2.1.5   Adjective + noun

It can be difficult to decide whether a given adjective + noun collocation is a compound or simply a noun phrase. The criterion taken as distinguishing between the two here is stress: nuclear stress on the adjective, when the collocation is spoken non-contrastively in isolation, indicates a compound; nuclear stress on the noun indicates a noun phrase. A collocation like *deep structure* is thus a compound if stressed '*deep structure*, but a noun phrase if stressed *deep* '*structure*. Adjective + noun phrases are frequently turned into compounds by a change in stress. Some recently coined compounds are *fast-food*, *hard-stuff*, *new town*, *software*. The range of adjectives that can occur in this construction is very limited: most of them are monosyllabic and of Germanic origin, although there are some disyllabic early Romance loans, too, as in *doubletalk* (see the discussion in §4.5.3.2).

7.2.1.6 Particle + noun

This is quite a productive pattern. Recent examples include *afterheat*, *in-crowd*, *off-islander*, *off-off-Broadway*, *over-kill*.

7.2.1.7 Adverb + noun

This is a very restricted pattern, partly because only adverbs of time or place occur in such compounds. It is possible that this class is not distinct from the previous class, since many of the particles can also be interpreted as adverbs showing time or place (for some discussion see Bauer, 1978d: §5.3.2). The only recent example of this pattern I have noted is *now generation*, where *now* could alternatively be interpreted as an adjective formed by conversion.

7.2.1.8 Verb + particle

The majority of words of this form are nominalizations of phrasal verbs, and it is arguable that these are not strictly compounds at all. Recent examples are *cop-out*, *drawback* 'withdrawal', *drop-out*, *press-down*, *put-down*, *put-on*. There is also a minor pattern, of much more restricted productivity, where the particle precedes the verb. This is illustrated by *throughput*. There are, however, a number of such formations which are not derived from phrasal verbs, although they may be coined by analogy with phrasal verbs. Recent examples of this type are *fallout*, *pray-in*, *teach-in*. Compounds with a second element -*in* are particularly productive at the moment. For some discussion of this type, see Bauer (1978d: §5.3.3) and references there.

7.2.1.9 Phrase compounds

There are several kinds of construction which might be included under this heading, constructions where an entire phrase seems to be involved in the formation of a new word. In some cases it may be questionable whether such formations should actually be considered to be compounds or lexicalizations of syntactic structures. A distinction can be drawn within this group between endocentric, dvandva and exocentric phrase compounds.

Among the endocentric phrase compounds there is a small, non-productive class with an initial head element, for example *lady-in-waiting*, *son-in-law*. A group with internal articles like *dog-in-the-manger* might also belong in this group (see Marchand, 1969: §2.49.2 for some discussion). More common, however, and very much more productive (though these compounds rarely become established) is the type where the head element is final and the first element is a phrase or sentence. Occasionally the first element is a sequence of words which could not be a constituent of an underlying sentence: consider, for example, *a pain-in-stomach gesture*.[1] The more usual pattern is illustrated by *a what-do-you-think-movement*,[2] where "what do you think" is a constituent (for further examples see above, §6.5.1).

The dvandva constructions discussed here differ from true dvandva compounds in including the word *and*. Of the formations in this section they seem the least like compounds and the most like syntactic phrases. Examples are *bubble-and-squeak*, *whisky-and-soda*. Some of this type also exist as adjectives: *milk-and-water*, *pepper-and-salt*.

The exocentric phrase compounds are a very mixed group, and include plant names such as *love-in-a-mist*, *love-lies-bleeding*, *forget-me-not* (note that the third looks like an imperative, which the others do not; some authorities make such imperative compounds into a separate group), words denoting people such as *has-been*, and occasional miscellaneous words like *I.O.U.* (see Marchand, 1969: §§2.49, 2.50).

7.2.2 *Compound verbs*

The majority of compound verbs in English are not formed by putting two lexemes together to form a new verb, but by back-formation or conversion from compound nouns (Adams, 1973: §7). However, despite this, the same type of classification by

[1] P. Mann. 1978. *Steal Big*. London, etc.: Granada Publishing, p. 134.
[2] Ibid. pp. 72–3.

form class is maintained in this section, and comments will be made as to the actual method of formation. Compound verbs are, in any case, rather rare.

7.2.2.1 Noun + verb

The vast majority of this group arise from back-formation, although a form like *to carbon-copy* is a conversion. There are plenty of this type of verb being coined in current English, some recent examples being *blockbust*, *carbon-date*, *colour-code*, *head-hunt*, *sky-dive*.

7.2.2.2 Verb + noun

I have only one example of this type, and it is converted from a member of a relatively unproductive series of compound nouns. The word is to *shunpike*. A noun *shunpiker*, which may or may not predate the verb, also exists.

7.2.2.3 Verb + verb

This type is exceedingly rare. The only word Marchand (1969) lists which might, but probably does not, belong here is *typewrite*. Adams (1973: 109) lists *test-market*, another dubious example, and *freeze-dry* does not unambiguously belong in this class either. I have found one recent example, *trickle-irrigate*, and even that could be either noun + verb or a back-formation from *trickle-irrigation*. There are some sequences of two verbs in English such as *make do*, *dare say* which are apparently felt by some speakers to be compound verbs (they are often hyphenated, for example), but it is not clear whether they are best treated as single lexemes or as sequences of two.

7.2.2.4 Adjective + verb

This type again generally arises through back-formation (or, occasionally, conversion). It is a relatively productive way of forming compound verbs. Recent examples are *double-book*, *fine-tune*, *free-associate*, *soft-land*.

7.2.2.5 Particle + verb

While some of this type may be back-formations, most of them seem to be genuine verbal formations. Recent examples are *outachieve*, *overachieve*, *overbook*, *overeducate*, *overmark* (an exam paper).

7.2.2.6 Adjective + noun

Compound verbs on this pattern are not common. Some can be seen as converted noun phrases, but others must be seen as forms created to be compound verbs. An example of each type is given here: *brown-bag* 'to bring one's own [liquor] to a restaurant, usually in a brown paper bag' and *bad-mouth*.

7.2.2.7 Noun + noun

This type, again not particularly common, generally arises from conversion of a compound noun. A recent example is *to breath-test*.

7.2.3 *Compound adjectives*

Compound adjectives are formed according to a large number of different patterns, though there may be some dispute about exactly what constructions should be termed compound adjectives. Some of these instances will be mentioned below.

7.2.3.1 Noun + adjective

This is the most frequent type of compound adjective, and there are a number of distinguishable semantic sub-types (see Adams, 1973: §6.3; Marchand, 1969: §2.17). Formally, it would be possible, as in all combinations with adjectives, to distinguish between participles and other adjectives, and there are some semantic relationships which are only found in one of these groups. For present purposes, however, this is not illuminating, and a list of some recent examples will provide some idea of the range of this type: *capital-intensive*, *card-carrying*, *childproof*, *clotheared*, *crashworthy*, *flightworthy*, *host-specific*, *leadfree*, *machine readable*, *space-borne*.

7.2.3.2 Verb + adjective

This type is not listed by Adams (1973) or Marchand (1969), and I have only one recent example: *fail safe*. It must therefore be assumed that the type is rare, and possibly new.

7.2.3.3 Adjective + adjective

These can be divided into two clear semantic groups: appositional compounds and endocentric ones. The classic examples of appositional compounds are *bitter-sweet* and *deaf-mute*. The type is productive, though not extremely so, and a recent example (clipped, it must be admitted) is *pro-am*. These appositional compounds, however, are rather rare, and adjective + adjective compounds are normally endocentric. In this group it may, in some cases, be difficult to tell whether the first adjective is really functioning adjectivally rather than adverbially, so that the label 'adjective + adjective' must be taken as referring to forms. Again, these compounds can be categorized formally according to whether or not they contain participles, and semantically in a number of ways. Recent examples are *double-helical*, *large-statured*, *open-ended*, *ready-made*.

7.2.3.4 Adverb + adjective

This type is not particularly common, but seems to be more frequent with participial second (head) elements. One recent example without a participle is *cross-modal* (always assuming that *cross* is indeed an adverb). A more common type has a particle as the first element. Recent examples are *over-qualified* and *uptight*. The majority of compounds in this group are simply participial forms of compound verbs.

7.2.3.5 Noun + noun

All the remaining compound adjectives are exocentric in that they function as adjectives but their second (head) element is not an adjective. In many cases these adjectives are converted nouns or verbs, and it often seems rather misleading to term them adjectives at all: a noun compound functioning as a modifier to another noun is probably not so much functioning as an adjective as forming a three-term noun compound. The argument against this position is that such modifying compounds become institutionalized and lexicalized as units, independent of their constituent parts, and in some cases are only ever used attributively, while in other cases they have very different connotations from the same forms used as non-attributive compound nouns. The problems inherent in the classification can be clearly seen in the following examples:

back-street (abortionist), *coffee-table* (book), *glassteel* (sky-scraper).

7.2.3.6 Verb + noun

The forms in this group are more obviously adjectival, since some of them do not appear to be used nominally. Recent examples are *break-bulk* (consignment), *roll-neck* (sweater), and *turn-key* (contract). Note that it was stated earlier (§7.2.1.2) that the type *turn-key* is only of marginal productivity in the generation of noun compounds; yet it is apparently more productive in the generation of adjective compounds.

7.2.3.7 Adjective + noun

This is perhaps the most productive set of those containing nouns. The confusing point here is that most of these compounds are not compounds, unless they are used attributively, but noun phrases. They change their stress pattern (orthographically become hyphenated, although this is not a trustworthy criterion) when they are used attributively. Recent examples are *broad-brush* (estimate), *grey-collar* (worker), *red-brick* (university), *solid-state* (physics).

7.2.3.8 Particle + noun

In these examples a prepositional phrase is converted to a modifier. Recent examples are *before-tax* (profits), *in depth* (study).

7.2.3.9 Noun + verb

This type does not appear to exist, since the verb invariably turns up as a present or past participle, and hence becomes classified as an adjective.

7.2.3.10 Verb + verb

This type is not discussed by Adams (1973) or Marchand (1969), although there are some modern examples. Most of the forms used here do not occur as compound verbs (although *make-believe* cited earlier is an exception). The type must be assumed to be new (consider also verb + verb compound nouns and verbs), and possibly growing. Recent examples are *go-go* (dancer), *pass-fail* (test), *stop-go* (economics). The type *make-believe*, which is rare, may arise through the conversion of the verb + verb compound noun.

7.2.3.11 Adjective/adverb + verb

This type of compound may be illustrated by the recent examples *high-rise* (tower) and *quick-change* (artiste). Their description is awkward because their first element is an adjective in form, but appears to function semantically as an adverb. Thus for consistency here they should be classified as adjective + verb, although Adams (1973: 92–3) treats them as adverb + verb. Neither Adams nor Marchand (1969) discuss this type of compound where the verb is a root rather than a participle.

7.2.3.12 Verb + particle

This type is very productive. In most cases it would seem that it is not phrasal verbs which are converted in this type, but verbs and prepositions or adverbial particles. Recent examples are *see-through* (blouse), *tow-away* (zone) and *wrap-around* (skirt).

7.2.4 *Compound adverbs*

The most common way of forming compound adverbs is by the suffixation of *-ly* to a compound adjective. However, other patterns are found, as is shown by *double-quick*, *flat-out*, *flat-stick*, *off-hand*, *over-night*. Some of these are also used in other form classes. It is not clear to what extent such formations are productive.

7.2.5 *Other form classes*

Compounds of other form classes are found as well, but they are rare and of extremely low productivity. Compound prepositions include *into*, *onto* and *because of*; compound pronouns are the *-self* forms and *somebody*, *anyone*, etc.; compound conjunctions include *whenever*, *so that* and even *and/or*.

7.2.6 *Rhyme-motivated compounds*

The majority of this class are noun compounds made up of two nouns, but other types do exist, so that a separate category can be set up. In these compounds, the rhyme between the two elements (one of which may not even be an independently existing form in English) is the major motivating factor in the formation. Established examples are *higgledy-piggledy*, *hobnob*, *hokey-pokey*, *hoity-toity*, *roly-poly*, *teeny-weeny*; recent examples (all of them nouns) are *brain-drain*, *culture-vulture*, *flower-power*, *gang-bang*, *nitty-gritty*, *stun-gun*.

7.2.7 *Ablaut-motivated compounds*

Similar in many ways to rhyme-motivated compounds are those involving ablaut, i.e. vowel change or alternation between the two elements. The most common patterns are /ɪ/~/æ/ and /ɪ/~/ɒ/ (Marchand, 1969: §8.2.1). Although I have noted no recent examples, I believe this process still to be productive, though not as productive as rhyme motivation. It may be most productive in nonce formations. Established examples are *flip-flop*, *riff-raff*, *shilly-shally*, *tick-tock*, *wishy-washy*, *zig-zag*.

7.3 **Neo-classical compounds**

In this section a type of word-formation will be considered which has received very scant attention in the literature on morphology. Accordingly, the discussion here will be much more concerned with basic theoretical issues than that in §7.2, which covered well-explored territory.

As was pointed out in §6.5.8, there are a number of elements in English word-formation which, while they function as affixes in some places, appear to be distinct from affixes in other facets of their behaviour. These elements, usually Greek or Latin in origin, are what the *OED* terms **combining forms**. Examples are *astro-*, *electro-*, *hydro-*, *-crat*, *-naut*, *-phile*, *-phobe* and so on.

The evidence for treating these combining forms as affixes is that they are sometimes added to lexemes just like any other affix. Parallels can be set up like the following:

an·electric	photo·electric
music·al	music·ology

where *an-* and *-al* are affixes, and thus *photo-* and *-ology* must also be affixes. However, as is pointed out in Bauer (1979c), there are also cases where this line of argumentation leads to the embarrassing conclusion that there are lexemes made up of a prefix and a suffix with no root; these are words like *biocrat*, *electrophile*, *galvanoscope*, *homophile*, *protogen*. This conclusion is embarrassing because affixes are frequently defined by their ability to co-occur with bases, which contain roots. The notion of a prefix and a suffix occurring together with no root thus leads to a contradiction.

Fortunately, there is some evidence that these combining forms cannot be normal affixes, because they behave differently from other affixes. A distinction can be made between Final Combining Forms (FCFs) like *-phobe* and suffixes, in that only the former can combine with Initial Combining Forms (ICFs). Thus while *electrolyte*, *electrophile*, *electrophonic* and *electroscope* all exist, **electroness*, **electroization*, **electroesque* and so on are all impossible.

There is also some evidence that FCFs should be considered as combining exclusively with ICFs. ICFs usually end in *-o* (/əu/), and almost invariably end in a vowel unless they combine with a formative that starts with a vowel. Forms which combine with FCFs usually end in *-o*, unless they are lexemes which end in a vowel (assuming *-er* to be a vowel in words like *sniperscope*): if a lexeme ends in a vowel it can be added before an FCF directly; if it ends in a consonant, then an *-o* is added to turn it into an ICF before it combines with the FCF. This is illustrated by the words *audiophile*, *jazzophile*, *negrophile*, *spermophile*. In fact these rules are not totally without exceptions, although the majority of the exceptions can be covered by other phonological generalizations. Some of these will be discussed in chapter 8. It seems, then, that on the whole a lexeme ending in a vowel can be made into an ICF by an identity operation (conversion), while other lexemes can be made into ICFs by adding *-o*. FCFs under this analysis combine only with ICFs, which may be listed in the lexicon as such or produced from lexemes.

The evidence that ICFs are a separate group is also the way in which they can collocate with FCFs. Firstly, there are a lot of prefixes which do not end in vowels, and these are prevented from combining with FCFs by the phonological restrictions mentioned above. Such prefixes are *arch-*, *circum-*, *dis-*, *en-*, *ex-*, *in-*, *mis-*, *non-*, *sub-*, *un-*, *vice-*, and so on. There are no ICFs which do not have a variant ending in a vowel. Secondly, even those true prefixes which end in a vowel cannot combine with FCFs, so that the following words are impossible: *acrat, *bephile, *co-ology, *delogical, *prephobe. While these particular examples may be excluded because there is nothing for them to refer to, this does seem to be a genuine restriction. Consider, for example, the formatives *hyper-* and *super-*. These are synonymous; but whereas *hyper-* acts as an ICF in words like *hyperbaric, hyperemia, hypergamy,* and *hypertrophy, super-* does not appear to be prefixed to FCFs at all.

In the majority of cases there is also a semantic difference between a prefix and an ICF, but this is much harder to specify. In general it seems that ICFs contain a higher density of lexical information than prefixes do, but this implies a measure of density of lexical information which is not actually available. The intention can be seen by comparing *socio-* or *eco-* with *pre-* or *un-*, where some reference to society and ecology is required for the specification of the meanings of the ICFs, but where the information for the prefixes can be expressed in terms of function words. Given pairs such as *hyper-* and *super-* mentioned above, it is clear that this distinction in terms of semantic density is no more than a tendency. There are also prefixes which have a relatively high density of lexical information: an example is *mini-*.

A further tendency which can help distinguish prefixes from ICFs is that ICFs in general produce more hyponyms of the base than do prefixes. This is again no more than a tendency, since it can be shown to be false in both directions: the ICF *pseudo-* very often produces lexemes which are not hyponyms of the base (a *pseudoacid* is not a kind of acid) and the prefix *arch-* does produce hyponyms of the base (an *archbishop* is a kind of bishop).

If combining forms are distinct from affixes, it must also be asked whether they are distinct from roots. The first thing to note about these forms is that if they are roots then they are bound roots. Generally speaking the productive use of bound roots in contemporary English is very restricted, but it is found, almost exclusively where the roots are classical in origin. Recent examples are *ebulism, ludic, phillumenist* and *viridian*. Established examples are *nautic* and *phobism*. Such words are awkward in the description of English word-formation. However, taking the elements of a word like *geology* as bound roots might provide a possible way of viewing the data. In this case, though, the words composed of combining forms would still provide a separate group, as there would then be a sub-set of bound roots which could only be used when attached before other bound roots. In other words, precisely this set of words is circumscribed even if these elements are treated as English bound roots.

My own preferred solution is to accept these combining forms for what they are etymologically: elements of the classical languages which are used in English word-formation. It must be stressed that they are used in English: the ancient Greeks never needed the word *telephone* although it is made up of Greek elements. It is because these elements are put together by speakers of English that it is possible for coiners to mix Greek and Latin as in *television*. Hence it is that such words are termed not 'classical compounds' but **neo-classical compounds**. It will be shown later that neo-classical compounds have some things in common with ordinary compounds, and since ICFs are used prefixed to English lexemes, they also have something in common with derivatives.

Recent examples of neo-classical compounds are *Anglophone*, *biocide*, *biocrat*, *electrophile*, *graphoscope*, *holograph*, *lysosome*, *oleophilic*, *selenodesy*, *stereology*, *synergamy*, *teleonomy*. Examples where an ICF is used with a lexeme are *acousto-electric*, *astro-dog*, *bio-science*, *geo-hygiene*, *megacity*. An example with a lexeme used as an ICF is *acidophilic*. With a form like *lunanaut* it is not clear whether it is a genuine neo-classical compound, or whether it is a blend (see below, §7.8.2). Neo-classical compounds are extremely productive in English, and are also used as bases in derivational processes, e.g. *holographic*, *prebiological*.

7.4 Prefixation

One of the results of defining ICFs as separate from prefixes (§7.3) is that the number of items to be dealt with as prefixes is considerably reduced. The vast majority of prefixes in English are class-maintaining; those that are not will be dealt with first, then those that are. In keeping with the rest of this chapter, prefixes will be considered in terms of the form class of the base to which they are added. However, the majority of prefixes can be added to bases of more than one form class. Some linguists (e.g. Chomsky, 1970) have suggested that the familiar form classes of noun, verb, adjective, etc., should not be considered as unitary wholes but as bundles of syntactic features. Adjectives have some nominal features (e.g. they agree for gender and number in a language like Latin), but also some verbal features (e.g. they can be classified for stativity, just as verbs can: see Lakoff, 1970a: 115ff), so that nouns might be classified as [+N, −V], verbs as [−N, +V] and adjectives as [+N, +V]. It might be possible to extend such an approach to include other form classes as well. If such an approach is taken, then it may be possible to specify the classes of base to which prefixes can be added more economically in terms of such features. This possibility will not be discussed in any further detail, but should be borne in mind when this section is considered.

7.4.1   *Class-changing prefixes*

a- /ə/   This prefix forms adjectives, mainly but not exclusively from forms which are ambiguous between nouns and verbs. The adjectives formed by this process are restricted to predicative position: *the house is ablaze*, *the ablaze house. Other examples are *asleep*, *astir*, *awash*. This prefix is still productive: recent examples are *aclutter*, *aglaze*, *asquish*, *aswivel*, *awhir*.

be-   This prefix forms transitive verbs from adjectives, verbs or, most frequently, nouns. Examples are *becalm*, *bespatter*, *bemoan*, *befriend*, *bewitch*. This prefix is probably no longer productive except in the sense seen in *bejewelled*, where the past participle of the verb is used adjectivally: the *OEDS* cites *bejeaned* from 1960 on this pattern.

en-   This prefix forms transitive verbs, mainly from nouns, as in *entomb*, *ensnare*, *enslave*. The meaning 'put into a N' is probably still productive, but the 'make into a N' meaning illustrated by *enslave* does not seem to be.

Other prefixes in this class are *de-* (*debark*), *dis-* (*disbar*), *non-* (*non-stick*), *un-* (*unhorse*). This list is not exhaustive.

7.4.2   *Class-maintaining prefixes*
7.4.2.1   Used exclusively with a noun base

arch-   This prefix is added particularly to human nouns to denote an extreme or pre-eminent person. It is still productive: Marchand (1969: §3.6.2) cites *arch-exponent* from 1951, and a more recent example is *archmonetarist*. Generally this prefix has a pejorative tone, which may limit its productivity.

mini- Several meanings of this prefix can be distinguished, but they all appear to be limited to noun bases. Recent examples are *minicomputer*, *minidress*, *minikilt*, *minipill*, *miniwar*. This prefix is very productive.

step- This prefix is probably no longer productive simply because all the available bases have been used. Interestingly, it is not used beyond the immediate family circle, although **stepgrandmother* and **stepcousin* would presumably be comprehensible.

Other prefixes in this class are *mal-* (*malnutrition*), *pro-* (*proconsul*) – though adjectives are sometimes derived from such prefixed forms – and *maxi-*.

7.4.2.2 Used exclusively with a verb base

This class is rare, and even the one prefix listed here is occasionally used with a noun base, but is then a class-changing prefix, not a class-maintaining one.

de- This prefix has a number of distinguishable meanings, and is often in competition with *dis-* and *un-* when added to verbs. Recent examples are *deaestheticize*, *deboost*, *decapacitate*, *deescalate*. The verbs produced by *de-* prefixation may subsequently be nominalized.

7.4.2.3 Used exclusively with an adjective base

a- /eɪ/ or /æ/ This prefix is added exclusively to adjectival bases, as in *amoral*, *apolitical*, *atypical*. It is still marginally productive – recent examples are *ahemeral* and *avaluative* – but seems to be losing ground to the much more productive *un-*, which even replaces *a-* in established words, so that *unpolitical* and *untypical* are frequently heard.

cis- This very rare prefix, meaning 'on this side of' (either spatially or temporally) is of very restricted productivity, although *cislunar* is a recent example.

Another prefix in this class is *extra-* (*extrasensory*).

7.4.2.4 Prefixes added to nouns and verbs

fore- This prefix is now only productive, if at all, when added to nouns (Marchand, 1969: §3.23.1). Established examples of it added to verbs are *foretell* and *forewarn*; established examples of it added to nouns are *foreground*, *forelock*, *foreman*.

re- This prefix is far more common with verbs than with nouns, and almost all of the nouns that begin with *re-* are nominalizations of verbs (e.g. *rearrangement*, *re-election*). Recent verbal formations are *reconfigure*, *recycle*, *resit* and *retribalize*.

Another prefix in this class is *mis-* (*mislead*, *misfortune*).

7.4.2.5 Prefixes added to nouns and adjectives

in- This prefix has a number of forms depending on the initial segment of the base: /ɪm/ before /p, b/; [ɪɱ] or /ɪm/ or /ɪn/ before /f, v/; /ɪ/ before /m, n, l, r/; /ɪn/ or /ɪŋ/ before /k, g/; and /ɪn/ before /t, d, s, tʃ, dʒ, j/ and vowels. It appears not to occur before /θ, ð, ʃ, ʒ, w/, presumably as a result of its restriction to Romance bases (Marchand, 1969: §3.26.1). Marchand (ibid.: §3.26.5) also notes that *in-* is not added to bases that begin with *in-*: **ininflammable*, **inintelligible*, **ininflected*. Although there are many words that can be analysed as containing this *in-* (e.g. *illegal*, *impossible*, *indefinite*, *inoperable*, *insane*, *intolerable*, *irreverent*, and nouns derived from these) it does not appear to be productive. The negative meaning has lost out to *un-* (e.g. an earlier *impopular* which has now been replaced by *unpopular*), and there are other prefixes with the form *in-* which are now productive, e.g. *in-joke*, *in-language*, *in-state* (see the entries in Barnhart *et al.*, 1973). The majority of nouns with *in-* are nominalizations of the adjectives, but a few, such as *incapacity* and *inutility* appear not to be. Very occasionally an adjective in *in-* is verbalized, as in *illegalize*.

mid- This prefix is of extremely limited productivity. Originally used exclusively with nouns (*mid-morning*, *mid-November*), it has relatively recently come to be used with adjectives (*mid-Victorian*).

Other prefixes in this group are *ex-* (*ex-president*, *exorbital*) and, according to the analysis given by Marchand (1969: §3.63), one of the meanings of *un-* (*unbeliever*, *unfair*).

7.4.2.6 Prefixes added to verbs and adjectives

This category is also rare, and even with the prefix given here, nominalizations of the verbs are common.

circum- This prefix is originally found in Latin words only, but is later used with English bases. Examples of verbs are *circumnavi-*

gate and *circumscribe*. Examples of adjectives are *circumjacent* and *circumpolar*, with a recent example *circumstellar*.

7.4.2.7   Prefixes added to nouns, verbs and adjectives
    counter-   Marchand (1969: §3.13) notes this prefix as being used with nouns and verbs with the occasional deverbal adjective. Recent examples, however, also include adjectives. Recent examples on a nominal base are *counterculture*, *countereffect*, *counterstrike*; on a verbal base *counterdemonstrate*; on an adjectival base *counterattractive*, *counterintuitive*, *counterproductive*. The prefix still seems to be extremely productive.
    dis-   Most productive, both now and throughout its history, in the formation of verbs, this prefix is also added to nouns and adjectives. Recent examples are *disbenefit*, *disinformation*; *disambiguate*, *disemplane*; *disbound*.
    Other prefixes in this category are *co-* (*co-author*, *co-articulate*, *co-equal*), *inter-* (*interdependence*, *intermix*, *interdigital*) and *sub-* (*subwarden*, *sublet*, *subconscious*).

7.5   Suffixation
    Various aspects of suffixation have already been discussed in this book: for example, the recursiveness of suffixation was considered in §4.2.2.2; the influence of suffixation on stress was discussed in §5.3; the problem of distinguishing suffixes was outlined in §5.3.2; and the specification of the meaning of suffixes was dealt with in §6.7. In this section, suffixes are classified according to the form class of the derivatives they produce. No attempt at exhaustiveness has been made in the lists of illustrations provided in each section.

7.5.1   *Suffixes forming nouns*
7.5.1.1   Nouns from nouns
    -dom   This suffix forms abstract, uncountable nouns from concrete, countable ones. For a long time it was thought that the suffix was moribund or totally non-productive, but Wentworth (1941) showed that it had never completely died out, and it is still productive in contemporary English, though not very much so. Recent examples include *Dollardom*, *fagdom*, *gangsterdom*, *girldom* (all *OEDS*).

-ess This suffix forms female human nouns from unmarked or male human nouns, showing either professional status or the status of the woman's husband. Of recent years, this suffix has met with a certain amount of disapproval from feminists, but it is still productive at the moment, though the productivity is limited because of competition from other patterns, notably compounds with a first element *woman-* and the (especially US) suffix *-ette*. The only word in *-ess* listed by Barnhart *et al.* (1973) is *astronautess*, but I have also attested *seeress*.[3]

-iana This suffix is added almost exclusively to human proper nouns to form uncountable nouns meaning 'things, especially literary facts, connected with the person in the base'. Recent examples listed in the *OEDS* include *Butterfieldiana, Etoniana, flunkeyiana, railroadiana*.

Other suffixes which produce nouns from nouns are *-er* (*Birch* > *Bircher*), *-ette* (*kitchen* > *kitchenette*), *-hood* (*man* > *manhood*), *-ism* (*absentee* > *absenteeism*), *-let* (*stream* > *streamlet*), *-ling* (*duck* > *duckling*), *-scape* (*sea* > *seascape*), *-ship* (*kin* > *kinship*). This list is not exhaustive.

7.5.1.2 Nouns from verbs

This is probably the most common type of derivation, although there are, of course, several different kinds of noun formed.

-ation Many words in *-ation* in fact show borrowing from Romance rather than English word-formation. Suffixation in *-ation* is extremely (possibly fully) productive where the base ends in the suffix *-ize* (*categorization, institutionalization, lexicalization*) but is also found with bases comprising simplex lexemes (*flirtation, formation, vexation*). Marchand (1969: §4.18.4) says that, by and large, verbs in *-ate* are formed from nouns in *-ation*, rather than vice versa. The suffix *-ation* is always stressed, and forms abstract nominalizations. Recent examples include *containerization, exfiltration, Finlandization, fracturation*. As has previously been mentioned (§5.4) there is currently dispute as to whether *-ation* should be seen as a single suffix or as a sequence of two. The facts listed above suggest a single suffix; parallelism with adjectives in *-atory*

---

[3] Meaning 'female clairvoyant'. C. Weston. 1977. *Rouse the Demon*. London: Gollancz, p. 70.

and *-ative* suggests a bimorphemic analysis might be more useful (Strauss, 1980).

-ee This suffix will be discussed in greater detail later (§8.2.1). It forms human patient nouns from verbs. It appears to be becoming more productive in current English, and recent words in *-ee* include *blackmailee, curee, vaccinee*.

-ure Like *-ation*, *-ure* forms abstract nominalizations from verbs, e.g. *close > closure*. Unlike *-ation*, however, *-ure* is no longer productive: the latest example cited by Marchand (1969: §4.77) is *licensure*, 1846.

Other suffixes which produce nouns from verbs are *-al* (*arrive > arrival*), *-ary* (*dispense > dispensary*), *-er* (*kill > killer*), *-ment* (*manage > management*). Again the list is not exhaustive.

7.5.1.3 Nouns from adjectives

-cy This suffix forms nouns particularly from adjectives ending in *-ant* or *-ent*: *excellent > excellency, militant > militancy*. It is probably no longer productive, having lost out to *-ce* (/s/): *dependent > dependence, elegant > elegance, excellent > excellence*. This *-ce* is probably no longer productive either. Many of the words using these suffixes represent loans from Latin or French rather than genuine cases of English word-formation.

-ness This is one of the most productive suffixes in the English language today. It is added predominantly, though not exclusively, to adjectives, and is used in nonce formations, and even established words, to replace other suffixes producing nouns from adjectives (note *certainty, certainness* discussed in §4.4). Semantically it is the simplest of these suffixes, and consequently it often gives rise to pairs of words which some speakers distinguish semantically, e.g. *sincereness/sincerity, productiveness/productivity*. For discussion of the productivity of this affix see Aronoff (1976: §3) and Williams (1965).

Other suffixes which produce nouns from adjectives are *-dom* (*free > freedom*), *-er* (*six > sixer*), *-hood* (*false > falsehood*), *-ist* (*social > socialist*), *-th* (*warm > warmth*).

7.5.2 *Suffixes forming verbs*

There are two main suffixes deriving verbs from nouns, *-ify* and *-ize*, and these are also used to derive verbs from adjectives.

The more productive of these is -*ize*. Recent words using these suffixes are *metrify*; *fishify* 'supply with fish'; *Cambodianize*, *instantize*, *marginalize*; *containerize*, *pedestrianize*, *structurize*, *Vietnamize*.

A third suffix deriving verbs is -*en* as in *shorten*, *whiten*, *widen*. This suffix is only marginally productive, if at all.

There do not appear to be any suffixes in English for forming verbs from verbs. There is no apparent reason for this, and such suffixes do exist in, for example, French: *chanter* 'to sing' > *chantonner* 'to hum'; *rêver* 'to dream' > *rêvasser* 'to muse, dream idly'; *morder* 'to bite' > *mordiller* 'to nibble at' (Guilbert, 1975: 170). The lack of such suffixes may correlate with the relative lack of hypocoristic and intensifying suffixes in English in general, when compared with the Romance languages.

7.5.3 Suffixes forming adjectives
7.5.3.1 Adjectives from nouns
-*al* This suffix is relatively unmarked semantically, providing adjectival forms with no major change in meaning, forms which can then be used to replace the attributive use of the corresponding noun, for instance: *education policy*/*educational policy*, etc. (see §6.7). The suffix is frequently added to already suffixed forms, especially where the earlier suffix shows nominalization: e.g. *environmental*, *transformational*. Indeed, -*al* seems to be extremely productive on bases which end in -*ation*. Historically, -*al* has also been added to simplex bases (e.g. *postal*, *tidal*) but it is not clear whether this use is still productive. Kiparsky (1972: 216) suggests that this suffix is not found with roots that contain the phoneme /l/, but that -*al* alternates with -*ar* under these conditions: there are, however, a great many examples which break this hypothesized constraint, which cannot therefore be accepted for this -*al*, although it does seem to hold for the -*al* which derives nouns from verbs (e.g. *arrival*, *recital*). Counter-examples to Kiparsky's claim include *dialectal*, *elemental*, *glottal*, *intellectual*, *labial*, *palatal*. Scholars seem to agree that -*ial* and -*ual* are allomorphs of -*al* (see e.g. Chomsky & Halle, 1968: 129; Marchand, 1969: §4.6). The factor conditioning the -*i*- or -*u*- is, however, obscure. Chomsky & Halle suggest that the extra vowel is

part of the base, and is deleted in other circumstances, so that the -*i* on the end of *presidenti* is only found in *presidential*, the -*u* on the end of *habitu* is only found in *habitual* and *habituate*, and so on. The existence of such pairs as *rectoral*, *rectorial* might argue against such a view-point, but pairs of this type are exceedingly rare. Indeed, the fact that this appears to be the only such pair in which there is a difference in meaning (other pairs such as *inspector(i)al*, *soror(i)al*, *sphincter(i)al* are synonymous) suggests that -*ial* and -*ual* are generally in complementary distribution with -*al*, and so the decision to treat them as allomorphs of -*al* is well motivated.

-*esque* This suffix is added both to common (*picturesque*) and to proper nouns (*Junoesque*), and is still productive in both usages, though more productive added to proper nouns which are the names of people.

-*less* This suffix is added very productively to common nouns, partly because there is no other affix which competes with it. Some recent coinages are *fieldless*, *flueless*, *flyless*, *furnitureless* (all OEDS).

Other suffixes which form adjectives from nouns are -*ate* (*passion* > *passionate*), -*en* (*wood* > *wooden*), -*ese* (*Pekin* > *Pekinese*), -*ful* (*doubt* > *doubtful*), -*ic* (*algebra* > *algebraic*), -*ly* (*friend* > *friendly*), -*ous* (*venom* > *venomous*), -*y* (*cat* > *catty*). This list is not exhaustive.

7.5.3.2 Adjectives from verbs

-*able* This is probably the most productive suffix in this group, forming adjectives from transitive verbs. The suffix is also found in conjunction with *un*- in words like *unbelievable*, *unthinkable*. In some cases the unprefixed form is actually more recent than the prefixed form (Marchand, 1969: §4.2.4): a recent example is *flappable* from *unflappable* (see §6.5.8).

-*less* This suffix is no longer productive when added to verbs, but a few established examples are current, such as *countless* and *tireless*.

Other suffixes which form adjectives from verbs are -*ant*/-*ent* (*absorb* > *absorbent*), -*atory* (*affirm* > *affirmatory*), -*ful* (*resent* > *resentful*), -*ive* (*generate* > *generative*).

7.5.3.3 *Adjectives from adjectives*

The clearest example of this type in English is -*ish* (*green* > *greenish*), which is productive, though not markedly so. Probably the clearest example of the productivity of this type is given by Marchand (1969: §4.50.6) who points out that one can say things like "This is an eight-ish essay" or "a sixty-nine-ish essay".

Other suffixes in this group are -*ly* (*good* > *goodly*) and possibly -*some* (*queer* > *queersome*: cited by Marchand, 1969: §4.72.3) neither of which seems to be productive in modern English.

7.5.4 *Suffixes forming adverbs*

The main suffixes forming adverbs are -*ly*, -*ward(s)* and -*wise*. With the phonological restriction discussed in §4.5.3.1, -*ly* is added totally productively to adjectives, as in *circadianly*; -*ward(s)*, previously added to particles, e.g. *afterward(s)*, *inward(s)* is now added mainly to nouns, as in *earthward(s)*, *homeward(s)*; and -*wise* is now productively added to nouns, e.g. *cornerwise*, *lengthwise*. For examples of -*wise* the reader is referred to Houghton (1968). Other suffixes used to form adverbs are -*fold*, -*way(s)* and -*fashion*, although it might be argued that all of these form adverbial compounds.

7.5.5 *Other form classes as bases*

Aronoff (1976: 21) claims that only nouns, verbs, adjectives and adverbs can be the product of word-formation, and that only these form classes can be used as bases in the formation of derivatives. The first part of this claim may be true – although prepositions and pronouns may be compound (*into*, *anyone*) – but there is plenty of evidence that minor form classes can be used as bases, in established forms like *iffy* and *uppity* and in recent formations like *downer*, *inness*, *muchness*, *suchness*, *thereness*, *thusly*,[4] *whyness*. (Words in -*ness* are from Williams, 1965.)

7.5.6 *English suffixation on foreign bases*

There are large numbers of words in English which are either analysable as derivatives though actually borrowed from other languages (usually Latin, Greek or French) or actually coined

---

[4] W. Goldman. 1976. *Magic*. London: Macmillan, p. 4.

in English using foreign bases. An example of the first type is *cavalcade*, which in the light of later examples such as *Beatlecade*, *camelcade*, *Hoovercade*, *motorcade* (Adams, 1973: 189) can be analysed as base *caval-* + suffix *-cade*. But *caval* is not a lexeme of English, although it might be analysed as a bound root, given *cavalier* and *cavalry*. Another example is *agent*, where *-ent* might be analysed as the same suffix as in *solvent*, but there is no lexeme *ag-* (in the appropriate sense). An example of a word coined in English using a Latin base is *terrestrial*, where the *-al* does not have a Latin etymon.

Both these types are current in English, though relatively rare. The first depends upon the reanalysis of some sequence as an affix, and is not of direct concern. The latter type is illustrated by the following recent coinages: *bariatrics* (from Greek *bar* 'weight') *cryonics*, *ebulism*, *laterize*, *ludic*, *phillumenist* and *viridian*.

7.6 **Conversion**
7.6.1 *Productivity*
Conversion is an extremely productive way of producing new words in English. There do not appear to be morphological restrictions on the forms that can undergo conversion, so that compounds, derivatives, acronyms, blends, clipped forms and simplex words are all acceptable inputs to the conversion process. Similarly, all form classes seem to be able to undergo conversion, and conversion seems to be able to produce words of almost any form class, particularly the open form classes (noun, verb, adjective, adverb). This seems to suggest that rather than English having specific rules of conversion (rules allowing the conversion of common nouns into verbs or adjectives into nouns, for example) conversion is a totally free process and any lexeme can undergo conversion into any of the open form classes as the need arises. Certainly, if there are constraints on conversion they have yet to be demonstrated. The only partial restriction that I am aware of is that discussed by Marchand (1969: §5.5). Marchand points out that derived nouns rarely undergo conversion, and particularly not to verbs. This is usually because of blocking. To take one of Marchand's examples, a derived noun like *arrival* will not be converted into a verb if that verb means exactly the same as *arrive*, from which *arrival* is derived. In cases where blocking is not a

relevant concern, even derived nouns can undergo conversion, as is shown by the series *a sign > to sign > a signal > to signal* and *to commit > commission > to commission*.

The commonness of conversion can possibly be seen as breaking down the distinction between form classes in English and leading to a system where there are closed sets such as pronouns and a single open set of lexical items that can be used as required. Such a move could be seen as part of the trend away from synthetic structure and towards analytic structure which has been fairly typical of the history of English over the last millennium. This suggestion is, of course, highly speculative.

7.6.2 *Conversion as a syntactic process*

Conversion is the use of a form which is regarded as being basically of one form class as though it were a member of a different form class, without any concomitant change of form. There are, however, a number of instances where changes of this type occur with such ease and so regularly that many scholars prefer to see them as matters of syntactic usage rather than as word-formation.

The most obvious cases are those where the change of form class is not a major one (such as from noun to verb or adjective to noun) but a change from one type of noun to another or one type of verb to another. The clearest example of this type is the use of countable nouns as uncountables and vice versa. In *some tea*, *tea* is used as an uncountable noun, while in *two teas* it is used as a countable noun; *goat* is normally a countable noun, but if a goat is being eaten it is quite in order to ask for *a slice of goat*, where *goat* is used as an uncountable noun. In general, given a suitable context, it is possible to use almost any noun in either way: for example, when the Goons took part in a mountain-eating competition, it would have been perfectly possible to ask whether anyone wanted *some more mountain*, using *mountain* as an uncountable noun. Similarly, proper nouns can be easily used as common nouns as in *Which John do you mean?* or *The Athens in Ohio is not as interesting as the Athens in Greece*. Intransitive verbs are frequently used as transitive verbs, as in *He is running a horse in the Derby* or *The army flew the civilians to safety*. Finally, non-gradable adjectives are frequently used as gradable adjectives, as in *She looks very French* or

New Zealanders are said to be more English than the English. Such processes are very near the inflectional end of word-formation.

Another case where it is not completely clear whether or not conversion is involved is with conversion to adjectives. This depends crucially on how an adjective is defined. For some scholars it appears to be the case that the use of an element in attributive position is sufficient for that element to be classified as an adjective. By this criterion *bow window*, *head teacher*, *model aeroplane* and *stone wall* all contain adjectives formed by conversion. However, it has already been argued (§5.2) that such collocations should be seen as compounds, which makes it unnecessary to view such elements as instances of conversion. Quirk *et al.* (1972: 1013) suggest that when such elements can occur not only in attributive position but also in predicative position, it is possible to speak of conversion to an adjective. On the basis of:

*This window is bow
This teacher is head
*This aeroplane is model
This wall is stone

they would thus conclude that, in the examples above, *head* and *stone* but not *bow* and *model* have become adjectives by conversion. But this introduces a distinction between two kinds of modifier which is not relevant elsewhere in the grammar and which masks a great deal of similarity (see the discussion in §5.2.2). It is therefore not clear that this suggestion is of any great value. This is not meant to imply that conversion to an adjective is impossible, merely that it is least controversial that conversion is involved where the form is not used attributively. Where the form is used attributively, criteria for concluding that conversion has taken place must be spelled out with great care. Apart from those mentioned, possible criteria are the ability to be used in the comparative and superlative, the ability to be modified by *so* and *very*, the ability to be used as a base for adverbial *-ly* or nominal *-ness* suffixation. It must be pointed out that very few adjectives fit all these criteria.

7.6.3 *Marginal cases of conversion*

There are cases of change in form class from a verb to a noun and from a verb to an adjective which do not involve any affixation, but which are not clearly instances of conversion. These are cases where there is a shift of stress, frequently with a concomitant change in segmental form, but no change in the morphophonemic form (or in the orthography). Established examples of verb > noun shift of this kind are *abstract, discount, import, refill, transfer* (Gimson, 1970: 234–6; Quirk *et al.*, 1972: 1018), and of verb > adjective shift: *abstract, frequent, moderate, perfect.* There is a certain amount of evidence that, at least in some varieties of English, these distinctions are no longer being consistently drawn, and such examples are becoming clear cases of conversion. Nevertheless, the pattern is still productive, particularly so in the nominalization of phrasal verbs: established examples are *show off, walk-over* and recent examples are *hangup, put-down*.

There is also a kind of partial conversion where a noun ending in a voiceless fricative (but excluding /ʃ/) is turned into a verb by replacing the final consonant with the corresponding voiced fricative. The historical reason for this was discussed in §5.4. The process is no longer productive. Examples are *belief/believe, sheath/sheathe, advice/advise*.

7.6.4 *Clear cases of conversion*

The least clear cases of conversion have been considered first, but there are innumerable perfectly clear cases. For many types a variety of subclassifications is possible. Thus instances of noun > verb conversion can be classified according to whether the noun shows location (*to garage the car*) or instrument (*to hammer a nail*) and so on, or according to formal criteria of whether the base is simplex or complex and so on. No attempt is made below to distinguish subgroups of these kinds. For further analysis of types the reader is referred to Adams (1973), Marchand (1969), Pennanen (1971) and Quirk *et al.* (1972).

The major kinds of conversion are noun > verb, verb > noun, adjective > noun and adjective > verb. Established examples of noun > verb conversion are *to badger, to bottle, to bridge, to commission, to mail, to mushroom, to skin, to vacation*. Recent examples are *to chopper, to data-bank, to leaflet, to network* and *to trash*. Established examples of verb > noun conversion are *a call, a command, a dump, a guess, a spy* and recent examples are *a commute, a goggle* and *an interrupt*. Established examples of adjective > verb conversion are *to better, to dirty, to empty, to faint*, *to open*, *to right* and a recent example is *to total* (a car). Established examples of adjective > noun conversion are relatively rare, and are frequently restricted in their syntactic occurrence. For example, *the poor* cannot be made plural or have any other determiner. Less restricted examples are *a daily*, *a regular*, *a roast*. This type seems to have become much more productive recently, and recent examples include *a creative*, *a crazy*, *a double*, *a dyslexic*, *a gay*, *a given*, *an inflatable*, *a nasty*.

Prepositions, conjunctions, adverbs, interjections and even affixes can all act as bases for conversion, as is shown by *to up* (prices), *but me no buts*, *the hereafter*, *to heave-ho* (a recent example) and *a maxi* (this might be a case of clipping). Moreover, most of these form classes can undergo conversion into more than one form class, so that a preposition *down*, for example, can become a verb (*he downed his beer*), a noun (*he has a down on me*) and possibly an adjective (*the down train*).

Exocentric phrase compounds, discussed in §7.2.1.8, might also be classified here as instances of conversion of a whole phrase. Established examples where the phrase acts as a noun are *an also-ran*, *a forget-me-not*, *a has-been*, and a recent example is *a don't-know*. An established example where the phrase acts as an adjective is *under-the-weather*.

7.7 Back-formation

The great majority of back-formations in English are verbs. Pennanen (1975: 217) gives a figure of 87 per cent, and explains this by saying that verbs "have a larger field of derivatives around them" than other form classes, so that there is a wider range of possible sources for a back-formation which is a verb.

Much has been made in the literature of the fact that back-formation is of mainly diachronic significance, since it is impossible to see synchronically that *editor* and *exhibitor* are not produced by identical processes from *edit* and *exhibit* respectively (see e.g. Marchand, 1969: 391ff and, following Marchand, Aronoff, 1976: 27; Quirk *et al.*, 1972: 977; Tietze, 1974: §4.1.1). It is therefore worth repeating here that back-formation is a synchronically productive process in English word-formation.

Some authorities (e.g. Marchand, 1969) prefer the term 'back-derivation' to 'back-formation'. However, it is not always a derivational process which is "reversed" .in back-formation. The classic example of this is the word *pea*, a back-formation from an earlier singular (uncountable) form *pease*, which was perceived as plural. Another is *cherry* which is a back-formation from the French *cerise*, again with the final /z/ perceived as a plural marker. A recent example of this type of formation is the form *alm* from *alms*.

The usual description of the process of back-formation is that a rule of word-formation (or in the light of the last paragraph, morphology) is reversed (see e.g. Adams, 1973: 105; Aronoff, 1976: 27). This is perhaps slightly misleading: the precise process can be seen from the formula below, which uses the examples of *editor* and *exhibitor*:

verb	PLUS	*-or*	→	noun
exhibit				*exhibitor*

verb		←	noun	MINUS	*-or*
edit			*editor*		

Or in more general terms, where X and Y are form classes of lexemes and A is a particular suffix:

Formation: $X + A \rightarrow Y$
Back-formation: $Y - A \rightarrow X$

Similar rules would apply to back-formations from prefixed forms. Note that for a process to be a back-formation, the appropriate formation rule must also exist.

The majority of back-formations are of this type. Some recent examples are *eutrophicate* < *eutrophication*, *lase* < *laser*, *lech* < *lecher*, *oneupman* < *oneupmanship*, *paramedic* < *paramedical*, *rotovate* < *rotovator* and *surreal* < *surrealist*. However, there are a number of formations, apparently back-formations, which do not fit this pattern. The first type can be illustrated with the recent formation *surveille* < *surveillance*. The nominalization of verbs with the suffix *-ance* is probably no longer productive, so that synchronically there is no formation rule of the form

verb + *-ance* → noun

If back-formation is the undoing of synchronic rules of word-formation, therefore, the form *surveille* cannot be accounted for. This implies that back-formation also has access to non-productive rules, or that back-formation is concerned with the deletion of suffixes rather than with the undoing of morphological rules.

Evidence that it is in fact the second of these which is the case, at least in some instances, is provided by the second type of unexpected back-formation. Recent examples of this type are *contracept* < *contraception* and *transcript* < *transcription*. Aronoff (1976: 27) also gives the examples *cohese* < *cohesion* and *self-destruct* < *self-destruction*. If the rules of back-formation led to the undoing of non-productive rules of word-formation, the expected forms of the verbs would be *contraceive* (also attested: Adams, 1973: 111), *transcribe*, *cohere* and *self-destroy*. The forms attested show that in these cases the back-formation has consisted of the deletion of a non-productive suffix, one which can be analysed in words like *collection*, *contribution* and *reaction*. In the formation *contraceive*, on the other hand, there is either a genuine undoing of a rule of word-formation, or an analogous formation with *conceive*.

In the light of the modern data, it might be better to redefine back-formation as the formation of new lexemes by the deletion of actual or supposed affixes in longer words. Back-formation would then become a special case of clipping (see §7.8.1).

7.8 Unpredictable formations

The words in this section are grouped together by Aronoff (1976: 20) as "oddities". Aronoff points out that many of the types listed here depend upon orthography to a greater or lesser degree, and thus cannot be universal, since orthography is not a prerequisite to linguistic behaviour. As far as English is concerned, though, these formations are so common (to judge by the word-list of Barnhart *et al.*, 1973) that it is misleading to consider them out of the ordinary. But however frequent these formations may be, they are very awkward from the point of view of generative grammar: it is by no means clear that the forms of these words can be predicted by rules without appealing to such ill-understood notions as euphony. Certainly it is true that if these forms can be predicted by rule, the rules will have to take a far wider range of factors into account than other rules of word-formation, although all the factors that have been discussed in relation to other types of word-formation will remain relevant.

7.8.1 *Clipping*

Clipping refers to the process whereby a lexeme (simplex or complex) is shortened, while still retaining the same meaning and still being a member of the same form class. Frequently clipping results in a change of stylistic level. The unpredictability concerns the way in which the base lexeme is shortened. The main pattern is for the beginning of the base lexeme to be retained as in the recent examples *bi* (< *bisexual*), *binocs* (< *binoculars*), *deli* (< *delicatessen*), *jumbo* (< *jumbo jet*), *mimeo* (< *mimeograph*), *narc* (< *narcotics agent*), *porn* (< *pornography*), *mike* (< *microphone*). It does not seem to be predictable how many syllables will be retained in the clipped form (except that there will be fewer than in the base lexeme), whether the final syllable will be open or closed, whether the stressed syllable from the base lexeme will be included or not.

While a clipping which retains the initial part of the word is easily the most common type, there are also others. In the following recent examples, it is the final part of the base lexeme which has been retained: *Cong* (< *Viet Cong*), *'Fro* (< *Afro*), *loid* (< *celluloid*), and *Yard* (< *Montagnard*). A much rarer type is where the middle of the word is retained, but both ends are clipped. Examples are *jams* (< *pyjamas*) and *shrink* (< *head-shrinker*). Adams (1973: §10.1) and Marchand (1969: §9) both give established examples of all three of these types.

Clipped forms are also used in compounds, as in *op art* (< *optical art*) and *org-man* (< *organization man*). It is also frequently the case that both halves of a compound are clipped as in *edbiz*. In these cases it is difficult to know whether the resultant formation should be treated as a clipping or as a blend (see §7.8.2); the border between the two types is not always clear. Perhaps the easiest way to draw the distinction (although it might be a bit *ad hoc*) is to say that those forms which retain compound stress are clipped compounds, whereas those that take simple word stress are not. By this criterion *bodbiz*, *Chicom*, *Comsymp*, *Intelsat*, *midcult*, *pro-am*, *sci-fi* and *sitcom* are all compounds made of clippings.

Clipping, particularly in scientific terminology, is often much more complex than in the examples that have been discussed so far. Consider, for example, the recent formations *parylene* < *paraxylene*, *phorate* < *phosphorodithioate*, *prepreg* < *preimpregnated*. In cases like these there seem to be no limitations on the clipping except that the clipped form should be a possible word, and such forms are as much instances of word manufacture (see §7.8.4) as of clipping.

7.8.2 *Blends*

When Alice asked Humpty Dumpty to explain the poem "Jabberwocky" to her, part of his explanation ran as follows:

Well, "slithy" means "lithe and slimy". "Lithe" is the same as "active". You see it's like a portmanteau – there are two meanings packed up into one word. (Lewis Carroll, *Through the Looking Glass*, 1872, ch VI)

Portmanteau words like *slithy* and *mimsy* are also called blends. A **blend** may be defined as a new lexeme formed from parts of two (or possibly more) other words in such a way that there is no transparent analysis into morphs. The question of analysis into morphs is the awkward part of this definition, since in many cases some kind of analysis can be made: for example, in some instances at least one of the elements is transparently recoverable.

The clearest examples of blends, however, are like the ones that Humpty Dumpty mentions, where the etymological root of the word is only clear when specifically explained. Recent examples are *ballute* (< *balloon* + *parachute*), *chunnel* (< *channel* + *tunnel*), *dawk* (< *dove* + *hawk*) and *shoat* (< *sheep* + *goat*). To see the unpredictability of this type of formation, consider *dawk* and *ballute*. A dawk is a person who is neither a dove nor a hawk in the extended sense of 'person who is opposed to/in favour of war'. Once it is decided to form a blend of these two lexemes, there are theoretically a number of possibilities open:

(i)	dʌk	(iv)	hɔv
(ii)	dɔk	(v)	hʌv
(iii)	dɔv	(vi)	hʌk

This excludes the possibility of forming a two-syllable blend, which should also be considered for the sake of completeness. However, taking only the monosyllabic possibilities into account, (i) and (vi) can be ruled out as real possibilities because of blocking – in particular (i) could lead to all sorts of misunderstandings. (iii) and (vi) can probably be ruled out, since blends normally take the first part of one word and the last part of another, rather than mixing phonemes at random, or inserting part of one word into the middle of another. This leaves (ii), (iv) and (v). The reason why (v) is not used seems to be orthographic rather than phonological or morphological. Although /h/ can occur before /ʌ/ as in *hull* and the sequence /ʌv/ can occur as in *love*, it is not clear how /hʌv/ would be spelled: *hove*, which would be the normal orthographic representation of the blend would be pronounced /həuv/, and the point of the formation would be lost. This leaves (ii) and (iv), and the choice of one rather than the other would appear to be fairly arbitrary, although the *Sprachgefühl* of the native speaker may find one more suitable than the other. In the case of *ballute*, the choice would seem to be even wider, since either a two- or three-syllable blend would appear to be possible. At least *paroon*, *paraloon* and *bala-chute* would seem to be permissible forms of this word. It seems likely that there is not a single "right answer" when searching for a blend, and that the blend chosen is at least partially random. To a certain extent this is also true in other kinds of word-formation, so that Barnhart *et al.* (1973) list both *skyjack* and *skyjacker* as synonymous, and also *judoist* and *judoman*, *jurimetricist* and *jurimetrician* and so on. However, in these other cases there are at least rules as to what the base must be and what the suffix must be for any given pattern: in blending, the coiner is apparently free to take as much or as little from either base as is felt to be necessary or desirable. As an example, consider Humpty Dumpty's own *mimsy* which, according to him, is from *flimsy* and *miserable*. *Flimserable*, *fliserable* and *misemsy* would presumably all have exactly the same content. This is, of course, not to say that there are not restrictions. *Flimerable*, *miseramsy*, *miserasy*, *miserlimsy*, *misimsy* would all appear less likely than *mimsy*. Exactly what the restrictions are, however, beyond pronounceability and spellability, is far from clear. One seems to be the rejection of forms that lead to the splitting up of consonant clusters from either of the original words, but this may be a spurious restriction.

There are other kinds of blend where the rules for blending are more obvious. In particular this is true of those blends where the two words used as the bases are both present in their entirety in the blend, though there is overlap. It should be noted that the overlap may be in pronunciation, in orthography or both. Recent examples are *glasphalt*, *octopush* and *wargasm*. Adams (1973: 154ff) adds *balloonatic*, *guestimate*, *slanguage* and *swelegant*.

A third kind of blend is the type where the new lexeme looks as though it is or might be analysable in terms of other word-formation processes, in particular as a neo-classical compound. Recent examples are *arcology* (< *architectural ecology*), *autocide* (< *automobile* + *suicide*), *electrodelic* (< *electro* + *psychedelic*), *molecism* (< *molecule* + *organism*), *pornotopia* (< *pornography* + *utopia*) and *stagflation* (< *stagnation* + *inflation*). Even if these are clearly seen as blends by the people who coin them, they are not always recognized as blends by the people who hear them, and in some cases may lead to the re-evaluation of some sequence of phonemes as an affix. This might happen with *autocide*, which is perhaps the most obviously analysable of the examples just cited, but *-topia* has now started to appear in more words (*dystopia*, *kakotopia*), and the element *-(o)holic* has now been taken out of *alcoholic* and is used as a suffix, although it probably started out in blends (on the suffix *-(o)holic*, see Kolin, 1979). Other elements which started out in blends and have recently become English suffixes are *-burger*, *-rama* and *-teria*.

Finally under blends, there is a set of formations whose precise status in the taxonomy is difficult to discern. These are words which function like blends, but which keep one of the two bases intact. As a result it is not clear whether they are in fact blends or compounds made up of one instance of clipping and one unaltered lexeme. Some examples, like *cremains* (< *cremate* + *remains*) and *carbecue* (< *car* + *barbecue*), have very much the effect of blends, while others, like *mocamp* (< *motor* + *camp*) and *frontlash* (< *front* + *backlash*), seem more like compounds. In between there is a whole range where it is difficult to take a decision: *Amtrack* (< *American* + *track*), *boatel* (< *boat* + *hotel*), *Nixonomics* (< *Nixon* + *economics*), *parawing* (< *parachute* + *wing*), *pulsar* (< *pulse* + *quasar*).

Generally speaking, the category of blends is not well-defined, and blending tends to shade off into compounding, neo-classical compounding, affixation, clipping and, as will be seen in the next section, acronyming. Nevertheless, it is a very productive source of words in modern English, in both literary and scientific contexts. For recent attempts at a typology of blends see Algeo (1977) and Soudek (1978), who consider the whole question in much greater detail.

7.8.3 *Acronyms*

An **acronym** is a word coined by taking the initial letters of the words in a title or phrase and using them as a new word, for example *Strategic Arms Limitation Talks* gives *SALT*. However, not every abbreviation counts as an acronym: to be an acronym the new word must not be pronounced as a series of letters, but as a word. Thus if Value Added Tax is called /vi eɪ ti/, that is an abbreviation, but if it is called /væt/, it has become an acronym. Further recent examples of acronyms are *BASIC* (Beginners' All-purpose Symbolic Instruction Code: other computer languages also have acronymic names), *FOBS* (Fractional Orbital Bombardment System), *GRAS* (Generally Recognized As Safe), *LEM* (Lunar Excursion Module), *REM* (Rapid Eye Movement), and *WASP* (White Anglo-Saxon Protestant). In some cases it seems that the name of a particular object is specially chosen to give a suitable acronym. This seems to be true of *BASIC* (quoted above) or, for example, the Federation of Inter-State Truckers, *FIST*. In other cases, the acronym spells something which seems to be appropriate in some metaphorical sense, as for example with *WASP*.

The lack of predictability in acronyms stems from at least two sources. Firstly, the phrase from which the acronym is taken is treated with a certain amount of freedom to permit the acronym to arise. For example, in *BASIC* only the first part of a compound adjective provides a letter for the acronym, while in *WASP* both parts of *Anglo-Saxon* provide a letter for the acronym; in *GRAS* the particle *as* provides the *A* in the acronym, but in *FIST* the particle *of* is not permitted to provide a letter (otherwise the acronym would be *FOIST*, which is presumably far less effective as the name of a trade union). It seems that the interests of the acronym are the deciding factor in what the "initial letters" of the phrase will be taken to include.

The second main reason for the lack of predictability in acronyms is that not every abbreviation which could be an acronym is treated as one, and there seems to be no particular reason why some abbreviations should be ignored. Clearly, *BBC* cannot be pronounced as a word, since it violates constraints on the phonological structure of English words, but the same is not true of *GOM* (Grand Old Man) or *OD* (Over-Dose). A particularly striking example is provided by the pair *JAL*, /dʒeɪ eɪ el/ (Japanese Airlines) and *IJAL*, /aɪdʒæl/ (*International Journal of American Linguistics*). Usage alone would seem to make the difference, and it is not clear what factors influence the variant usages.

Occasionally, unusual acronyms are found where the letters are not strictly speaking initial letters in the words in a phrase. One notable example is *KREEP*, a type of moonrock, where the *K* is the chemical symbol for potassium, and the acronym means 'potassium, rare earth elements, phosphate'.

Far more common is the case where more than one letter is taken from the beginning of one or more of the words in the phrase which is the base of the acronym. Recent examples of this are *Arvin* (Army of the Republic of VIetNam), *GHOST* (Global HOrizontal Sounding Technique), *HILAC* (Heavy Ion Linear ACcelerator) and *rejasing* (REusing Junk As SomethING else: alternatively, *rejaser* (REuse Junk As Something Else + suffix -*er*)). In some cases it may no longer be clear whether the new word is an acronym or a blend: consider, for example, *linac* (LINear ACcelerator). It is certainly unusual for blends to use the beginnings of the two words which are to be blended, but it cannot be ruled out as impossible; and while it is normal for acronyms to use the beginnings of words, the clearest cases use only the initial letters.

Finally, it must be stressed that acronyming is very much orthographically-based, and as such differs considerably from most other word-formation processes. Consider, for example, *PERT* (Program Evaluation and Review Technique). If the phonetic value of each initial letter as it is used in the base of the acronym were taken as the starting point of the acronym, a pronunciation /pɪrt/ would be expected, that is /pɪət/ in dialects of English that do not have post-vocalic /r/. The pronunciation /pɜt/ shows the expected pronunciation of the orthographic sequence *er*. Similarly with *WASP*. If the acronym were based on the pronunciation of the elements, the expected pronunciation would be /wæsp/ (or possibly /hwæsp/) rather than /wɒsp/.

7.8.4 *Word manufacture*

The purest cases of **word manufacture** are when a word is created *ex nihilo*, with no morphological, phonological or orthographic motivation whatsoever. This is rare, except in brand names like *Kodak*. Bareš (1974: 181–2) reports, however, that computer programs have been used to provide new names which do not have etymologies. In fact, since a human being makes a choice from a list provided by a computer, some of these invented words end up looking as if they had an etymology. For example, Bareš cites *Antron*, *Dacron*, *Krylon*, *Orlon* and *Teflon* as instances of computer-produced words, and yet the *-on* at the end of such formations begins to look like a suffix, and might well be analysed as representing a morpheme with the meaning 'artificial, synthetic'. The only clear non-commercial words I have found in this category are *grok* 'to communicate sympathetically' (from Robert Heinlein's (1961) novel *Stranger in a Strange Land*), *wampeter*, *foma* and *grandfalloon* (which all feature in the title of a (1974) book by Kurt Vonnegut), and *quark* (which had its origins in James Joyce's (1939) novel *Finnegan's Wake*). *Scag* 'heroin' may be another example.

More marginal are the words, particularly scientific words, that are abstracted from long technical phrases in a manner which is reminiscent of blending and acronyming, but where the motivation is far less clear than in those cases. For example, consider *pemoline* < *phenylimino-oxazolidinone* or, an even more extreme example, *picloram* < *aminotrichloropicolinic acid* where the groups of letters borrowed from the base have been reversed in the final word. Such formations, while motivated, in that the chemical names provide the source of the letters in the new word, are far less obviously motivated than the other categories that have been discussed in this section, and may be best described as instances of word manufacture. They certainly do not obviously fall into any other category, and they are not obviously subject to rules other than phonotactic rules of English.

7.8.5 *Mixed formations*

There are some formations which appear to be a mixture of two or more of the processes described in this section or of the product of one of the processes described in this section and an unaltered lexemic base or a normal affix. Since it is obviously possible to mix these processes productively, the coiner is not restricted to one or another of them, and this makes the words produced by these methods even less predictable. Examples are *poromeric* < *porosity* + *polymer* with the English suffix *-ic*; *scramjet* < *supersonic combustion ramjet*; and *molechism* < *molecule* + *chemical* + *organism*. Extreme examples of this type look very much like word manufacture, and are possibly best treated as such.

7.9 Avoidance of word-formation

As Aronoff (1976: 35) stresses, word-formation rules are always optional. This means that it is always possible to avoid using a process of word-formation. Typically, this will be done by providing a description rather than the name which word-formation gives (see §6.1.1). Where the head word is a noun, the description may occur in a relative clause; where the head word is a verb, the description may occur in one or more adverbials. For instance, it would be a description to talk about the 'person who was arrested', but word-formation to talk of the *arrestee*.[5]

One frequent occurrence where nouns are concerned is that a whole noun phrase becomes established as a name, even though no process of word-formation is undergone: the noun phrase fits all the rules for a normal noun phrase, but is used in the same way as a lexeme, and, like a lexeme, cannot be interrupted or have its elements reordered (see §5.2.2). Recent examples are *new town* and *women's liberation*. In this context it is interesting to compare the phrase *women's liberation* with an apparently equivalent phrase *children's shoes* in a number of syntactic contexts:

women's liberation	children's shoes
the liberation is women's	the shoes are children's
women's summer liberation	children's summer shoes
women's first liberation	children's first shoes
all women's liberation	all children's shoes

Although these phrases are probably all acceptable, the semantic coherence of *women's liberation* is lost in the other syntactic

[5] Joseph Wambaugh. 1975. *The Choirboys*. London: Weidenfeld and Nicolson, p. 61.

contexts, whereas there is no equivalent semantic coherence in the phrase *children's shoes*.

The fact that lexemes can arise diachronically without any word-formation process being undergone, and the fact that word-formation can always be avoided, are points which should not be forgotten in the study of word-formation.

8

Theory and practice

We are pleading here for the systematic description of synchronically
productive word-formation processes in individual languages, with the
conditions of the creation, use and understanding of so-called 'nonce-
formations' as the main aim.

(Brekle, 1978: 70)

8.1 Introduction

Although the general points discussed in the first six
chapters of this book were illustrated with individual examples, the
general tenor of those chapters was theoretical. Chapter 7, while
less theoretically oriented, was mainly concerned with illustrating
the range of patterns that are found in English rather than with
applying the theory to those patterns. In this chapter the main
emphasis shifts to the detailed study of word-formation, to see how
well the theoretical points discussed in the main body of this book
hold in practice. Further theoretical points will emerge from the
consideration of actual data.

Each section in this chapter is based on a corpus of attested cases
of word-formation, and discusses the problems raised by the
attested data for the elaboration of lexical entries. The particular
examples have been chosen to illustrate a range of limitations on
productivity. While these may look unfamiliar and even, in some
cases, unlikely, all the forms given have been attested (though not
necessarily by me), and it is often the unfamiliar items which show
the productivity of the process in question. Recent neologisms are
also taken as evidence for the productivity of a process. It is
assumed that all the processes described in this chapter are at least
marginally productive.

Since long references, illustrative quotations and definitions for
each of the several hundred words that will be listed in this chapter
would be too space consuming, words will frequently be listed with
a parenthesized symbol following them, thus: *minicrat* (A). These
symbols refer to the academic works and lexica listed below, where

the appropriate word can be found. Note that those marked (ALD) or (W) can be assumed to be established. The same is true for the majority of those marked (L), since Lehnert (1971) is a reverse dictionary of words listed in a number of English dictionaries, including the *OED* and *Webster's*.

(A)	Adams, 1973
(Al)	Algeo, 1971
(ALD)	Hornby, 1974
(B)	Barnhart *et al.*, 1973
(F)	Foster, 1964
(H)	Harder, 1966
(J)	Jespersen, 1942
(K)	Kiparsky, 1964
(L)	Lehnert, 1971
(Ly)	Lyons, 1977
(M)	Marchand, 1969
(Mi)	Minton, 1958
(OED(S))	(*Supplement to the*) *Oxford English Dictionary*
(R)	Rudnyckyj, 1959
(W)	*Webster's Third New International Dictionary*

Some explanation is required of the format of the descriptions of word-formation processes that will be used in this chapter. No rules will be specified in the strict sense of the term 'rule' used by generative grammarians. However, it is hoped that sufficient information will be provided in the discussion for it to be clear in general terms how such rules might work. Whether the rules introducing affixes should be phrase structure rules or transformational rules and what, if any, special notation might be required to formulate them are questions which will not be considered. Instead, lexical entries will be specified for the various affixes, following the pattern suggested in §6.8, and the discussion will centre on matters necessary for the specification of these entries: matters such as the nature of the limitations on productivity and how best to specify the apparent meanings of the affixes discussed. Suffixes will be discussed first, and in greatest detail, then neoclassical compounds and prefixes.

8.2 **Suffixation**

8.2.1 *The suffix '-ee'*

The *-ee* suffix that will be considered in this section is the one which is used to form patient nouns like *appointee* (L), *evacuee*

(F, L), *examinee* (L), *kissee* (L), etc., and not the diminutive *-ee* also spelled *-ie* and *-y* as in *doggy* and *weepie* (for which see Harder, 1964), nor the equally homophonous *-ee* of *bargee*, *coachee* etc. (see Marchand, 1969: §4.24.5), where the *-ee* is apparently a diachronic diminutive. While this suffix is productive in English, my corpus of productively formed examples is quite small, so rules will be formed on the basis of established forms, and it will then be shown that there are productive examples which fit some of the rules.

Although this *-ee* suffix originated in loans from Old French, and was originally a legalistic suffix (Marchand, 1969: §4.24.1), in its more recent productive use it is frequently playful or whimsical in tone (Barnhart *et al.*, 1973; Marchand, 1969: §4.24.3), particularly in contexts where the formality of legal style is inappropriate. Consider the following examples, all of which must be considered established since they are listed by Lehnert (1971):

(1)	flirtee (L)	laughee (L, M)
	kickee (L)	shavee (L)
	kissee (L)	
(2)	appointee (L)	parolee (L)
	indictee (L)	payee (L)
	licensee (L)	

Those in (1) show the whimsical usage, those in (2), which occur in quasi-legal contexts, show the serious usage. In the productive series, there are far more whimsical formations (3) than serious ones (4):

(3)	huggee (F)	rushee (M)
	meetee (B)	squeezee (M)
(4)	franchisee (B)	? slanderee (M)

This, then, is the basic stylistic value of the suffix, although other stylistic effects which can be attributed to word-formation as a whole rather than to this particular suffix should not be ignored. These include compactness, and the value that is achieved by giving something a name as opposed to a descriptive label.

With the single possible exception of *absentee*, which might be derived from an adjective or a verb (the *OED* says from a verb), the base is a verb in all the established examples I have found. Phonologically it must be noted that the suffix takes the stress in the new complex form, although in disyllabic complex forms the base and the suffix sometimes have equal stress.

This implies a lexical entry for the suffix -*ee* which includes the information set out below. The roman figures refer to the various boxes in the lexical entry outlined in Figure 6.10, §6.8.4. Semantic information, which is missing below, will be provided later.

(i) Segmental form: /i/
 Suprasegmental form: stress on suffix (or equal stress on base and suffix) [that is, general stress rules apply to the whole derivative]
(ii) Suffix forming [+ Human] nouns
(v) Whimsical in contexts where not (quasi-)legal
(vii) Base must be a verb

In this particular case, the limitations on the base (apart from the fact that the base must be a verb) and the meaning of the complex form are inextricably entwined, and they will accordingly be discussed together.

The most common meaning (in both established and nonce forms) seems to be 'one who is Ved' where the verb is transitive. This meaning implies a limitation on the base of the following kind:

$$\begin{bmatrix} + \text{ Verb} \\ + \text{ Transitive} \\ + \begin{bmatrix} + \text{Noun} \\ + \text{Human} \end{bmatrix} \text{DO} \end{bmatrix}$$

As elsewhere, the notation here is not intended to make theoretical claims about the model of syntax that must be used, and different models will mark the noun phrase that is the direct object (DO) of the verb in different ways. It is merely meant to illustrate the kind of thing that will have to be possible in any theory of syntax if it is to cope adequately with this type of word-formation. Established examples of the pattern generated with this limitation include:

consultee (L)   persecutee (L)
examinee (L)   toastee (L)
internee (L)   trainee (L)
interviewee (L)

The second most common pattern permits exactly the same meaning, but is formed from a di-transitive (or tri-valent) verb rather than from a transitive verb, such that the person who is denoted by the complex form would be the indirect object of the verb in question. Using the same kind of notation as above, this base limitation may be written as:

$$\begin{bmatrix} + \text{ Verb} \\ + \text{ Di-transitive} \\ + \begin{bmatrix} + \text{Noun} \\ + \text{Human} \end{bmatrix} \text{IO} \end{bmatrix}$$

Established examples of this pattern include:

grantee (L)	promisee (L)
payee (L)	sendee (L)

The third group consists of verbs which permit a prepositional phrase including a human noun. The meaning in these cases is 'one who is Ved preposition', so that *experimentee* is 'one who is experimented on', a *flirtee* is 'one who is flirted with' and so on. The verbs used as bases in this kind of formation appear to be both transitive and intransitive. The limitation on the base seems to be of the following kind:

$$\begin{bmatrix} + \text{ Verb} \\ + \begin{bmatrix} + \text{Noun} \\ + \text{Human} \end{bmatrix} \text{O Prep} \end{bmatrix}$$

Further established examples are:

appellee (L)	jestee (L)
depositee (L)	objectee (L)

In cases like *signal(l)ee*, 'one to whom a signal is made or transmitted' (*OED*), it may not be clear whether this pattern or the indirect object pattern is the model for the formation. A stronger hypothesis might be that this group should be merged with either the direct object group or the indirect object group, possibly on the basis of the deep case of the argument of the verb which includes the appropriate human noun. While I would not wish to rule out such a hypothesis, I can see little immediate evidence for this particular one. A more likely hypothesis is that the unifying factor is the ability of all the nouns to appear as subjects of verbs with passive form.

The final meaning is much rarer. In this one, *-ee* seems to be synonymous with *-er*, since the human noun concerned is the subject of the base verb. This means a limitation of the following kind:

$$
\begin{bmatrix}
+ \text{ Verb} \\
+ \begin{bmatrix}
+ \text{ Noun} \\
+ \text{ Human}
\end{bmatrix} \text{Su}
\end{bmatrix}
$$

but somehow an extra limitation must be built into the grammar to show that this process of word-formation is not a preferred method of forming derivatives. There is, in fact, only one absolutely clear case of this in Lehnert (1971), *escapee*. Other words may fit the same pattern: *absentee* (L), *infiltree* ('one who has entered another country or territory in a manner resembling military infiltration' (W)) and *parkee* (L). *Absentee* might be glossed as 'one who absented himself', *infiltree* might equally be glossed as 'one who has been infiltrated into another country' and the meaning of *parkee* is obscure, so it is difficult to tell which group it belongs to, or whether it is even a relevant example.

There is also a formal limitation on the base of *-ee* words. If the verb being used as a base ends in *-ate*, this is normally deleted. Established examples are:

evacuee (L)   nominee (L)
liberee (L)

The *-ate* is not deleted, however, if the final consonant of the base would then be /k/ in a word of Romance origin (i.e. spelled with a *c*). To avoid the velar softening of /k/ to /s/ before the /i/ of the suffix, the *-ate* is kept in these cases:

allocatee (L)   dedicatee (L)

The process is thus:

#X [+ segment] + -ate# → #X [+ segment] + ϕ#
Condition: [+ segment] $\neq$ [k] and X [+ segment] $\neq$ [+ Romance] (where X is a variable over strings of segments, and # is a word-boundary)

In all, then, there are four separate patterns which have been productive in the formation of established -*ee* derivatives. There are also some words in -*ee* which are almost certainly lexicalized, in that they do not fit with any of these patterns. These include *amputee*, *lessee* and *trustee*. These are lexicalized for different reasons: *amputee* is semantically lexicalized, since it does not fit the meanings of any of the above groups, nor of any other series of forms; *lessee* is phonologically lexicalized, since the expected form of the base would be /lis/ rather than /les/; and *trustee* is morphologically lexicalized since the verb from which the meaning is derived is *entrust*, not *trust*. The question now is which of the four major patterns are still productive. If any of the patterns is no longer productive, then the forms listed above which were generated according to that pattern must be classed as lexicalized. For each of the patterns, the -*ate* limitation may also apply. Words where it has applied are marked in the lists below with an asterisk. The words listed below are all from recent sources, and must be assumed to be productive uses of the suffix.

Pattern 1: Direct object
blackmailee (B)
congratulee* (M)
curee (B)
deferee (B) 'person who is not drafted to the army'
designee*[1] 'designated hitter'
franchisee (B) [*to franchise* also listed in (B)]
huggee (F)
kidnapee[2]
educatee (M)
honoree (M)
holdupee (M) [cf. somebody was held up]
pumpee[3]
retardee (B)
rushee (M)
seducee (L, M)
slanderee (M)
squeezee (M)

[1] *American Speech* 46 (1971) 294.
[2] Alistair Maclean. 1977. *Goodbye California*. London: Collins, p. 25. Spelling as original.
[3] Ben Bova. 1977. *The Multiple Man*. London: Gollancz, p. 66. 'Someone who is pumped for information': "I decided to be the pumper not the pumpee."

vaccinee* (B, L)
visitee (M)

Pattern 2: Indirect object
None in sample

Pattern 3: Object of preposition
laughee (L, M) [quotation in the *OED* for 1829]

Pattern 4: Subject
charteree[4]
dilutee (F) 'unskilled worker used to dilute a skilled work-
force'
standee[5]

There are also a number of examples where it is not totally clear
whether pattern 1 or pattern 4 is being used:

adaptee (B)	mergee (B)
embarkee (B)	retiree (F)
meetee (B)	

In fact, Foster comments on the ambiguity of the last item. In the
case of *meetee*, this might be an instance of pattern 3 in American
English, where one *meets with* a person. The most likely interpretation, it seems to me, is one with a conjoined plural subject, as in
The management and union representatives met last night, where
everyone concerned is a meetee. Foster also lists another interesting
item:

resignee 'person who resigns from a job'

The *OED* marks *resignee* as obsolete with the meaning 'one to
whom anything is resigned', but Foster gives a reference from 1959
where, he says, pattern 4 is used.

There is one final item in my corpus and it is irregular:
biographee (F). This seems to be an analogical formation from
biographer, since it implies a non-existent verb **to biograph*. While
the existence of a parallel *-er* formation is often an important cue for
the formation of an *-ee* word, the vast majority of these still imply
the existence of the base verb (for an example, see fn. 3, p. 248).

The results here are quite dramatic. They seem to indicate the

---

[4] Antony Trew. 1975. *The Zhukov Briefing*. London: Collins, p. 72. 'A person
who charters a yacht'.

[5] Helen McCloy. 1976. *Cruel as the Grave*. London: Gollancz, p. 99. 'A person
who stands in a subway train'.

demise of patterns 2 and 3, though with the small sample it might just be that they are not very productive. They also indicate an increase in the productivity of pattern 4. Why this should be when there is such a plethora of suffixes for indicating persons without a 'patient' meaning (*-er*, *-ist*, *-ite*, *-man*, etc.) is far from clear. One suggestion (made to me by Bernard Comrie) is that it shows a trace of ergative-absolutive patterning in English: that *-ee* is coming to be used to mark the object of a transitive verb and the subject of an intransitive verb, like the absolute case in ergative languages. Whether or not this is the case (and there are a couple of examples which cannot be explained by this), it may be true that such formations in *-ee* show a coming trend in word-formation patterns.

8.2.2 *The suffix '-ese'*

The *-ese* suffix that will be discussed here is the one denoting a "characteristic jargon" (Marchand, 1969: §4.33), and no mention will be made of the homophonous suffix for deriving nationality adjectives from noun bases. Again the sample is fairly small, but in this case it seems rather easier to work out the rules. The corpus of *-ese* words on which the discussion is based is listed here:

Afro-Americanese (B)	journalese (M)
Americanese (M, *OEDS*)	linotype-ese (*OEDS*)
cablese (M, *OEDS*)	Meredithese (*OEDS*)
Carlylese (M)	Nabokovese (B, under *-ian*)
childrenese (B)	newspaperese (*OEDS*)
computerese (B)	New Yorkese (M)
educationese (B)	novelese (M, *OEDS*)
golfese (*OEDS*)	officialese (M, *OEDS*)
guide-bookese (*OEDS*)	Ruskinese (*OEDS*)
headlinese (*OEDS*)	sociologese (B)
jargonese (M)	telegraphese (M)
Johnsonese (M)	Washingtonese (*OEDS*)

The lexical entry for the suffix provides little difficulty, but the limitations on the base are interesting here. As far as the lexical entry is concerned, only one point requires discussion, and that is the form class of the base. In the vast majority of instances, the base is clearly a noun. There are, however, three examples where the base could be considered an adjective: *Afro-Americanese*, *Americanese*, *officialese*. In each of these cases, however, it is also possible to view the base as a noun, and semantically this makes rather more sense: *officialese* is the characteristic jargon of officials, rather than of things official. It will thus be assumed that the base in derivatives with *-ese* is always a noun. This allows the postulation of a lexical entry on the following lines:

(i)	Segmental form: /iz/
	Suprasegmental form: stress on the suffix [that is, general stress rules apply to the whole derivative]
(ii)	Suffix forming [− Concrete], [− Count] nouns
(iv)	Characteristic jargon connected with or produced by the entity named in the base
(v)	Derogatory
(vii)	Base must be a noun

In the words under consideration, there also appears to be a phonological limitation on the base. This is exemplified by *sociologese*. It seems that the final /ɪ/ or /i/ of *sociology* has been deleted under the influence of the /i/ in the suffix (compare *educationese* for the assumption that the base is, in fact, *sociology*). This deletion in suffixation will be illustrated again in later sections. Nowhere in the data considered in this book is there a large enough corpus of words where this happens to allow the formulation of rules on the subject. Suffice it to say at this point that it is probably not entirely automatic: I suspect that if an *-ese* derivative were to be formed from McCawley, the result would be *McCawleyese* and not *McCawlese* (see the *OED*: *Macaulayese* [erron. *Macaulese*]), but what the precise constraints on such deletion are, I do not know.

The other limitations on the base are interesting because they show preferences. It is clearly not a strict limitation that the base should denote a person or typical source of the printed word, yet over half of the words listed fall into one of these two groups. There also seems to be a slight preference for proper nouns as the base of these formations. Such factors have to be listed as positive factors conducive to the choice of a suffix with a particular base noun. These limitations are rather different from the limitations on the type of verb listed above for *-ee* formations. There it was possible to specify exhaustively all the classes that could act as bases. Here no exhaustive specification is possible.

It is by no means self-evident that an affix which allows two or more formal or semantic classes as its base has to show a significant preference for one, and certainly not to the extent which both *-ese* and *-ee* seem to. Accordingly, this should be seen as a significant fact about these particular affixes, and one which has to be noted somehow. This could be done with some kind of variable rule, for instance, with a marking alongside the limitations on the base of a structural preference factor. Psychologically, this would not seem to have any great reality, since the individual speaker is not coining enough words to be able to operate according to criteria of this kind. As a descriptive factor applying to *langue* rather than to competence, such a procedure can be seen as relevant, though. That is, preference patterns may be a statement about how such processes happen to have been used in a particular society rather than anything to do with competence (even that of the ideal speaker-listener). It is thus a descriptive problem to decide how or whether such factors should be treated in a grammar that aims to reflect competence. If they are listed, they seem to be going beyond competence, and if they are not listed, some important facts about word-formation seem to be lost. On the other hand, such tendencies are not generally discussed in the transformational literature: for example the tendency for passives in English to occur with no agent or with a long agent phrase is never built in as a filter on the passive transformation. For some discussion of the status of such tendencies see Aronoff (1976: 55), Chambers & Trudgill (1980: 155–61), the works of Labov and, particularly, Romaine (1981), where it is argued that such tendencies are not reflections of competence.

Part of the reason for the semantic preferences in the base of *-ese* formations mentioned above is presumably the factor of hypostatization (or requirement of existence, see §4.5.1.1), in that a characteristic jargon must be related to language users in some guise. These preferences are thus at least partially pragmatic. On the other hand, the apparent preference for proper nouns in the base is a grammatical factor which ought possibly to be listed. This is not the only suffix to show a preference for proper nouns. For instance, the suffix *-iana* can be added to common nouns, as is shown by the existence of *railroadiana* (*OEDS*) and *whaleiana* (*OEDS*), but these are the only two examples of *-iana* being added to something other than a proper noun among the sixteen examples of *-iana* listed by the *OEDS*.

The converse of the listing of preference factors, the listing of non-preference factors, presumably also has to be considered. Since preference factors do not necessarily provide an exhaustive list of all possible formations from a given process, it is possible that there are also other types of base which, while productive, are productive to a very limited degree, not because of phonological, morphological or semantic limitations, nor because of problems of hypostatization, but simply because there is a preference not to use that particular pattern. The use (prior to the present century) of *-ee* to correspond to the meaning of the subject of the base verb, might be a case in point. If a decision is taken to list preferences as part of the grammar, it will also have to be decided whether such non-preference factors must be listed as well, or whether the listing of preferred types automatically implies that all other types are of lesser productivity. The difficulty will only really arise where there are several non-preferred types, all of different degrees of productivity.

8.2.3 *The suffix '-i'*

In this section the nationality forming suffix *-i* will be discussed, though for a number of reasons a lexical entry for it will not be specified. This suffix illustrates yet another kind of limitation on the base in word-formation processes.

The suffix *-i* appears to be fairly new in English, and surprisingly enough the *OEDS* does not discuss its etymology. It would appear that it originally came into English in loan words and has subsequently become an English suffix in its own right: according to the *OEDS* neither *Iraqi* nor *Kashmiri*, for example, are loans. This does, however, point to a problem in dealing with this suffix. It is not clear to what extent *-i* can be said to be a productive English suffix – at least partly because it is not clear how many of the words in which *-i* appears are English formations. The number is certainly small, and the English formations are certainly a minority of the words in which the suffix *-i* can be analysed. The list below is not necessarily exhaustive, and does not distinguish between native formations and loans:

Adeni (M)	Iraqi (M)
Afghanistani (ALD)	Israeli (M)
Bahraini (ALD)	Kashmiri (M)

Bangladeshi [attested in radio interview]	Kuwaiti (M)
	Pakistani (M)
Bengali (M)	Punjabi (M)
Bhutani (ALD)	Yemeni (M)
Bihari (*OEDS*)	Zanzibari (M)

The question is whether such of these words as are English formations are formed by analogy or by productive rule, and the borderline between the two is evidently not as clear as was suggested in §4.5.6.

In all these formations, the base is the name of a country or region (Marchand, 1969: §4.79.9 adds "quasi-state"), and the derivative denotes the human inhabitants of the state or region, or the national of the state. In every case the derivative is also used as an attributive adjective (although in the case of *Israeli* this seems to be officially frowned upon: see the *OEDS* under *Israel*, quotation for 1972). The major reason for the queries about the productivity of the suffix -*i* is the small number of new words using it. This can be explained by the small number of new countries emerging and the consequent small demand for new words showing nationality. Derivatives in -*i* are not formed for established states because of blocking: *Egyptian*, *Iranian* and *Lebanese* block **Egypti*, **Irani* and **Lebanoni* (although *Kashmirian* has not prevented the formation of *Kashmiri*, no doubt because both words are so rare, and *Kashmirian* was not well enough established to act as a block).

One consequence of this is that generalizations made on the basis of the available data about -*i* are automatically suspect. This is the prime reason for not providing a lexical entry for this suffix here. In particular it is not clear whether there are any phonological restrictions on the bases of this suffix, although it seems likely that there are: consider the potential words *Lebanoni, Libyai, Moroccoi*.

However, it does seem fairly clear that there is at least one important limitation on the base. As the *OEDS* notes, the country has to be in the East or Near-East. In practice this appears to mean in an area bounded by approximately the following degrees of latitude and longitude: 10°S, 40°N, 30°E, 100°E. Now obviously it is absurd to claim that the speaker coining new words must have a mental picture of the world including degrees of latitude and longitude. On the other hand, the area delimited above does not correspond to any clear geographical area. Perhaps the best that can be said is that certain areas, notably the Indian sub-continent and the Arabian peninsula, are seen as centres in which the -*i* suffix can be applied, and that the use of the suffix radiates from these centres, weakening as it goes.

However this limitation is conceived or formulated, it is clear that it is a type of limitation that has not been discussed previously in this book. The examples of semantic limitations discussed in §4.5.3.4 were ones where a semantic feature or set of semantic features (in one case a superordinate) defined the set of bases that could undergo the word-formation process in question. In this case the semantic or pragmatic information required is not whether the base belongs to a general category, but whether it has a precise location in the real world.

Finally, it is worth noting that although the class of -*i* derivatives is very small, there is still room for lexicalized forms in it. *Israeli* must be taken to be phonologically lexicalized for every pronunciation of *Israel* except /ˈɪzreɪl/. In all other -*i* derivatives, the form of the base remains unchanged. But in /ɪzˈreɪli/ there is vowel deletion (from /ˈɪzreɪəl/ or /ˈɪzreɪel/) or vowel change (from /ˈɪzrɪəl/), and there is also stress shift.

Israeli is also unusual semantically in that it contrasts with *Israelite*, 'an inhabitant of the Israel of Biblical times'. No other -*i* word contains a similar implicit contrast. However, this is not crucial, since the prior existence of *Israelite* can be seen to block the extension of *Israeli* to all natives of Israel at all points in its history, and so restrict the meaning to an inhabitant of modern Israel. It should be noted that no other country has a similar lacuna in its history to make a distinction such as that between *Israelite* and *Israeli* necessary.

8.2.4 *The suffix '-nik'*

Consideration of the suffix -*nik* recapitulates many of the problems that have been considered in the last three sections, but adds more because of the size of the sample and the complexity of the semantics of -*nik*. It also illustrates some of the difficulties there can be in dealing with word-formation from a purely formal angle. It turns out that there are several kinds of -*nik* suffix which have to be kept separate. The fact that a single form can have more than one meaning is frequently a problem in the study of word-formation, since it is not always clear what status should be given to the various meanings. Diachronically they may be explicable as extensions of a unified original form, as coincidentally homonymous, or as derived from two homonymous forms; synchronically such distinctions are not necessarily relevant. It is not necessarily obvious whether it will be preferable to list such forms as different affixes or as slightly different (or radically different) meanings of a single affix. Factors such as the form class of the derivative produced by the affix, the form class of the base (where relevant), and limitations on the base might be expected to distinguish between these two categories, so that homonymous affixes would provide or apply to different form classes and show different phonological limitations on the base, while extensions of the same affix would produce forms of the same form class from bases of the same form class with the same limitations on the base. However, even such criteria will not always provide clear answers to the problems raised by such forms. Alternative approaches to word-formation where this kind of fact would not create any problem at all are, of course, quite feasible – in fact one will be discussed briefly below (§8.5). Discussion of *-nik* will show, though, how such matters can complicate the analysis of a word-formation process within the approach that is being used here.

8.2.4.1   '-nik' as in 'sputnik'
        Many of the earliest coinages in *-nik* have bases which end in

$$-X\begin{Bmatrix}[\Lambda]\\[\upsilon]\end{Bmatrix} [+ \text{Obstruent}]\#$$

and are evidently based directly on *sputnik*. The variation in the base reflects variation in the pronunciation of *sputnik*: either /spʌtnɪk/ or /spʊtnɪk/. English coined words which fit with this limitation include:

dudnik (R)	phutnik (Mi, R)
enoughnik (Mi, R)	puffnik (Mi, R)
jutnik (R)	pupnik (R)
kaputnik (A, K, Mi, R)	rebutnik (Mi, R)
muttnik (A, K, Mi, R)	whuffnik (R)
nutnik (R)	woofnik (R)

and also, since it was coined in American English, where *what* is pronounced /hwʌt/,

> whatnik (A, R)

At this stage, a lexical entry for -*nik* can be postulated as follows:

(i)   Segmental form: /nɪk/
   Suprasegmental form: stress on base; no stress change [that is, -*nik* is preceded by a # boundary]
(ii) Suffix forming [+ Concrete], [+ Count] nouns
(iv) Satellite
(v)   Used especially in slightly jokey words
(vii) Base may be a noun, interjection or adjective
   Base has form

$$X \left\{ \begin{matrix} [ʌ] \\ [ʊ] \end{matrix} \right\} [+ \text{Obstruent}] \#$$

If only one such word had existed, it would have been possible to speak of an analogical formation. With so many it seems fairer to speak of a rule, even though many of the words were coined independently and at about the same time.

It would create a neat diachronic succession if it could be shown that the next stage followed this stage, but unfortunately the two appear to have been synchronous. At stage I, -*nik* was isolated as a suffix, at stage II, -*nik* was added to bases which were not phonologically restricted. In particular, words were coined for two events: (1) the launching of a satellite with a dog inside in November 1957 and (2) the failure of an American satellite (a *Yanknik* (A, K)) to be launched in December 1957.

(1)   dognik   poochnik (A, R)
   and examples quoted above with [ʌ]/[ʊ]

(2)   flopnik (A, Mi, *OEDS*, R)   pfftnik (R)
   goofnik (A, Mi, R)   sputternik (A, H, K, R)
   ifnik (Mi, R)   stallnik (Mi, R)
   latenik (Mi, R)   stayputnik (Mi; in H, R
   oopsnik (Mi)   'fixed satellite')

At this stage the lexical entry for -*nik* might be modified in the following way:

(iv) Satellite connected with the base
(vii) Base may be any lexeme or interjection

Note that at this stage there still seems to be a preference for the base to end in an obstruent, but this restriction did not last long. The connection with the base tended to be looser than in the examples already quoted. As far as I can tell (though not all of the sources cited give definitions in all cases) the *-nik* formations listed below still fit this revised lexical entry. (In this list, * marks those bases which do not end in an obstruent, and † marks the examples in which the form appears to have been influenced by the original *sputnik*.)

beepnik (R)	samnik* (R)
disputnik† (H)	spacenik (H, R; in Mi 'spaceman')
frasnik (R)	spoofnik (Mi 'hoax sputnik'; R 'hoax
hoaxnik (R)	spaceman')
icenik (R)	spooknik (R)
Ike-nik (H)	stayputnik† (H, R 'fixed satellite'; Mi
lightnik (R)	'December 1957, failed satellite')
lunnik* (H, R)	Uncle Samnik* (R)
moonik* (R)	USnik (R)
mousenik (K, Mi, R)	

In at least two cases, creativity seems to have operated simultaneously with productivity to give *Bronxnik* (R) and *milknik* (R), where the entity denoted is like a sputnik, rather than being a satellite – in *Bronxnik* because it flies ('flying manhole cover') in *milknik* because of its appearance ('rocket-like machine for experimenting with milk'). There are also two formations which are interesting in different ways. *Churchnik* (R) is a model rocket used by a minister to illustrate his sermon. If a strict account of the meanings of these formations is kept in terms of what is located where, then *churchnik* 'the sputnik is in the church' is just the inverse of, say, *muttnik* 'the mutt is in the sputnik'. The vague "connected with" used in the lexical entry above – which seems to be fairly typical of word-formation – means that this does not become a problem. The other formation is *pednik* (R) 'a toy sputnik driven by a pedal' where the *ped-* element can only marginally be said to be a base at all (in words like *biped*), and certainly not a lexeme. This suggests that box (vii) in the revised lexical entry above should be further modified to read:

(vii)   Base may be any lexical base

Alternatively, it might be taken to mean that /nɪk/ had itself become re-analysed as a stem, and that formations like *churchnik* should really be treated as compounds. This conclusion might be supported by formations like *cutnik* (R) and *jetnik* (R) where the semantic relationship between the two parts is a "like" relationship, which is common in compounds. A *cutnik* is a hair-cut that looks like a sputnik, a *jetnik* is a car fitted with an ejector seat which, presumably, puts someone in orbit like a sputnik. Yet another alternative is that the preference for a vowel + obstruent pattern at the end of bases before *-nik* should have led to the deletion of the [l] in *pedal* and the [k] in *(e)ject*.

Other formations which clearly come under the *sputnik* umbrella are humorous punning formations which are analogous formations, remotivated morphologically because of the existence of the *-nik* suffix. There are three of them in the corpus: *bottlenik* (R) 'satellite delayed by a bottleneck in production'; *picnik* (R) 'a pic(ture) of a (sput)nik'; *saintnik* (R) 'reindeer, belonging to Saint Nick, which fly through the sky'. These, while depending on the existence of *-nik* for their remotivation, should not be expected to be generated by the *-nik* rule. The same is true of the cartoon character *demonik* (A, H, R). All of these words can be seen as blends motivated by puns, and thus as non-rule-governed.

8.2.4.2 '-nik' as in 'beatnik'

There has been a certain amount of discussion in the literature about whether the *-nik* in *beatnik* is "the same" *-nik* as in *sputnik* or a different suffix (see e.g. Adams, 1973; Barnhart *et al.*, 1973; Kiparsky, 1964). If it is a different suffix, then it is a suffix borrowed from Yiddish and found in (American English) *nudnik* or *nudnick* 'tedious person' (first quotation in the *OEDS* for 1947). I believe that there are two *-nik* suffixes, for the following reasons:

1. The *OEDS* lists *stuck-upnik* with a reference to 1945, before the sputnik era. This seems totally parallel to *far-outnik* (A, H) which is a postsputnik (H, Mi, R) formation. It seems nonsensical to say that these two should have different suffixes, only the latter being the *-nik* from sputnik.

2. The *sputnik -nik* apparently stopped being productive early in the 1960s (possibly when sputniks were replaced by space probes and artificial satellites). The person suffix *-nik* as in *beatnik* is still productive. Rudnyckyj, writing just past the height of the sputnik era, lists a clear preponderance of *sputnik*-type formations in *-nik*. A few years later still,

Barnhart *et al.* list only *beatnik*-type words. The last quotation for a -*nik* word in Barnhart *et al.* (1973) is for 1970. The suffix may have died since then.

3. Rex (1975) cites a letter from the person he claims first coined the word *beatnik*, where the coiner states that he believes -*nik* to be a Yiddish suffix. This assumes, of course, that Rex has actually found THE coiner of the word, and not A coiner of the word.

This is not to deny that the two -*nik* suffixes have had a considerable influence on each other. If it is THE coiner of *beatnik* who has been contacted by Rex, then he admits to having been influenced by the then (early 1958) current craze for *sputnik* -*nik* words. It seems that *sputnik* gave *nudnik* a new lease of life, and *nudnik* has since gone on to outlive *sputnik*.

Whether the *beat* in *beatnik* means 'tired' or 'rhythm' is not really relevant for the argument here. However it started life, though, it seems likely that at one stage it was understood as 'rhythm', and there is a whole series of other musical -*nik* words which may have been motivated by this reading.

Just as *sputnik* formed a phonetic pattern for later formations, so *beatnik* (not *nudnik*) formed a phonetic pattern in /i/ + obstruent, though this pattern can never have provided more than a preference:

beachnik (A, H, R)	elitenik (H)
beaknik[6] (H)	greasenik (A, H)
bleatnik (H)	peacenik (A, B, H)
cheatnik (H, R)	

Chicnic (H) may or may not belong in this group, depending on how Frenchly it is pronounced. The quotation in Harder (1966: 151) suggests a pronunciation /ʃiknɪk/. Otherwise it is obviously motivated in part, at any rate, by internal rhyme, along with *sicknik* (H, *OEDS*) and *slick-nik* (H).

The other preferred patterns for this -*nik* suffix concern (1) fans of a particular kind of music and (2) rebels against the established order.

---

[6] Also June Kay. 1970. *The Thirteenth Moon*. London: Hutchinson, p. 88, where it means 'white headed vulture'.

(1)   drumbeatnik (R)   popnik (A)
         folknik (A, H)   rocknik (A, H)
         jazznik (B)   soulnik (H)

(2)   draftnik (H, *OEDS*)   so-whatnik (H)
         limpnik (A, H)   Vietnik (B, H, *OEDS*)
         protestnik (A, B, H, *OEDS*)

Following from group (1), the meaning 'fan, supporter of' seems to be quite widespread:

boatnik (A, H)   knitnik (H)
cinenik (B)   OOB-nik (H) [*OOB* is
computernik (B, *OEDS*)   an acronym for
discothequenik (A)   'off-off-Broadway']
fashionnik (H)   Shakespearenik (A, H)
filmnik (B)   Spaaknik (R)
Freudnik (*OEDS*)   sportnik (H, R)

By far the largest group is the one where *-nik* appears to mean simply 'person'. Despite the fact that this is where the meaning appears to come closest to the Yiddish original, this requires some explanation. The difficulty is to explain why the suffix *-nik* should have been used rather than some other word-formation process, for instance, suffixation of *-er*, *-ist*, *-ite* or compounding. Adams (1973) points out that many of the people who use these words are Jewish, thus probably familiar with Yiddish, and this might provide a partial explanation, though it cannot explain the use of *-nik* by gentiles. Limitations on other kinds of suffixes may help in the explanation here, but cannot provide the whole story: in particular they cannot account for the use of *-nik* in preference to compounding. The explanation seems to reside partly in the craze for words in *-nik* which seems to have existed in the early 1960s in particular, so that other things being equal a *-nik* formation was felt to be more fashionable. Part of the explanation also lies in the style of words in *-nik*. They tend to be slightly "derogatory, inviting disparagement or ridicule" (Barnhart *et al.*, 1973), to sound rather slangy or jargony, or to have overtones of hippiedom and youthfulness brought over from the meanings listed above:

allrightnik (A)   passnik (R)
beautnik (H)   phonnik (R) [< *phoney*]

butnik (Mi, R) [for meaning
see below]
citynik (B)
courtnik (H)
dotnik (Mi, R) [for meaning
see below]
failnik (R)
far-outnik (A, H)
flipnik (H) [meaning obscure,
?flip person]
goodwillnik (B)
holdupnik (A)
hutnik (Mi, R) [for meaning
see below]
jobnik (B)
monknik (A)
nogoodnik (A, B, H, R)
nudenik (H, K)
poetnik (A)
popcornik (R) 'salesman of

popcorn'
prutnik (Mi) [for meaning see
below]
putnik (Mi, R) [for meaning
see below]
scholarnik (R)
straightnik (A 'conventional
person trying to be
unconventional'; *OEDS*
'heterosexual')
subnik (H) [*sub* =
'submarine']
sweetnik (K; H gives a
different meaning, see
§8.2.4.6)
tigernik (R) 'tiger keeper in a
zoo'
way-outnik (A, H)
yutnik (Mi, R) [< *youth/
young*]

As far as this kind of *-nik* formation is concerned, the lexical entry would be rather complex, but would have to have something of the following form:

(i)   Segmental form: /nɪk/
(ii)   Suffix forming [+ Human] nouns
(iv)   Relatively young; fan, supporter; <anti-authority>
(v)   Derogatory, inviting ridicule; trendy; slangy
(vii)   Base may be a lexeme or idiomatic phrase

– where the angle brackets only apply when the angle brackets in the following list of preference factors conducive to the use of a particular base in *-nik* formations also apply:

$$X\begin{bmatrix} i \\ + \text{ Stress} \end{bmatrix} [+ \text{ Obstruent}]$$

Semantics: connected with music
<Semantics: connected with protest movement>

The term "idiomatic phrase" is used in (vii) because all of the bases which are phrases seem to be either phrasal verbs (*holdupnik*) – which are arguably one lexeme – or phrases which have collocational cohesion, if not idiomatic status (*allrightnik, goodwill-*

nik, faroutnik, nogoodnik, stayputnik, stuckupnik, wayoutnik).
This fits in well with what seems to happen in *-er* formations on
phrasal bases, where the same cohesion is found (Bauer, 1979d).

The only formation that may have a root rather than a lexeme as
its base is *cinenik*, where *cine* is probably a bound form, though
some speakers use it as a clipped form of *cine-camera*. It might be
possible for an extra category, bound root, to be added under (vii)
in the lexical entry. This might also apply to *phonnik*, though it
seems more likely here that a clipped form is being used as a base.
Butnik, dotnik, prutnik, putnik and *yutnik* are formed on created
bases which seem to have little in common with their presumed
etymologies (*business, dormitory, program, physical* and *youth*
respectively) other than their initial consonant or consonant cluster
in the written form. These formations are all from a single source
(YMCA Brooklyn, November 1957) and may have been formed
before *beatnik*. It is noteworthy that the vowel in these formations
(and *hutnik*, which comes from the same place, but is apparently
rather more motivated) is mainly /ʌ/, and that they all end in /t/,
under the influence of *sputnik* – indeed, this seems to have been a
major factor in their formation. Formally these words belong in the
first list in §8.2.4.1, and they only fit here semantically, where they
are virtual anachronisms.

8.2.4.3 Mixed '-nik's

There are a few formations where the *sputnik -nik* and
the *beatnik -nik* seem to have become confused. These are:

lizardnik (R)	spacenik (H, Mi, R) [also listed above]
mannik (R)	spoofnik (R; Mi has another meaning)
peoplenik (R)	titnik (R)

There may also be others that I have inadvertently listed in the
sputnik group. A *lizardnik* is a passenger [which is a lizard?] in a
toy sputnik; a *mannik* is the person in the sputnik rather than a
sputnik containing a man; *peoplenik* are the kind of people you
would like to see shot into outer space; a *spacenik* may be a
spaceman or someone who claims to associate with spacemen; a
spoofnik is a spaceman; and *titnik* is a woman riding on a rocket. In
each of these the 'satellite' meaning and the 'person' meaning seem
to have become confused. While three of these might be generated

by the rules for *beatnik* *-nik* formations, *lizardnik* and *peoplenik* appear to be totally perverse formations, and I do not know how they would be best dealt with.

8.2.4.4 "Russian" '-nik's

In a very limited number of formations, the *-nik* suffix seems to be used partly to make the new word sound Russian, or sound as if it refers to Russians. The items concerned are:

> Ivan Birchnik (H, specified as being Russians in the quotation) [see also *(John) Bircher, Birchite* (Barnhart *et al.*, 1973)]
> snuffnik (R) 'Russian preparation to guard against influenza, which is sniffed'
> speednik (Mi, R) 'TU 114 aircraft'
> sportnik (R; H gives a quotation which does not appear to refer to Russians)

In *Nureyevnik* (H) the Russianness implied by the *-nik* would seem to be totally redundant.

The otherwise totally irregular formation *fufnik* (H; adjective; meaning unclear) may be used in a similar way to show Jewishness, though there is not enough information to be sure about this.

8.2.4.5 Playful formations

There are a very few *-nik* derivatives which are not formed according to the rules, and probably not by analogy (as defined in §4.5.6) either. They are coined (especially by headline writers) to be eye-catching rather than meaningful. These include:

> daynik (A, R) "every dognik has its daynik"
> deadnik (R) "Sputnik may be deadnik"
> neatnik (H, R) "beatnik goes neatnik"
> offshootnik (Mi) "*Sputnik* and some of its offshootniks"

For want of a better term, these may be called **playful formations**. The only rule here, if it is sensible to talk in terms of rules at all, seems to be:

> lexeme + *-nik* → lexeme / another *-nik* formation

This may also be true of *spotnik* (Mi, R) where *sputnik* is present by implication, though a pun is also involved here. The context is a cartoon showing the US President by the bedside of a sick NATO which has earth satellites orbiting its head, and the patient is saying

"I keep seeing spotniks before my eyes" (Minton, 1958: 117). In this category I would also class *shmunik* (H) "lunik shmunik". In such formations the phonetic sequence [nɪk] is more important than any semantic content associated with that sequence. Nonetheless, it seems to be important for most of these (though not for *shmunik*) that *-nik* can be isolated as an affix.

8.2.4.6 Other '-nik's

This does not exhaust *-nik* formations. One meaning of *beachnik*, for example, is 'shorts', where the *-nik* seems to be remotivated from *knickers* (Adams, 1973). This meaning also seems to be involved in *completenik* (H) 'a sweater to go with trousers' and possibly, though this is not clear, with *chicnik* (H), which is listed above under a 'person' meaning. An alternative is that *tunic* may be the remotivating force in these formations, as it is in one meaning of *sweetnik* (H), not to mention the formation *tune-ik* (H) 'a tunic for tuned-in people'.

Other formations cannot be explained by this kind of remotivation. In some of these formations the style seems to be the only motivating force. In others, it is not even clear that the style allows the formation.

> bellnik (R) 'stomach ache'
> Eucnic (R) ' large [Euclid?] tractor'
> loconik (H) meaning unclear
> oatnik (R) 'race horse'
> smoochnik (R) 'kissing date'
> smugnik (R) ?'smug'
> splitnik (H, R) [meaning unclear, possibly 'duplex apartment']
> yulenik (R) 'Christmas test'

It is not clear to what extent these formations can or should be accounted for by rules. Nor do they seem to be playful or analogical formations in the senses in which these have been defined. This has quite serious consequences for a theory of word-formation, because if it is always the case that there is a residue of "irregular" formations, then it is not clear how successfully word-formation can be treated as rule-governed behaviour. Admittedly, these words are only about 5 per cent of those listed in this section, but that is too high a proportion for them simply to be ignored. There may be several reasons for this "irregularity".

1. The analysis provided here might not be the best possible. This is quite likely, but it is not clear to me how the analysis would have to be changed to accommodate these examples.

2. It might be possible to extend the notion of playful formation to cover these formations. While this would undoubtedly be able to cope with the range of formations, it is not clear that it should be extended in this way. In particular it is not clear how far the notion can be extended if it is to remain a principled factor in word-formation.

3. There might be one or more further regularities which the data have not shown up.

4. There might be other homophonous *-nik* suffixes.

5. There might always be "incompetent" formations, which do not catch on precisely because they break the rules, but which can be recorded when *hapax legomena* are being recorded. This would fit with the (rather dismissive) comments in Bauer (1978d: §§1.1.4, 5.5.2) that rules for compounding are rather more relaxed in newspaper headlines than elsewhere. Part of the reason for such incompetent formations might be that the people who coin them make generalizations on the basis of a very small amount of data, without knowing what patterns are going to become accepted in society. In favour of this analysis it should be pointed out that only formations listed in §§8.2.4.1–2 appear to have become established; that is, only the major patterns have provided more than nonce words. In advertizing and headline writing the demand for an eye-catching label might over-rule the normal constraints on word-formation processes. How big a problem this irregularity is for word-formation will not be known until more studies have been done, but it is potentially a huge stumbling block for a generative theory.

8.2.5 *The suffix '-esque'*

All the suffixes that have been considered so far have been noun-producing suffixes (with the marginal case of *-i* which also produces adjectives). In this final section on suffixes, the adjective-producing suffix *-esque* will be considered, and it will be seen that the same kinds of problem exist here, though the limitations discussed will be slightly different.

Although the suffix *-esque* is found in many words where it has been added to a common noun base (*picturesque*, *statuesque*), it seems that this is a process of marginal productivity. Productively, *-esque* appears mainly to be added to proper nouns, and moreover, proper nouns which are surnames. The following list illustrates this:

Audenesque (*OEDS*)	Disneyesque (B, *OEDS*)
Browningesque (*OEDS*)	Garboesque (J, M)
Caravagg(i)esque (*OEDS*)	Gershwinesque (B)
Carlylesque (*OEDS*)	Hemingwayesque (M)
Casanovesque (J)	Kiplingesque (J, M)
Chandleresque (B)	McCarthyesque (B)
Chaplinesque (*OEDS*)	McLuhanesque (B)
Dantonesque (*OEDS*)	Molieresque (J)
Dickensesque (*OEDS*)	Shawesque (J)

There are also a few words where the suffix is added to a common noun base:

goblinesque (B)	robotesque (B)
lawyeresque (M)	teacheresque (M)

Whether *-esque* is added to a common noun or a proper noun, the meaning is 'in the manner or style of the person in the base' (Jespersen, 1942: 326), 'having the (artistic, bizarre, picturesque) style of the person in the base' (Marchand, 1969: §4.34).

There seems to be a preference for the base to be polysyllabic (*Shawesque* is the only monosyllabic base above), and, as Jespersen remarks, "if the word from which the adj is derived ends in a vowel this is dropped (Casanov(a)esque), if semantic reasons do not prevent this (Garboesque)". There are two points of interest here. Firstly, although it is fairly clear that the "semantic reasons" referred to have to do with the recognizability of the base (*Garbesque* would not obviously be related to *Garbo*), it is by no means clear how this is to be formalized for a generative grammar. Secondly, the vowel referred to by Jespersen must be orthographic and not phonetic: *Chandler*, *Disney* and *Shaw*, for example, end in phonetic vowels, but not in orthographic vowels. This seems to suggest that the orthography of an element can in some cases be as important as the phonological structure of that element, and is thus another instance of the orthographic form of an item being basic to the spoken form, although the norm is for the spoken form to be primary (Lyons, 1968: §1.4.2, 1970: 18).

All this can be captured with a lexical entry like that given below; but it should be noted that some of the terms in the lexical entry demand the application of human intuition for their correct interpretation:

(i)   Segmental form: /esk/
                Suprasegmental form: stress on suffix
(ii)   Suffix forming adjectives
(iv)   'Having the manner or style characteristic of the person in the base'
(vii)   Base denotes a person
                Where the base is a [− Common] noun, monosyllabic bases tend to be avoided
                Bases which end in an orthographic vowel delete that vowel provided that the base remains recognizable

This kind of formulation allows the analyst to make predictions about which bases will and which bases will not be able to undergo *-esque* suffixation, but there is another problem with *-esque* which this kind of approach can never solve. The problem is to decide, in any given case, which of several competing suffixes will be added to a given base to form an adjective. When adjectives derived from personal names are considered, it is fairly clear that *-ian* is the commonest suffix: a count of adjectives derived from personal names in the letters B, C and F of the *OEDS* reveals that about 60 per cent of them use *-ian*. The rest are distributed among seven suffixes as follows:

	per cent
-ese	2·8
-esque	15·4
-ic	2·8
-ine	1·4
-ish	5·6
-ist	4·2
-ite	8·4

There do not appear to be any phonological factors determining which of these suffixes is used – in fact, there are several cases where there are alternative suffixed forms from the same base, so the suffixes are clearly not in complementary distribution determined by the phonological structure of the base. Such semantic criteria as may distinguish between the suffixes are extremely weak. For example, in this small sample from the *OEDS* and in the word-list of Barnhart *et al.* (1973) the suffix *-ist* is used only to form adjectives showing a connection with political groups. It is, however, not the only suffix used in this way (*-ite* is another) and examples can be found outside this small corpus where *-ist* is not used in this way. Even stylistic differentiation of the various suffixes cannot be motivated from the citations in my sources. Many speakers apparently feel that *-esque* and *-ite* in particular are derogatory in tone, but this is not supported by the following citations:

> The most spectacular Caravaggioesque [*sic*] light and shade (A. Huxley, cited in the *OEDS*)
> All over America these pretty Disneyesque buildings proliferate (P. H. Johnson, cited in the *OEDS*)
> The formation of the 'new woman' of the Ibsenite and Shavian period (*The Listener*, cited in the *OEDS*)

While it would be foolish to deny that such connotations may be found in some words formed with these suffixes, it does not seem to be the case that they are the inevitable consequence of these particular suffixes. Perhaps the most typical situation is for adjectives derived from the same proper name to be synonymous, at least in some usages. Thus Chapman (1939: 76f) lists *Dickensian*, *Dickensesque*, *Dickenesque*, *Dickensish*, *Dickensy* and *Dickeny* as synonymous, although there are undoubtedly speakers who would distinguish between *a Dickensian slum* and *a Dickensesque novel*. The *OEDS* lists *Ibsenesque*, *Ibsenian*, *Ibsenish*, *Ibsenist* and *Ibsenite* as synonymous (note that *Ibsenist* does not have anything to do with a political movement, despite the use of *-ist*). Other sets listed as synonymous in the *OEDS* include *Browningesque*, *Browningese*, *Browningite*; *Carrollese*, *Carrollian*, *Carrolline*; *Casanovaish*, *Casanovesque*, *Casanovian*; *Chamberlainic*, *Chamberlainite*. Barnhart *et al.* (1973) contains the set *Zhdanovian*, *Zhdanovist*, *Zhdanovite*. Theoretically, this situation should not pose any problem for a generative account of word-formation, since it is rarely the case that a surface structure is uniquely determinable from a particular deep structure; what is crucial is that the deep structure is uniquely recoverable from the surface structure. Nevertheless it is awkward because there do not appear to be any consistent correlates of the various patterns, as there would be for most syntactic rules. The conclusion that the various suffixes are distributed strictly according to probabilistic patterns once again seems inevitable, given the level of our present knowledge, but it is not an attractive conclusion. The discussion here is merely intended to show that there are problems connected with suffixation which are not discovered by an analysis of each suffix separately.

8.3 Combining forms

Combining forms and neo-classical compounds have already been discussed at length in §§6.5.8, 7.3. In this section three combining forms, one Initial Combining Form (ICF) and two Final Combining Forms (FCFs) will be considered in more detail, and some of the problems raised by combining forms, particularly ICF's, will be discussed.

8.3.1 *The combining form '-naut'*

The first combining form to be considered here is *-naut*. Originally from Latin NAUTA 'a sailor', this made its way into English through the mythical *Argonauts* and then, because it had connotations of exploration and adventure, spread, with the advent of ballooning, to *aeronauts* (Adams, 1973: 183). Preliminary rules for the phonological form of ICFs were discussed in §7.3: either the ICF ends in a vowel, usually *-o*, or it is formed from a lexeme, by conversion if the lexeme ends in a vowel, otherwise by adding *-o*. Both of the words mentioned so far are loans rather than English coinages, yet the presence of the *-o* makes them look as though they might have regularly formed ICFs. The existence of *aeronaut* gave rise to a whole series of flying nauts:

astronaut (L)	luna(r)naut (A, B)
cosmonaut (L)	stratonaut (L)

and, whether because of the original Latin meaning of *nauta*, or whether because *-naut* became reinterpreted as meaning 'person enclosed in the way that an astronaut is' with the connotations of exploration and adventure persisting, to a series of sailing nauts:

aquanaut (A, B, L)	hydronaut (A, B, L)
bathynaut (A, L)	oceanaut (A, B, L)
hovernaut (A)	

All these, with the exception of *oceanaut*, are either formed by combining with established ICFs or according to the rules given above. *Oceanaut*, according to the rules discussed above, might be expected to have the form *oceanonaut*, but the /n/ at the end of *ocean* and the one at the beginning of *naut* appear to have coalesced instead. The question of whether this is rule-governed or not will be taken up again below.

I have found three formations which appear to belong to this series but which require further comment. The first of these is *plastinaut* (A, L) 'artificial astronaut made of plastic'. The most important point here is the form of the ICF. It cannot have been created from *plastic* by the rules discussed above, nor can it have been created by truncation of the *-ic* ending, since the predicted form would then be *plasto-* (cp. *electro-*) or possibly *plastio-* (cp. *physio-*). Both *plasti-* and *plasto-* exist in other combinations, but both are rare, *plasti-* more so than *plasto-*. *Webster's* lists only *plastisol* with *plasti-* (*plastidome* is from *plastid + ome*) but several forms with *plasto-* including *plastomer*, *plastometer*, *plastotype*, *plastochron*. The question of exactly how ICFs are formed when they are not formed by the simple addition of *-o* is one of the problems which will have to be solved if this type of word-formation is to be accounted for by rule. For the moment the problem will be allowed to remain unresolved, and other similarly awkward forms will be pointed out later.

The other interesting point concerning *plastinaut* is that the semantic relationship between the two elements is different here from that in all the other words listed. Previously the first element has always been a locative, giving the area of exploration or the vehicle being 'sailed' in. Here the *plasti-* element gives the material from which the passenger is made. In this, words made up of combining forms can again be seen to resemble compounds closely.

The same can be seen to be true with the next example, *chimponaut* (A, L), where there is yet another semantic relationship between the two elements (the astronaut is a chimpanzee). Here the form of the ICF is unproblematical, although there is a variant here, *chimpnaut* (L), which seems to be totally irregular. This is the third form, and provides a direct counter-example to the rules which have been proposed.

With the exception of *chimpnaut* and *oceanaut*, all the forms discussed so far can be generated using the information provided in the following lexical entry, along with a few general rules:

(i)   Segmental form /nɔt/
         Suprasegmental form: stress on the ICF

(ii)   FCF forming [+ Human] nouns

(iv)   Person travelling in an enclosed vehicle; connotations of exploration, adventure

General rules:

(1)   FCFs combine only with ICFs

(2)   The semantic interpretation of neo-classical compounds follows the same rules as the interpretation of compounds

(3)   The form of an ICF is either:
        (a) lexically listed
        (b) lexeme + -*o* (Condition: the final phoneme of the lexeme is not a vowel)
        (c) lexeme (Condition: the lexeme must normally end in a vowel)
        (d) The -*o* at the end of the ICF may be truncated when the FCF begins with a vowel

There are three more words in my corpus denoting persons. *Brokernaut* (A) comes from an advertisement where insurance brokers were said to be "able to get you off the ground with your insurances (*sic*)", so that the formation is definitely based on *astronaut*, with the ICF formed regularly. The lexical meaning of -*naut* is completely lost at the expense of its connotations, even if it is assumed that a *brokernaut*, like a *chimponaut*, actually goes into orbit himself. A *cybernaut* (A) is an explorer and innovator in the area of cybernetics. Again the 'enclosed traveller' part of the meaning has disappeared, and the connotations have become the most important part. Finally, *responaut* was the title of a periodical for people living in breathing apparatus (Adams, 1973: 186). The -*naut* element here seems to focus on the 'enclosed' part of the meaning. The *respo*- element apparently comes from *respiratory* or *respiration*. *Respiro*- might have been the expected form here (cp. *respirometer*), and this is another case where the method of formation of the ICF is not clear, and where it is questionable whether it could have been predicted.

As far as the -*naut* element is concerned, it seems that in these final examples the semantic reading has been changed to something like:

(iv)   (adventurer, explorer) (travelling) (especially in space) (in an enclosed space)

where any combination of the parenthesized elements is possible.

Such a reading is, of course, still compatible with the words listed earlier. As Adams (1973: 186) points out, words in *-naut* seem to imply favourable judgements of the people involved, and this information could be added to the lexical entry for this element, in box (v).

This does not exhaust the formations in *-naut*, however, though the remainder do not denote persons. The most familiar of these is *Juggernaut* (L), and the others may be based on this word. It should be noted that the *-naut* in *Juggernaut* is not a morpheme in its own right, and etymologically has nothing to do with the other *-naut* that has been discussed here. *Juggernaut* is a loan from Hindi, and originally referred to an idol drawn on a huge cart, under whose wheels devotees sacrificed themselves. The extension of the term to cover heavy lorries in Great Britain provides a clear example of creativity as opposed to productivity.

The other two vehicular *-nauts* are *aluminaut* (A) and *telenaut* (A). Both are underwater vehicles, and the *tele-* in the second refers to the TV cameras with which it is equipped. Whether *Juggernaut*, *astronaut* or *Nautilus* is the motivating force behind these formations is not clear, and there are not enough forms to allow prediction of trends. The form of the ICF in *aluminaut* is interesting, though. Presumably it comes from the American English form *aluminum*, with the deletion of the *-um*. The expected form might then be *aluminonaut* (cp. *aluminotype*, *aluminothermic*). But here again, as in *oceanaut*, the two /n/s seem to merge rather than be repeated, and this suggests (though the number of examples is too small to be conclusive) that this might be a regular way of forming the ICF before *-naut*. This suggests the following revised rules for the formation of the ICF:

(a)   ICF lexically listed
(b)   lexemic base → ICF [there is a possibility that this could be more precisely formulated as an instruction to delete a few specific endings such as *-ic* and *-um*]
(c)   base of form XV(n) → ICF of form XV
(d)   base of form XC + *-o* → ICF (Condition: C≠ /n/)

These revised rules, which should be read as applying only before *-naut* because of the specificity of the /n/, still do not account for the form of the ICF in *plastinaut* and *chimpnaut*, and do not account for the deletion of more than suffixes in the ICF of *responaut*. Just how general rules of this type are, and whether any of these last three forms can be said to be regular, are problems which can only be solved when a far larger sample is analysed in detail.

As an FCF, *-naut* is not very productive, and only about 20 examples have been considered here, of which some (*Argonaut*, *Juggernaut* at least) must probably be said to be lexicalized, and others (*astronaut*, *cosmonaut* at least) are institutionalized. The sample is really too small to allow any hard and fast conclusions. Nonetheless, there is sufficient information to show that some of the problems (e.g. the semantic extension of the FCF) are similar to those found in suffixation (note the treatment of *-nik* above), but that this kind of word-formation also brings up new problems, notably the form of the ICF. In the next section another, slightly more productive FCF will be considered, to show how general these problems are.

8.3.2 The combining form '-crat'

As far as institutionalized words in *-crat* are concerned, there is almost always a corresponding form in *-ocracy*. This gives rise to a preliminary problem, which is to decide whether the existence of a *-crat* word presupposes the prior existence of an *-ocracy* word, or indeed the converse. Quirk *et al.* (1972: 995), for example, assume that *-crat* words are derived from *-ocracy* words. While this may be true of established words, it does not seem to be the case with productive uses of the forms. There are a number of new *-crat* words where there is no preceding *-o-*, which is always present in the *-ocracy*, e.g. *educrat* (B) and *minicrat* (A). Conversely, there are many *-ocracy* words which do not have a corresponding *-crat* word, especially, but not exclusively, when the first element in these words denotes a person: *cottonocracy*, *foolocracy*, *hagiocracy*, *hierocracy*, *meritocracy*, *pornocracy*, *strumpetocracy* (all L). This suggests that productively *-crat* and *-ocracy* may be considered as two independent combining forms, even though they have a lot in common both formally and semantically.

Many formations in *-crat* are quite old, going back at least to the sixteenth century (notably *aristocrat* and *democrat*), but *bureau-crat*, which seems to have given a new lease of life to the combining form, is a relatively recent formation (mid-nineteenth-century). There is a problem in deciding whether these old formations are lexicalized or only institutionalized. It will be assumed here that they are only institutionalized, unless evidence is uncovered for lexicalization.

Many of the formations in *-crat* have standard ICFs, i.e. ones which might be expected to be listed in the lexicon. These are:

aristocrat (L)	monocrat (L)
autocrat (L)	ochlocrat (L)
biocrat (B)	physiocrat (L)
chemocrat (L)	plutocrat (L)
democrat (L)	technocrat (L)
Eurocrat (A)	thalassocrat (L)
gyn(a)ecocrat (L)	theocrat (L)

As far as *democrat* is concerned, this could very well be the source of *demo-* as an ICF, a fairly rare ICF, occurring also in *demography* and possibly in *demotic*. All of these could be learned loans. Another word which might belong in this list is *pantisocrat* (L), where there are actually two ICFs *pant(o)-* and *iso-*, both of which are frequently found in other combinations.

Semantically, all those marked (L) might be glossed as 'supporter of a (political) system'. It is only a small step from that to 'member of a ruling faction or elite' which seems to be the more usual meaning (not only in more recent formations based primarily on *bureaucrat*, but also in some of the words above: *aristocrat*, *plutocrat*, *theocrat*). It might be argued that this in itself shows that these forms are actually lexicalized.

The next set of forms all have *-crat* added to a lexeme + *o* except where the lexeme ends in a vowel. These words are:

bankocrat (M)	mobocrat (M)
bureaucrat (L)	pedantocrat (L)
Dixiecrat (A)	shamocrat (L)
landocrat (L)	shopocrat (M)
millocrat (L)	slavocrat (L)

As far as *slavocrat* is concerned, (L) lists an alternative spelling for *slaveocracy*, though not for *slavocrat*. As far as can be seen, *-crat* in these formations has the meaning 'member of a ruling faction or elite', rather than merely 'supporter of a system'.

This leaves three forms to be accounted for:

educrat (B)   minicrat (A)
Eisencrat (A)

Educ- might be taken to be the root of *education*, with /kk/ being reduced to /k/ in the same way that /nn/ was reduced to /n/ in the -*naut* formations. *Eisen-* (from *Eisenhower*) cannot, however, be explained in the same way. It is doubly awkward, firstly because of the deletion of -*hower* which is not a morpheme, and secondly because it ends in a consonant which is not homorganic with the initial consonant of the FCF. What appears to have happened is that *Eisenhower* was clipped, possibly for reasons of conciseness, and that no modification was made to the form for reasons of recognizability (see the discussion relating to *Garbo* above, §8.2.5). *Minicrat* looks as though it might belong in the first group with established ICFs, except that the context makes it seem likely that it is meant as a contraction of *minister* or *ministry*, possibly with an intentional pun on the normal meaning of *mini-*: "These records . . . are also going to be available to any Jack-in-office working for the Minister of Health . . . Once again, the fact that these minicrats would have to get permission from their boss before they snoop affords no protection" (cited in Adams, 1973: 184). The influence of the normal *mini-* would seem to be the only possible influence on the form of the ICF here. In all of these three, the meaning is either the same 'member of a ruling faction or elite' or 'bureaucrat connected with ICF'. This meaning might also be given to some members of the previous series, e.g. *biocrat, bankocrat, Dixiecrat, Eurocrat*. This seems to be the latest development in the meaning, though it is difficult to say whether other meanings have ceased to be productive or not. The style of -*crat* words with this meaning is clearly derogatory.

The rules provided for the creation of forms with the FCF -*naut* can be modified in obvious ways to provide the rules for the creation of forms in -*crat*. The problems associated with the two FCFs can be seen to be very alike, the major one still being the form of the ICF.

8.3.3 *The combining form 'bio-'*

The extremely productive form *bio-* has been chosen here as an example of an ICF. All the words in this section are taken from Barnhart *et al.* (1973). While it would be a simple matter to expand this corpus, there are more words considered in this section than there were in either the section on -*naut* or the section on -*crat*.

The majority of forms with *bio*- have an unmodified lexeme as their second element. That is, *bio*- acts just like any other prefix:

bio-acoustics	biogeology
bio-contamination	biohazard
biocybernetics	biomathematician
biodegradability	biomedicine
biodegradable	bio-parent
biodegradation	biopolitical
biodegrade	bioproductivity
biodestructible	biorhythm
biodeterioration	biosatellite
bioengineer	bioscience
bioengineering	bioscientific
bioethics	bioscientist
bioexperiment	biotelemetric
biofeedback	biotelemetry

One notable factor here is that when one lexeme with a given root is prefixed by *bio*-, the other derivatives with the same root also occur prefixed by *bio*-. The clearest example in this corpus is *biodegradability*, *biodegradable*, *biodegrade*, *biodegradation*, but there are also others. To a certain extent, it seems misleading to say that *bio*- is prefixed to each of the lexemes independently, and yet the alternative, to set up a root *biodegrad* and then add suffixes is even less satisfactory, and clearly counter to the actual historical process involved: -*ation* is probably no longer a productive nominalization suffix where the base does not end in -*ify* or -*ize*. The most useful idea here seems to be one of **word families** (the term is taken from Orsman, 1979). The existence of one prefixed form in a word family tends to imply the (at least potential) existence of the prefixed form for all other members of the word family, and the new word families thus formed may be seen as the result of a single simultaneous prefixing operation, even though the new words will obviously emerge in some kind of serial order in the language.

Semantically, it is hard to improve on Barnhart *et al.*'s definition of this element: 'biological; relating to living things'. The relationship between the ICF and the second element is variable, as in compounds (see the discussion above with reference to -*naut*):

compare *biodestructible* where the *bio-* is instrumental with *bio-science* where the science is biological, and *biosatellite* where the satellite carries life.

The second, much smaller, group is made up of an ICF and an FCF:

biocidal	biocrat
biocide	biomorphism

Bio- here is semantically identical with *bio-* as prefixed to lexemes, and the relationship between the two combining forms is still variable.

There is not really enough data here to be sure about the form of the ICF. It appears to be completely stable, but there are no examples in this corpus of it appearing before an *o* (cf. institutionalized – and possibly lexicalized – *biology*). The *OEDS* lists only two forms which might be of relevance here, and both were probably coined before the First World War: *biome* (from *bio* + *ome*, first citation 1916) and *biopsy* (from *bio* + *opsis*, 1895). The dislike of pairs of identical vowel letters brought about by the collocation of two combining forms is obviously not complete: *Webster's* lists *retro-ocular*, *retro-operative*, *photooxidation*, *para-anesthesia* among others. Yet the dislike seems to be as much for two identical LETTERS to occur together as for two identical SOUNDS to occur together, note the occurrence of *polyimide*, for speakers of varieties of English where *poly-* ends in /ɪ/, and *polyestrous*, *polyene*, for speakers of varieties of English where *poly-* ends in /i/. The form of the ICF thus remains a problem even, in some cases, with established ICFs.

It is interesting to note the relatively small number of formations where *bio-* is added to an FCF. This does not seem to be simply coincidental. Of 87 *bio-* formations in the *OEDS*, only nine are composed of combining forms, *biocide* (which was also listed in Barnhart *et al.*) and:

biogen	biomorph
bioherm	biophor(e)
biolith	biostrome
biolysis	biotope

The significance of this is, however, not clear to me.

8.4 **Prefixation: the prefix 'non-'**

The prefix *non-* shows immense productivity. The *OEDS* alone lists over 500 "of the more frequently occurring formations", and less frequently occurring formations can be found without difficulty in technical, semi-technical and journalistic writing. *Non-* is always added to a lexeme, and almost always to a noun or an adjective, where 'adjective' is taken to subsume participles (two classes of exceptions will be mentioned below).

The basic meaning of *non-* is negation or 'lack of' (Algeo, 1971), such that the prefixation of *non-* divides the world up into two classes: those things denoted by the non-prefixed lexeme, and those denoted by the prefixed lexeme. In this way, prefixation with *non-* often provides a contrast with other kinds of negative prefixation, especially on adjectives, because other kinds of negative prefixation frequently give rise to antonymy rather than to complementarity (see Lyons, 1968: 461 for the terms). Algeo (1971: 90) gives the following examples:

A Moslem is a *non-Christian*, but only a Christian can be *un-Christian* in behavior. A *nonrealistic* novel is one whose goal is other than a realistic view of the world, but an *unrealistic* novel is likely to be one that aims at, and fails to achieve, realism

He points out that similar distinctions can be made for other pairs, e.g. *nonbeliever* ('Person without religious beliefs' – W) and *unbeliever* ('One who does not accept a particular religious belief, an infidel' – *OED*). Lyons (1977), like many others, produces new technical terms in accordance with this distinction, and one passage (1977: 154) is worth quoting at length as a clear example of the type of distinction there is between *non-* and other negative prefixes:

To be distinguished from asymmetrical, intransitive and irreflexive relations are non-symmetrical, non-transitive and non-reflexive relations. A relation, R, is non-symmetrical if and only if it is not symmetrical: i.e. if for some (though not necessarily all) values of x and y, $R(x, y)$ holds, but not $R(y, x)$. It follows that (except for the empty relation, which is both symmetrical and asymmetrical), all asymmetrical relations are non-symmetrical, but not conversely. The terms 'non-transitive' and 'non-reflexive' are distinguished from 'intransitive' and 'irreflexive' in similar fashion.

This meaning of *non-* can be termed the 'exclusive' meaning. It seems that only the exclusive meaning of *non-* is applicable when *non-* is prefixed to non-participial (!) adjectives. *Non-* with exclusive meaning can be added to compound adjectives with a participle in final position, although none of these were found in the corpus provided below. The *OEDS* lists a few, such as *non-English-speaking* and *non-habit-forming*, and *non-rule-governed* is used just below. It seems curious that there should be so few examples of exclusive *non-* added to nominal compounds, particularly given the size of the sample below and of that in the *OEDS*. To a certain extent, this is a result of lexicographic method. *Nonmember bank* (W) is likely to be listed simply as *nonmember*, and so appear as if *non-* is prefixed to a non-compound base. However, it is still odd that *non-* is so rarely attested as a prefix on a compound which is written as one word (*non-householder* (M) is the only example in the corpus). If this is a genuine preference, it is the first sign that there might be some sort of difference between single and double stressed compound nouns. It seems equally likely, however, that these forms are not listed in dictionaries simply because they look like nonce words, and are not among "the more frequently occurring formations". *Non-blackbird*, for instance, does not strike me as an impossible word, and *non-classroom teaching* seems perfectly acceptable, though *non-slumlord* from *slumlord* (B) does sound slightly less probable.

The second meaning of *non-* can be termed the 'pejorative' meaning. Algeo (1971) glosses this meaning as 'possessing the superficial form but not the values of'. Algeo suggests that the earliest examples of this meaning are *nonbook* and *nonevent* from the early 1960s, but the *OEDS* gives a quotation with this meaning for *nonlecture* as early as 1953. Whereas *nonactor* with the exclusive meaning of *non-* means simply 'someone who is not an actor' (see the *OEDS* quotation from 1937), *nonactor* with the pejorative meaning of *non-* means 'someone who is in a situation where an actor is called for, but who does not actually act' (see Barnhart *et al.*'s quotation). A *nonbook* is a volume with no literary or scientific merit: coffee-table books often count as nonbooks. This particular meaning of *non-* grew rapidly in the 1960s and 1970s, as the examples cited by Algeo show. Pejorative *non-* seems to be exclusively prefixed to nouns. The counter-examples cited by Algeo are both playful formations:

> The sheer nothingness to which Republicanism, under the Tribune's leadership and that of other *like-minded* or *non-minded* men, has been reduced

> It is a *non-book*, so to speak, *non-written* by Andy Warhol

If these are taken as non-rule-governed playful formations, the note above on participial adjectives can be deleted, so that when *non-* is prefixed to an adjective it always has the exclusive reading.

The third meaning of *non-* is what Algeo terms the 'dissimulative' meaning. He glosses this as 'possessing the value, but not the surface characteristics or acknowledged identity of', and points out that lexemes with dissimulative *non-* are not necessarily pejorative in tone. This meaning should be compared with the meaning of pejorative *non-*, of which it is virtually the converse. The clearest example of this usage is probably *noncandidate*. The illustrative quotation below is taken from Barnhart *et al.* (1973):

> One of the most maddening candidates in the political race is the noncandidate . . .
> He is the fellow who is being talked for the race but who will just never admit his candidacy until the last minute.

That is, the person being discussed is really a candidate, but denies the appropriateness of the label *candidate*; if *noncandidate* were used in the pejorative sense it would mean that the person concerned claims to be a candidate, but for some reason (e.g. he is not expected to appeal to the voters) is not a serious contender for the post. Algeo is, as far as I know, the only scholar to have commented on the dissimulative use of *non-*, and he does not provide very many examples of it. Some forms appear with both pejorative and dissimulative readings (e.g. *nonhero*, as a synonym for *antihero* in the pejorative reading, and referring to Vietnam veterans with the dissimulative reading), and in many cases an exclusive reading and a dissimulative reading seem fairly close. These words are difficult to spot, but may well be on the increase.

A fourth meaning of *non-* creates adjectives from verbal bases, with the reading 'that does not V' or 'that is designed not to V'. In the corpus provided here, only one such form was found (*nonstick* (B)) but the *OEDS* adds *noncrease*, *noncrush*, *nondazzle*, *non-shrink*, *nonskid* and *nonslip*.

There are a few adverbs with a *non-* prefix, but remarkably few.

My corpus includes only one: *nonspecifically* (Ly). The *OEDS* lists eight. But presumably an adverb can be formed from any *non*-prefixed adjective, so that the productivity of adverbs with *non*-must be seen as fairly unrestricted.

The corpus that was used in arriving at these generalizations is given below. In order to keep the corpus down to a manageable size, forms listed only in the *OEDS* are not included here. This does not appear to make any difference to the semantic categories that are established, though it does mean that the proportion of *non*- words in the various categories is not representative. The list in the *OEDS* suggests that the currently most productive use of *non*- is as an exclusive prefix added to adjectives, but the data in Algeo's paper virtually ignored this reading. A few forms are listed in more than one place, when they appear with more than one reading of *non*-. These forms are followed by an asterisk. For illustrative quotations, the reader is referred to Algeo (1971), Barnhart *et al.* (1973) and the *OEDS*.

A. Exclusive *non*-

1. Prefixed to an adjectival base:

nonabsorbent (Al)	nongenerative (Ly)
non-active (M)	nonhuman (Ly)
nonbelligerent (M, *OEDS*)	nonlinguistic (Ly, *OEDS*)
nonbiodegradable (B, *OEDS*)	nonmodal (Ly, *OEDS*)
nonbreakable (Al, M)	nonnative (Al)
noncompetent (M)	nonnuclear (B)
nonconstative (Ly)	nonopen (Ly)
noncontributory (Al, *OEDS*)	nonpast (Ly, *OEDS*)
nondefensive (M)	nonporous (Al, *OEDS*)
nondefinitive (Ly)	nonprejudicial (Al)
nondegradable (B)	nonprosodic (Ly)
nondeictic (Ly, *OEDS*)	nonproximal (Ly)
nondescriptive (Ly, *OEDS*)	nonreflexive (Ly, *OEDS*)
nondisposable (B)	nonstandard (Al)
nondisruptive (B, *OEDS*)	nonsymmetrical (Ly, *OEDS*)
nonefficient (M)	nontransformational (Ly)
nonelectronic (B, *OEDS*)	nontransitive (Ly, *OEDS*)
nonepistemic (Ly)	nontrivial (B, *OEDS*)
nonethnic (B)	nonuniversal (Ly)
nonfiscal (M)	nonverbal (Ly, *OEDS*)
nongaseous (M)	nonvocal (Ly, *OEDS*)

Where the adjective is participial:

nonaligned (B)
nonanalysed (M)
noncommitted (B, *OEDS*)
nongraded (B)
noninterrupted (M)
noninvolved (B)

nonirritating (M)
nonisolating (Ly)
nonliving (Al, *OEDS*)
nonpolluting (B, *OEDS*)
nonsalaried (Al)

2. Prefixed to a nominal base:

nonabstainer (M)
nonaccomplishment (Ly)
nonactor (*OEDS*)*
nonaddict (B, *OEDS*)
nonadherence (M)
nonaerospace (B)
nonaggression (M, *OEDS*)
nonastronaut (B)
nonbeliever (Al, M)
nonbelligerence (M)
nonblack (B, *OEDS*) [noun]
noncolour (B)
noncombustion (M)
noncommitment (Ly)
nonconviction (M)
noncreditor (M)
nondealer (M)
nondemand (?) (M)
nondepositor (M)
nonestablishment (B)
nonexercise (?) (M)

nonexistence (Ly)
nonfactive (Ly)
nonfriend (B)
nonheathen (M)
nonheritor (M)
nonhouseholder (M)
nonkernel (Ly, *OEDS*)
nonlanguage (Ly, *OEDS*)*
nonlead (B)
nonmusician (B)
nonparishioner (M)
nonproducer (M)
nonproliferation (B)
nonremoteness (Ly)
nonresident (M, *OEDS*)
nonstudent (Al, M)
nonsympathizer (M)
non-U (Al)
nonviolence (Al)
nonwhite (Al, *OEDS*) [noun]

B. Pejorative *non-*

1. Prefixed to a nominal base:

nonaction (Al)
nonactor (B)*
nonanswer (Al, *OEDS*)
nonarchitecture (Al, *OEDS*)
nonart (Al)
nonauthor (Al)
nonbook (Al, *OEDS*)
noncampaign (Al)
noncase (Al)
noncommunicating (Al,
   OEDS) [noun]
noncommunication (Al,
   OEDS)

nonleader (Al)
nonliving (Al) [noun]
nonmeaning (Al)
nonmoney (Al)
nonmovement (Al)
nonmovie (Al)
nonmusic (Al, *OEDS*)
nonname (Al)
nonnation (Al)
nonnetwork (Al)
nonnewsconference (Al)
nonnovel (Al, M)
nonpainting (Al)

nonconclusion (Al)
noncountry (Al, *OEDS*)
noncourse (Al)
noncrime (Al)*
nondance (Al)
nondebate (B)
nondiscipline (Al)
nondrama (Al, *OEDS*)
nonemergency (Al)
nonending (Al)
nonestate (Al)
nonethic (Al)
nonevent (Al, B, *OEDS*)
nonexperience (Al)
nonexpose (Al)
nonface (Al)
nonfact (Al)*
nonfood (Al)
nongovernment (Al)
nonhappening (Al, B)
nonhero (Al, *OEDS*)*
nonhistory (Al)
nonhomily (Al)
noninformation (B)
noninterview (Al)
nonissue (Al, B)
nonlanguage (Al)*

nonperson (Al, *OEDS*)
nonplanning (Al) [noun]
nonplay (Al, B)
nonpoems (Al)
nonpolicy (B)
nonpolitician (Al)
nonproblem (Al, *OEDS*)
nonprogram (Al)
nonreply (Al)
nonromance (Al)
nonscript (Al)
nonshow (Al)
nonsolution (Al)
nonstate (Al)
nonstatement (Al)
nonstory (Al, B)
nonsupper (Al)
nonsystem (Al)
nonteacher (Al)
nontheology (Al)
nonthinking (Al) [noun]
nonthought (Al)
nontitle (Al)
nonword (Al)
nonworker (Al)
nonwriter (Al)

2. Playful formations prefixed to a participial base:
nonminded (Al) nonwritten (Al)

C. Dissimulative *non-*
nonacting (Al)
nonbuilding (Al)
noncampaign (Al)
noncandidacy (Al, B, *OEDS*)
noncandidate (Al, B, *OEDS*)
noncrime (Al)*
noneclipse (Al)
nonfact (Al)*

nonfamily (Al)
nonhero (Al)*
nonmagazine (Al)
nonprofit (Al)
nonschool (Al)
nonsuit (Al)
nonwar (Al)
nonwatch (Al)

D. Adjective-forming *non-* on a verbal base

nonstick (B, *OEDS*)

E. Adverb in *non-*

nonspecifically (Ly)

The considerable lack of overlap in the bases to which the different kinds of *non-* can be prefixed might lead one to the conclusion that separate prefixes are involved here rather than one polysemous prefix, the possible exception being the pejorative and dissimulative meanings which, while in some sense the negation of each other, are clearly closely related semantically, and they both apply to the same classes of base.

The lexical entries for the various types of *non-* should be deducible from the discussion above, but they are summarized here:

(1) (i)   Segmental form: /nɒn/
     (ii) Prefix, class-maintaining
     (iv) Complementary of the base
     (v)   Technical, objective
     (vii) Base must be an adjective or a noun

(2) (i)   Segmental form: /nɒn/
     (ii) Prefix, class-maintaining
     (iv) Possessing the superficial form, but not the value of the base
     (v)   Pseudo-technical, pejorative
     (vii) Base must be a noun

(3) (i)   Segmental form: /nɒn/
     (ii) Prefix, class-maintaining
     (iv) Possessing the value, but not the surface characteristics or acknowledged identity of the base
     (v)   ?Whimsical
     (vii) Base must be a noun

(4) (i)   Segmental form: /nɒn/
     (ii) Prefix forming adjectives
     (iv) That is designed not to perform the action described by the base
     (v)   Predominantly advertising and commercial
     (vii) Base must be a verb

Pattern (1) is the preferred pattern, patterns (3) and (4) are both weakly productive.

8.5 Subject nominalizations

There is a class of nominalizations which is sometimes given the name 'agentive nominalization' in the literature (e.g. Lees, 1960; see above, §6.7). This class is made up mainly of forms such as *baker*, *examiner*, *killer*, where the suffix *-er* is added to a verbal base. 'Agentive nominalization' is actually a misnomer because such forms do not always denote agents, in any normal sense of the term 'agent'. In words like *curler*, *opener*, *synthesizer* the derivative in *-er* denotes an instrument; in words like *lover* the derivative denotes an experiencer or patient. These various semantic effects, however, can be given a unitary explanation if it is said that the derivative is a lexeme which is a typical subject for the verb used in the base: a curler curls, an opener opens, a lover loves, and so on. A better name for this group of nominalizations, therefore, is **subject nominalization**, although this label will cover more than just *-er* suffixation. In this section, subject nominalizations which are also animate nouns will be considered.

When subject nominalizations are considered in the literature, the word-formation process that is usually discussed is *-er* suffixation. This is not, however, the only word-formation process involved in subject nominalizations. Others are *-ant* suffixation (*attendant*), *-ee* suffixation (*escapee*, see above, §8.2.1) and conversion (*nurse* n, v). At least two of these are still productive, though neither of them is as productive, in this meaning, as *-er* suffixation.

In earlier sections of this chapter the processes of word-formation have been considered from a very restricted viewpoint: it has generally been assumed that the affix to be used is known, and that the class of bases that may be used with that affix is restricted in various ways by the affix concerned. Little attention has been paid to the question of how it is known which affix should be used. In some cases this is not a problem: *-able* is the only affix with a meaning of the type 'able to be Ved', and *-ee* is the only suffix with the meaning 'person who is Ved'. In other cases, as was shown with the competing adjectival suffixes (§8.2.5), the problem can be considerable. In this section word-formation will be approached from a rather different point of view: rather than taking the word-formation process as a given, the question will be posed as to whether it is possible to predict which word-formation process will be used in any given formation. To the extent that it is possible to do this on the basis of semantic or stylistic information, this will lend support to a theory of word-formation that takes its starting point in some kind of semantic or cognitive structure (as is hinted at in Bolinger, 1975: 109).

A priori, a theory which starts with the notion of having

"something to say" and works towards the way in which that something is expressed seems very satisfactory. This is perhaps particularly true in the field of word-formation, where it is frequently possible to catch the native speaker in the act of coining a new lexeme to fit a concept. Moreover, in some cases at least, it does seem possible to begin with the semantic notion to be expressed and to predict the word-formation process that will be used on the basis of the base chosen and the semantic modification required: this is perhaps particularly true where there are very few affixes used to provide a particular semantic effect. The question is, then, whether this is always possible.

It is clearly the case that in any absolute sense such a hypothesis will not hold. This is shown by the numerous instances of synonymous derivatives formed by contrasting word-formation processes. Examples from Barnhart *et al.* (1973) are *jurimetricist* and *jurimetrician*; *juicehead* and *juicer*; *optical artist*, *op artist* and *opster*; and so on. The discussion of adjectival suffixes in §8.2.5 provides further counter-examples. On the other hand, it is not clear whether such examples are the exception or the rule. This will now be considered on the basis of data from subject nominalizations formed in *-ee*, *-er* or by conversion from a verb base.

The data on which the discussion is based are given below. Most of the words in *-ee* have been listed earlier (§8.2.1), and sources for these are not given. All the cases of *-er* suffixation and conversion are taken from Barnhart *et al.* (1973).

-ee suffixation:

adaptee	meetee
attendee[7]	mergee
charteree	resignee
dilutee	retiree
embarkee	returnee[9]
escapee	standee
knockee[8]	waitee[10]

---

[7] Isaac Asimov. 1976. *Authorised Murder*. London: Gollancz, p. 9. 'Person attending a conference'.

[8] Attested in conversation, 1980. 'Person knocking at a door'.

[9] Leon Uris. 1958. *Exodus*. New York: Doubleday. 'Person returning to the homeland [Palestine]'.

[10] Heard on Radio New Zealand's National Programme, 9 June 1980. 'Person waiting in a waiting-room'.

-er suffixation:

blitzer	petnapper
blockbuster	rapper
converger	scrambler
defuser	skinny-dipper
diverger	skyjacker
dropper-in	speed-reader
floater	swinger
hyper	trasher
jostler	

conversion:

drop-in	orienteer
drop-out	skyjack
lech	

There are a number of points to note about this body of data. Firstly, the relatively high number of *-ee* formations listed here is due less to the inherent productivity of the suffix in this meaning than to my personal awareness of the suffix, which has led to my noting down a lot of scattered examples. Since I have not noted examples of the other two patterns to the same extent, but have drawn the examples purely from Barnhart *et al.* (1973), the comparative productivity of the patterns is not accurately reflected in the data: in real terms the *-er* class is by far the largest, even more so than is shown by the data here. Secondly, there are two instances in the data here of pairs where the same meaning is provided by two forms: *dropper-in* and *drop-in*; *skyjacker* and *skyjack*. Since these cannot be distinguished semantically, the question must be posed as to whether they can be distinguished in any other way.

The obvious way to make the distinction is in terms of style. This seems to work quite well for the first case, *dropper-in* vs. *drop-in*. There is great difficulty in forming *-er* subject nominalizations from phrasal verbs, and there are five competing patterns. The first is to add *-er* to the verbal base before the particle, as in *dropper-in*, *finder-out*, *see-er-off*. The second, a very rare one, is to add *-er* to the particle, as in *come-outer*. The third is to prepose the particle and add the *-er* to the verb, as in *onlooker* (see Jespersen, 1942: 236 for all these). The fourth is to add the *-er* to both the verb and the

particle, as in *breaker-inner*,[11] *cleaner-upper*.[12] The fifth is to omit
the particle completely, as in *waiter* (from *to wait on somebody*)
(Jespersen, 1942: 236). Of these, the first and fourth tend to feel
very clumsy, and as a result tend to be used mainly in colloquial
speech; the second, as I said, is very rare, because the suffix seems
to be added in the wrong place; the third and fifth both lose the
coherence of the verb + particle unit: in particular the fifth would
probably not be connected with the phrasal verb. Both the
awkwardness of the patterns and the fact that there is such a wide
choice of patterns provide excellent reasons for avoiding the
problem if possible, and the conversion option allows the whole
problem to be avoided. One result of this is that the converted form
drop-in sounds rather less colloquial than the *-er* form *dropper-in*.

The same is not so obviously true with *skyjacker* and *skyjack*. I
am not personally familiar with the word *skyjack*, and find myself
unable to predict any stylistic difference between it and *skyjacker*.
The entries in Barnhart *et al.* (1973) do not allow any conclusions
to be drawn. This looks like a case of free variation, although it
should be noted that the *-er* variant appears to be the more
common.

To the extent that there is any general principle operating in this
set of data (or perhaps more accurately, to the extent that I am able
to detect any general principle operating here) it seems to be that
-er should be used unless there is a reason not to use it. The reasons
for not using *-er* vary from word to word.

In four cases blocking appears to prevent the use of *-er*: *adaptee*
(*adaptor* is an instrument), *knockee* (*knocker* is an instrument),
mergee (*merger* is what the mergees are a party to) and *waitee*
(*waiter* is a profession). *Attendee* is awkward, since the established
form here is *attendant*, not *attender* (although this form is listed by
the *OED* with quotations up to the nineteenth century, while
attendee is listed with the appropriate meaning in *Webster's*). If
this is a case of blocking, it is blocking of a very different type.
Meeter might have been blocked by the homophonous *meter/metre*,
and further stylistic reasons may also have played a role here.

It might be expected that *lech* would be blocked by the synony-

---

11 L. Egan. 1978. *A Dream Apart*. London: Gollancz, p. 63.
12 Heard on Radio New Zealand's National Programme, 9 June 1980.

mous *lecher*, given that Aronoff (1976: 56) predicts that it will be impossible for there to "be two words with the same meaning and the same [root] in the same person's lexicon at the same time". The key to this might be the phrase "in the same person's lexicon" – it might be that *lech* was used by somebody who did not have *lecher* in his vocabulary (perhaps only temporarily, due to a momentary recall problem). Another possibility is that the two are distinguished in style, *lech* being more colloquial than the fairly formal *lecher*. If this is the case, then Aronoff's statement quoted above will need to be modified to allow stylistic variants based on the same root.

It is probably misleading to list the word *escapee* here at all, since it is not an English formation but a nineteenth-century loan from French. Its etymological source explains why *-er* was not used.

Some of the words seem to have the form they have because of analogy (see §4.5.6 for a discussion of analogy). These are *orienteer* (possibly on analogy with *volunteer*; the existence of an *-eer* suffix denoting persons seems important here), *resignee* (possibly on analogy with *designee*) and *returnee* (possibly on analogy with *internee*). The use of *charteree* rather than *charterer* may be due to a phonological constraint. Despite the existence of a few words like *adulterer*, *plasterer*, *poulterer* and *sorcerer* which end in /ərə/, Marchand (1969: §4.30.17) shows that the pattern is fairly rare, and most of the words he cites with this pattern came into English before the seventeenth century. The pattern of *drop-out* has already been discussed in connection with *drop-in*.

This leaves four forms unexplained: *dilutee*, *embarkee*, *retiree* and *standee*. The only reason I can think of for why these should use the *-ee* suffix rather than *-er* is that, although the people concerned are potential subjects for the verbs in the bases, they are felt to be affected by circumstances rather than acting of their own free will. This "explanation" is far less convincing for *embarkee* than for the other three items.

It can be seen that this type of approach to the study of word-formation deals far more with imponderables than the approach which has been taken in the larger part of this chapter, and there are a number of gaps which are left unexplained. None the less, it does seem to be possible to show why certain affixes are chosen in particular cases. The danger with this kind of approach, of course, is that it is far easier to justify the use of a particular word-formation process *post hoc* than it is to predict which process will be used before the event. This means that this type of approach is far less satisfactory in a generative model than the approach which has been used earlier in this book. It should also be noted that a crucial assumption was made at the outset, namely that animate subject nominalizations provide a coherent area of study. While this may be so, it has certainly not been shown to be so.

The conclusion of this section must be that it is by no means always possible to predict which word-formation process will be used to form a new lexeme in any particular instance, but that the formation of new lexemes is, nevertheless, far from random. Despite the dangers of posthockery implicit in the approach that has been taken here, it can cast some light on word-formation which other approaches would not be able to.

9
Conclusion

Trotz beträchtlicher Fortschritte ist die Bemerkung Wilhelm von Humboldts auch heute noche gültig, dass die Wortbildung den "tiefesten, geheimnisvollsten Teil der Sprache" bilde. [Despite considerable advances, Wilhelm von Humboldt's remark that word-formation is the "deepest, most secret part of language" is still valid even today.]

(Motsch, 1977: 201)

In the past, the majority of studies of word-formation or word-formation processes have not distinguished between productive processes and lexicalized material. While such studies provide a wealth of extremely valuable data, it has been suggested here that the only realistic way of gaining a proper understanding of the way in which word-formation works is by ignoring lexicalized forms and concentrating on productive processes.

Those scholars who have distinguished between productive and non-productive formations have usually taken the distinction no further. It has been shown that there is a vast number of factors, not all of them linguistic, which can limit productivity, and that productivity must be viewed as a cline, with some processes being more or less productive than other processes.

Some of the theoretical linguistic factors involved in word-formation have been discussed, and it has been shown how lexicalization and productivity affect the syntactic and phonological descriptions of word-formation that have been proposed in the literature.

An outline of the possibilities that are, or have been, available in English word-formation was given, showing just how wide a range of patterns can be found. Finally, a few examples of productive processes were considered in greater detail, to show how the theoretical points that had been discussed in earlier chapters influence the study of actual data. It was pointed out that other methods of analysis can be used in the study of word-formation, and are valuable in that they throw a different light on the subject. Accordingly, it should not be assumed that the approaches used in this book are necessarily the best for any particular purpose, although they do provide a framework within which students can continue to make their own discoveries about word-formation.

One fact should be stressed: despite the amount of study of word-formation since the ancient grammarians described Sanskrit, word-formation study is still in its infancy, and word-formation is still a "most secret" area of language study. There are innumerable questions to which science has not yet provided answers. These involve not only the study of individual processes – the study of de-verbal nominalizations, the study of forms in *-esque* and *-ian* – but also general questions of theoretical interest. A number of questions have been posed in this book, some of which are:

(1)   How precisely is the meaning of a word-formation process constrained?

(2)   Is there a correlation in word-formation between productivity and precision in meaning?

(3)   Is the specification of syntactic constraints on the configurations used in the generation of instances of word-formation possible or necessary?

(4)   What part does orthography play in word-formation?

(5)   Is stress in compounds regular and predictable?

(6)   How are ICFs formed?

By far the most important question that has been raised in the course of this book (and particularly in chapter 8) is the question of irregularity in word-formation. To what extent is it true to say that the processes of word-formation are rule-governed? It has been assumed throughout this book that word-formation is rule-governed, but that the rules are complex and far from obvious. However, a number of points have been made which seem to suggest that word-formation, at least in some areas, may not be rule-governed at all. For example, in the discussion of *-nik* suffixation (§8.2.4) there was a residue of unexplained forms which, it was suggested, might be incompetent formations. In the discussion of subject nominalizations (§8.5) there was a small residue of non-*er* derivatives which could not be satisfactorily explained. In the discussion of neo-classical compounds (§8.3) there were several examples of ICFs which did not appear to have been formed according to the usual rules, and for which there was no apparent generalization to be made. The discussion of such processes as acronyming, clipping and blending (§7.8) made it clear that where there were generalizations to be captured they frequently depended upon notions such as euphony, which it may not be possible to formulate in generative terms. In all these cases it was suggested that the examples under consideration were exceptions to the general principle of regularity in word-formation – that they were possibly creative rather than productive, and so on. However, it might seem that rather too much is being swept under the carpet in this way, and it must be asked whether the processes of word-formation are in fact not rule-governed, whether they are in principle irregular.

If instances of word-formation are not produced by rules, then there must be some other process which allows them to be coined. This process is probably analogy (the term 'analogy' used now in a much wider sense than previously in this book). An "irregular" formation like *resignee*, according to this view, is not formed by a rule of *-ee* suffixation. Its form might, for instance, be determined by *resignation*. *Resignation* without the nominalization suffix is /rezɪg'n/, and the speaker, looking for a form to encapsulate the meaning 'one who hands in a resignation', a form with stress on the suffix, thinks of *resig'nee*. Had the speaker thought of the concept as 'one who resigns', *resigner* might well have been coined instead. There are thus two analogies determining *resignee* on this view: the phonological pattern of *resignation*, and the stress on the suffix *-ee*. In the case of the "irregular" formation *chimpnaut* the analogy might not be with other neo-classical compounds, but with a compound like *maid-servant*, with *naut* seen as a bound stem like *monger*. If instances of word-formation arise by analogy then there is in principle no regularity involved, and each new word is produced without reference to generalizations provided by sets of other words with similar bases or the same affixes: a single existing word can provide a pattern, but there is no generalization. The reader is invited to return to the irregularities mentioned in chapter 8 and consider them from this point of view, as possible cases of analogy. If it is true that there are in principle no generalizations, then a generative account of word-formation is at best a convenient fiction and at worst an irrelevancy.

Of course, it can be seen that there is regularity in word-formation: after all, most of the words discussed in this book have been attributable to regular patterns. But while such regularity is necessary if word-formation is seen as a rule-governed process, it is merely coincidental if word-formation is seen as an analogical process. This raises the question of whether it is possible to distinguish between a theory based on analogy and one based on rule-governed productivity. In Bauer (1979b: 366) I stated, perhaps rather prematurely, that the two are equivalent. They may be so in their results, but they are not necessarily so in their implications. The best evidence that rules rather than analogies are at work seems to me to lie in the fact of lexicalization of word-formation processes and in the existence of unacceptable forms for which there is an obvious analogy. If it is true that *bluen*, analogous to *redden*, is impossible, this suggests that rules are applying. Unfortunately, it is not absolutely clear that such a form is totally impossible.

At the moment, when comparatively little is known about word-formation, it is not even clear how big a problem this is. It may be assumed that it will always be possible to provide a model for a particular formation in terms of analogy, and that it will not always be possible to provide a rule to account for every formation. To a certain extent, this has been predicted by the discussion here, in that the emergence of new patterns has been allowed for. Only when more data have been analysed, however, and only when data from a wider range of languages have been analysed, will it become clear how large a proportion of formations the apparent irregularities make up, whether or not there are further subregularities which can account for all or some of them, and whether the subregularities are in fact any more than the linguist's constructs. It is by making the assumption that word-formation is regular (as has been done here) and pushing that approach to the extreme that linguists are most likely to discover whether the regularity hypothesis, the analogy hypothesis, or some compromise between the two is most suitable to account for the types of word-formation actually found. Consideration should also be given to the question of whether any solution here would have implications in the study of phonology and syntax, and if so, how far such parallels can be taken.

A second possible line of approach is through psychological testing. Such work as has been done so far is inconclusive, some of it seeming to suggest that productivity has psychological correlates

(Dressler, 1977; Whitaker & Whitaker, 1976), other projects seeming to suggest that analogy is a more likely basis for word-formation (Gleitman & Gleitman, 1970; Ohala, 1974; Wheeler & Schumsky, 1980). But these projects were not aimed specifically at this particular problem, and it is possible that psychological testing could show results that would give a better idea of how speakers actually use word-formation. It might, in this context, be worth speculating whether language users work by analogy whereas linguists interpret such behaviour in terms of rules, so that a linguist's description is inevitably a fiction.

With major questions like this still to be answered, it is obvious just how much research there still is to be done in word-formation, and why it should be the "deepest, most secret part of language". Nevertheless, there are grounds for optimism, since even such basic problems do not appear to be insoluble in principle. Word-formation seems to offer the opportunity for valuable and fruitful linguistic research, and a challenge which more and more linguists are taking up.

BIBLIOGRAPHY AND
CITATION INDEX

Adams, V. 1973. *An Introduction to Modern English Word-Formation*. London: Longman. *pp.* 2, 3, 5, 32, 33, 39, 43, 44, 82, 97, 98, 105, 140, 162, 184, 201, 202, 207, 208, 209, 211, 212, 226, 229, 231, 232, 233, 236, 243, 259, 261, 265, 270, 272, 273, 276.

Aitchison, J. & Bailey, G. 1979. Unhappiness about not unhappy people. *Journal of Linguistics* 15, 245–66. *p.* 68.

Aldrich, R. I. 1966. The development of "-scape". *American Speech* 41, 155–7. *p.* 96.

Algeo, J. 1971. The voguish uses of *non*. *American Speech* 46, 87–105. *pp.* 243, 279–85.

Algeo, J. 1977. Blends, a structural and systemic view. *American Speech* 52, 47–64. *p.* 237.

Anderson, J. & Jones, C. (eds.) 1974. *Historical Linguistics II*. Amsterdam: North Holland. *See* papers by Hudson and Ohala.

Aronoff, M. 1976. *Word Formation in Generative Grammar*. Linguistic Inquiry Monograph 1. Cambridge, Mass.: MIT Press. *pp.* 2, 24, 26, 58, 62, 87–8, 90, 91–2, 93, 95, 98, 115, 123, 124, 136, 170, 174–6, 189, 222, 225, 230, 231, 232, 240, 252, 290.

Bach, E. 1968. Nouns and noun phrases. In Bach & Harms (eds.), 90–122. *pp.* 150, 153.

Bach, E. & Harms, R. T. (eds.) 1968. *Universals in Linguistic Theory*. New York: Holt, Rinehart & Winston. *See* papers by Bach and Fillmore.

Bareš, K. 1974. Unconventional word-forming patterns in present-day English. *Philologica Pragensia* 17, 173–86. *p.* 239.

Barnhart, C. L., Steinmetz, S. & Barnhart, R. K. 1973. *A Dictionary of New English*. London: Longman. *pp.* 36, 42, 54, 55, 63, 65, 87, 91, 96, 114, 164, 175, 176, 201, 219, 221, 232, 235, 243, 244, 259, 260, 261, 264, 268, 269, 276–8, 280, 281, 282, 287, 288, 289.

Basbøll, H. 1975a. Grammatical boundaries in phonology. In Hovdhaugen (ed.), 35–54. *pp.* 48, 49, 84.

Basbøll, H. 1975b. Det rigsdanske stød i generativ belysning. *Selskab for nordisk filologi. Årsberetning 1971–73*, 17–22. *pp.* 51, 52.

Bauer, L. 1977. On teaching compound nouns. *Moderna Språk* 71, 325–36. *pp.* 51, 103, 105, 108.

Bauer, L. 1978a. On lexicalization. *Archivum Linguisticum* 9, 3–14. *pp.* 48, 51, 53.

Bauer, L. 1978b. Compounding the difficulties – a look at some nominal compounds in Danish. *Acta Philogica Scandinavica* 32, 87–113, *pp.* 54, 101.

Bauer, L. 1978c. Productivity in word-formation. In Gregersen (ed.), 333–7, *pp.* 62, 65, 67, 70, 82.

Bauer, L. 1978d. *The Grammar of Nominal Compounding with special reference to Danish, English and French*. Odense University Studies in Linguistics 4. Odense: Odense University Press. *pp.* 35, 38, 47, 48, 61, 62, 80, 85, 94–5, 105, 148, 158–9, 160, 162–3, 164, 165, 167, 171, 174, 184, 202, 206, 266.

Bauer, L. 1978e. Remarks on "Remarks . . .". *Prepublications of the English Institute of Odense University* 12. *p.* 75.

Bibliography and citation index

Bauer, L. 1979a. On the need for pragmatics in the study of nominal compounding. *Journal of Pragmatics* 3, 45–50. *pp.* 85, 142, 160.

Bauer, L. 1979b. Review of Brekle & Kastovsky (eds.) (1977a). *Journal of Linguistics* 15, 364–9. *pp.* 6, 65, 295.

Bauer, L. 1979c. Against word-based morphology. *Linguistic Inquiry* 10, 508–9. *pp.* 175, 213.

Bauer, L. 1979d. Patterns of productivity in new formations denoting persons using the suffix -er in modern English. *Cahiers de Lexicologie* 35, II, 26–31. *pp.* 175, 263.

Bauer, L. 1980a. Deux problèmes au sujet des noms composés comprenant un premier élément verbal en français moderne. *Français Moderne* 48, 219–24. *p.* 205.

Bauer, L. 1980b. In the beginning was the word. *Te Reo* 23, 73–80. *p.* 175.

Bauer, L. To appear. Stress in compounds: a rejoinder. *English Studies.* *pp.* 103–4.

Bazell, C. E. 1945. On some asymmetries of the linguistic system. *Acta Linguistica (Hafniensia)* 5, 139–45. *p.* 16.

Bazell, C. E. 1953. *Linguistic Form.* Istanbul: Istanbul Press. *pp.* 24, 26, 27.

Beard, R. 1976. Once more on the analysis of ed-adjectives. *Journal of Linguistics* 12, 155–7. *p.* 93.

Beard, R. 1977. On the extent and nature of irregularity in the lexicon. *Lingua* 42, 305–41. *pp.* 62, 72–4, 170, 189.

Beard, R. 1981. On the question of lexical regularity. *Journal of Linguistics* 17, 31–7. *p.* 189.

Bernard, J. & Delbridge, A. 1980. *Introduction to Linguistics: an Australian perspective.* Sydney: Prentice-Hall. *p.* 44.

Bierwisch, M. & Heidolph, K. E. (eds.) 1970. *Progress in Linguistics.* The Hague: Mouton. *See* papers by Lees and Motsch.

Bloomfield, L. 1935. *Language.* London: George Allen & Unwin. *pp.* 3, 9, 26, 105, 190.

Boas, H. U. 1974. On Halle's "Prolegomena to a theory of word formation" or what is a linguistic generalization?. *Linguistics* 134, 5–8. *p.* 170.

Bolinger, D. L. 1975. *Aspects of Language.* 2nd edn. New York: Harcourt, Brace & Jovanovich. *pp.* 87, 286.

Bowers, F. 1969. The deep structure of abstract nouns. *Foundations of Language* 5, 520–33. *pp.* 5, 83.

Brekle, H. E. 1970. *Generative Satzsemantik und transformationelle Syntax im System der englischen Nominalkomposition.* München: Wilhelm Fink Verlag. pp. 3–4, 5, 149, 158, 162, 184, 202.

Brekle, H. E. 1975. Zur Stellung der Wortbildung in der Grammatik. In H. Rix (ed.) *Flexion und Wortbildung.* Wiesbaden, 26–39. *pp.* 48, 149, 151.

Brekle, H. E. 1976. Foreword to second edition of Brekle (1970). *p.* 156.

Brekle, H. E. 1977. Die Stellung der Wortbildung in F. Schmitthenners (1796–1850) Grammatiksystem. In Brekle & Kastovsky (eds.), 32–8. *p.* 2.

Brekle, H. E. 1978. Reflections on the conditions for the coining, use and understanding of nominal compounds. In Dressler & Meid (eds.), 68–77. *p.* 242.

Brekle, H. E. & Kastovsky, D. (eds.) 1977a. *Perspektiven der Wortbildungsforschung.* Bonn: Bouvier Verlag Herbert Grundmann. *p.* 6. *See also* papers by Brekle, Brekle & Kastovsky, Burgschmidt, Coseriu, Dressler, Geckeler, Karius, Leitner, Ljung, Motsch, Neuhaus and Stein.

Brekle, H. E. & Kastovsky, D. 1977b. Wortbildungsforschung: Entwicklung und Positionen. In Brekle & Kastovsky (eds.), 7–19. *pp.* 2, 4, 48, 59.

Brown, E. K. & Miller, J. E. 1980. *Syntax: a linguistic introduction to sentence structure.* London: Hutchinson. *pp.* 12, 15.

Bruck, A., Fox, R. A. & LaGaly, M. W. (eds.) 1974. *Papers from the Parasession on Natural Phonology.* Chicago: Chicago Linguistic Society. *See* papers by Skousen and Vennemann.

Burgschmidt, E. 1977. Strukturierung, Norm und Produktivität in der Wortbildung. In Brekle & Kastovsky (eds.), 39–47. *pp.* 62, 87.

Carroll, J. M. 1979. Complex compounds: phrasal embedding in lexical structures. *Linguistics* 17, 863–77. *p.* 164.

Chambers, J. K. & Trudgill, P. 1980. *Dialectology*. Cambridge: Cambridge University Press. *p.* 252.

Chapman, R. W. 1939. *Adjectives from Proper Names.* SPE [Society for Pure English] Tract 52. Oxford: Oxford University Press. *p.* 269.

Chomsky, N. 1957. *Syntactic Structures.* The Hague: Mouton. *pp.* 3, 66, 71.

Chomsky, N. 1965. *Aspects of the Theory of Syntax.* Cambridge, Mass.: MIT Press *pp.* 2, 16, 67, 78, 87, 143–7, 160, 177, 190.

Chomsky, N. 1966a. *Cartesian Linguistics.* New York: Harper & Row. *p.* 66.

Chomsky, N. 1966b. *Topics in the Theory of Generative Grammar.* The Hague: Mouton. *p.* 71.

Chomsky, N. 1970. Remarks on nominalization. In Jacobs & Rosenbaum (eds.), 184–221. *pp.* 5, 75–81, 145, 177, 197, 216.

Chomsky, N. & Halle, M. 1968. *The Sound Pattern of English.* New York: Harper & Row. *pp.* 4, 109–11, 116, 119, 122, 124, 129, 223.

Clark, E. V. & Clark, H. H. 1979. When nouns surface as verbs. *Language* 55, 767–811. *pp.* 48, 85, 87, 97.

Coseriu, E. 1977. Inhaltliche Wortbildungslehre (am Beispiel des Typs "coupe-papier"). In Brekle & Kastovsky (eds.), 48–61. *p.* 60.

Dansk Sprognævn. 1972. *Ny ord i dansk 1968–69.* København: Gyldendal. *p.* 79.

Dansk Sprognævn. 1978. *Ny ord i dansk 1970–71.* København: Gyldendal. *p.* 42.

Derwing, B. 1973. *Transformational Grammar as a Theory of Language Acquisition.* Cambridge Studies in Linguistics 10. Cambridge: Cambridge University Press. *p.* 44.

Dik, S. C. 1967. Some critical remarks on the treatment of morphological structure in transformational generative grammar. *Lingua* 18, 352–83. *pp.* 28, 84.

Downing, P. 1977. On the creation and use of English compound nouns. *Language* 53, 810–42. *pp.* 48, 85, 95, 105, 142, 153, 158.

Dressler, W. 1977. Wortbildung bei Sprachverfall. In Brekle & Kastovsky (eds.), 62–9. *p.* 296.

Dressler, W. & Meid, W. (eds.) 1978. *Proceedings of the Twelfth International Congress of Linguists, Vienna, August 28–September 2, 1977.* Innsbruck. *See* papers by Brekle and Soudek.

Dubois, J. 1962. *Etude sur la dérivation suffixale en français moderne et contemporain.* Paris: Larousse. *p.* 36.

Dubois, J. & Dubois, C. 1971. *Introduction à la lexicographie: le dictionnaire.* Paris: Larousse. *p.* 36.

Ettinger, S. 1974a. *Form und Funktion in der Wortbildung. Die Diminutiv- und Augmentativmodifikation im Lateinischen, Deutschen und Romanischen. Ein kritischer Forschungsbericht 1900–1970.* Tübingen: Tübinger Beiträge zur Linguistik 47. *pp.* 26, 48, 89, 92.

Ettinger, S. 1974b. *Diminutiv- und Augmentativbildung: Regeln und Restriktionen.* Tübingen: Tübinger Beiträge zur Linguistik 54. *pp.* 89, 92, 94.

Fiengo, R. & Lasnik, H. 1972. On nonrecoverable deletion in syntax. *Linguistic Inquiry* 3, 528. *p.* 160.

Fillmore, C. 1968. The case for case. In Bach & Harms (eds.), 1–88. *pp.* 144–6, 149, 154.

Fleischer, W. 1975. *Wortbildung der deutschen Gegenwartssprache.* Tübingen: Niemeyer. Reproduction of the 4th rev. edn. Leipzig: VEB Verlag. *pp.* 48, 67.

Fleischman, S. 1977. *Cultural and Linguistic Factors in Word-Formation.* University of

California Publications in Linguistics 86. Berkeley and Los Ángeles: University of California Press. *p.* 23.

Foster, B. 1964. *The Changing English Language*. Harmondsworth: Penguin. *pp.* 98, 243, 249.

Fraser, B. 1970. Some remarks on the action nominalization in English. In Jacobs & Rosenbaum (eds.), 83–98. *pp.* 47, 186.

Fudge, E. 1975. English word stress: an examination of some basic assumptions. In Goyvaerts & Pullum (eds.), 277–323. *pp.* 123, 125.

Geckeler, H. 1977. Zur Frage der Lücke im System der Wortbildung. In Brekle & Kastovsky (eds.), 70–82. *p.* 85.

Geddie, W. (ed.) 1968. *Chambers's Twentieth Century Dictionary*. Edinburgh: Chambers. First published 1901, new edn. 1959. *p.* 82.

Gimson, A. C. 1970. *An Introduction to the Pronunciation of English*. 2nd edn. London: Edward Arnold. *pp.* 125, 229.

Giraud, J., Pamart, P. & Riverain, J. 1974. *Les nouveaux mots dans le vent*. Paris: Larousse. *p.* 42.

Giurescu, A. 1972. El método transformacional en el análisis de los nombres compuestos del español moderno. *Revue Roumaine de Linguistique* 17, 407–14. *pp.* 5, 59.

Gleason, H. A. 1955. *Workbook in Descriptive Linguistics*. New York, etc.: Holt, Rinehart & Winston. *p.* 18.

Gleitman, L. R. & Gleitman, H. 1970. *Phrase and Paraphrase: some innovative uses of language*. New York: Norton. *pp.* 5, 48, 296.

Goyvaerts, D. L. & Pullum, G. K. (eds.) 1975. *Essays on "The Sound Pattern of English"*. Ghent: Story-Scientia PVBA. *pp.* 116, 123. *See also* paper by Fudge.

Greenberg, J. 1966. *Universals of Language*. 2nd edn. Cambridge, Mass.: MIT Press. *p.* 26.

Gregersen, K. (ed.) 1978. *Papers from the Fourth Scandinavian Conference of Linguistics*. Odense University Studies in Linguistics 3. Odense: Odense University Press. *See* papers by Bauer and Hakulinen.

Grévisse, M. 1964. *Le bon usage*. 8th edn. Gembloux et Paris. *pp.* 37, 39.

Gruber, J. S. 1976. *Lexical Structures in Syntax and Semantics*. Amsterdam: North Holland. *pp.* 32, 99–100.

Guilbert, L. 1975. *La créativité lexicale*. Paris: Larousse. *pp.* 19, 23, 43, 48, 62, 223.

Gunter, R. 1972. English derivation. *Journal of Linguistics* 8, 1–19. *p.* 64.

Hakulinen, A. 1978. Some unsolved problems in the lexicon. In Gregersen (ed.), 325–32. *pp.* 1, 2, 70, 97.

Halle, M. 1973. Prolegomena to a theory of word formation. *Linguistic Inquiry* 4, 3–16. *pp.* 5, 28, 170.

Hanks, P. (ed.) 1971. *Encyclopedic World Dictionary*. London, etc.: Hamlyn. *pp.* 80, 151.

Hanks, P. 1979. To what extent does a dictionary definition define? *ITL* 45–6, 32–8. *p.* 189.

Harder, K. B. 1964. The suffix "-ee". *American Speech* 39, 294–6. *p.* 244.

Harder, K. B. 1966. More instances of "-nik". *American Speech* 41, 150–4. *pp.* 243, 260.

Hasselrot, B. 1972. *Etude sur la vitalité de la formation diminutive française au xxe siècle*. Acta Universitatis Upsaliensis. Studia Romanica Upsaliensia 8. Uppsala: Almqvist & Wiksells. *p.* 88.

Hatcher, A. G. 1960. An introduction to the analysis of English noun compounds. *Word* 16, 356–73. *pp.* 105, 149, 184, 202.

Henzen, W. 1947. *Deutsche Wortbildung*. Halle. *p.* 38.

Hill, A. A. 1974. Word stress and the suffix -*ic*. *Journal of English Linguistics* 8, 6–20. *pp.* 114–16.

Hirtle, W. H. 1969. -ed adjectives like "verandahed" and "blue-eyed". *Journal of Linguistics* 6, 19–36. *p.* 93.

Hockett, C. 1947. Problems of morphemic analysis. *Language* 23, 321–43. Reprinted in M. Joos (ed.) 1957. *Readings in Linguistics* 1. Chicago: University of Chicago Press, 229–42. *pp.* 15, 17.

Hooper, J. B. 1976a. *An Introduction to Natural Generative Phonology*. New York, etc.: Academic Press. *pp.* 135–7.

Hooper, J. B. 1976b. Word frequency in lexical diffusion and the source of morphophonological change. In W. M. Christie (ed.) *Current Progress in Historical Linguistics*. Amsterdam: North Holland, 95–105. *p.* 71.

Hooper, J. B. 1979. Substantive principles in Natural Generative Phonology. In D. A. Dinnsen (ed.) *Current Approaches to Phonological Theory*. Bloomington and London: Indiana University Press, 106–25. *p.* 7.

Hornby, A. S. (ed.) 1974. *Oxford Advanced Learner's Dictionary of Current English*. 3rd edn. London: Oxford University Press. *pp.* 46, 73, 103, 104, 243.

Houghton, D. E. 1968. The suffix *-wise*. *American Speech* 43, 209–15. *p.* 225.

Hovdhaugen, E. (ed.) 1975. *Papers from the Second Scandinavian Conference of Linguistics*. Oslo: Oslo University Department of Linguistics. *See* papers by Basbøll and Pennanen.

Hsieh, H. 1976. On the unreality of some phonological rules. *Lingua* 38, 1–19. *p.* 42.

Hudson, G. 1974. The representation of non-productive alternation. In Anderson & Jones (eds.), 203–29. *pp.* 42, 135.

Hudson, R. A. 1975. Problems in the analysis of ed-adjectives. *Journal of Linguistics* 11, 69–72. *p.* 93.

Jackendoff, R. 1975. Morphological and semantic regularities in the lexicon. *Language* 51, 639–71. *pp.* 5, 57, 86, 170.

Jacobs, R. & Rosenbaum, P. (eds.) 1970. *Readings in English Transformational Grammar*. Waltham, Mass.: Ginn. *See* papers by Chomsky and Fraser.

Jensen, J. T. 1974. How abstract is abstract?. *Glossa* 8, 247–60. *p.* 133.

Jespersen, O. 1909. *A Modern English Grammar on historical principles. Part I. Sounds and Spelling*. London and Copenhagen: George Allen & Unwin and Ejnar Munksgaard. *p.* 52.

Jespersen, O. 1924. *The Philosophy of Grammar*. London: George Allen & Unwin. *p.* 40.

Jespersen, O. 1942. *A Modern English Grammar on historical principles. Part VI. Morphology*. London and Copenhagen: George Allen & Unwin and Ejnar Munksgaard. *pp.* 3, 32, 38, 52, 62, 98, 202, 243, 267, 288–9.

Johannisson, T. 1958. Tendenser i nutida svensk ordbildning, *Modersmålslärarnas Förening Årsskrift*, 7–22. *p.* 143.

Karius, I. 1976. Zur Beziehung zwischen Wortbildung und Alltagswissen. In K. Braunmüller & W. Kürschner (eds.) *Grammatik*. Tübingen: Niemeyer, 59–68. *p.* 85.

Karius, I. 1977. Instrumentalität und denominale nulsuffigierte Verben des Englischen. In Brekle & Kastovsky (eds.), 104–15. *p.* 85.

Kastovsky, D. 1977. Word-formation, or: at the crossroads of morphology, syntax, semantics and the lexicon. *Folia Linguistica* 10, 1–33. *p.* 6.

Katz, J. J. & Fodor, J. A. 1963. The structure of a semantic theory. *Language* 39, 170–210. *pp.* 141, 191.

Kiefer, F. 1972. A propos derivational morphology. In F. Kiefer (ed.) *Derivational Processes*. Stockholm, KVAL, 42–59. *p.* 48.

Kingdon, R. 1958. *The Groundwork of English Stress*. London: Longman. *pp.* 103, 105, 106, 108, 114, 121, 180, 181.

Kiparsky, P. 1972. Explanation in phonology. In S. Peters (ed.) *Goals of Linguistic Theory*. Englewood Cliffs, N.J.: Prentice-Hall, 189–227. *p.* 223.

Bibliography and citation index

Kiparsky, V. 1964. Les aventures d'un suffixe. *Revue des Etudes Slaves* 40, 114–18. *pp.* 23, 243, 259.

Koerner, E. F. K. (ed.) 1975. *The Transformational-Generative Paradigm and Modern Linguistic Theory*. Amsterdam: Benjamins. *See* papers by Lipka and Steinberg & Krohn.

Kolin, P. C. 1979. The pseudo-suffix *-oholic*. *American Speech* 54, 74–6. *pp.* 23, 236.

Koziol, H. 1937. *Handbuch der englischen Wortbildungslehre*. Heidelberg. *pp.* 3, 32, 35, 201.

Kruisinga, E. 1911. *A Handbook of Present-Day English*. 5th edn. 1932. Groningen. *p.* 35.

Kürschner, W. 1974. *Zur syntaktischen Beschreibung deutscher Nominalkomposita*. Tübingen: Niemeyer. *p.* 184.

Lakoff, G. 1970a. *Irregularity in Syntax*. New York, etc.: Holt, Rinehart & Winston. *pp.* 5, 75, 186, 217.

Lakoff, G. 1970b. A note on vagueness and ambiguity. *Linguistic Inquiry* 1, 357–9. *pp.* 159,187.

Leben, W. R. & Robinson, O. W. 1977. "Upside-down" phonology. *Language* 53, 1–20. *pp.* 133–5.

Leech, G. 1974. *Semantics*. Harmondsworth: Penguin. *pp.* 5, 48, 56, 141, 192.

Lees, R. B. 1960. *The Grammar of English Nominalizations*. 5th edn. 1968. The Hague: Mouton. *pp.* 2, 3–4, 47, 59, 62, 67, 82, 104, 105, 107–9, 149, 159, 161, 162, 167, 171, 184, 186, 202, 285.

Lees, R. B. 1970. Problems in the grammatical analysis of English nominal compounds. In Bierwisch & Heidolph (eds.), 174–86. *pp.* 5, 160.

Lehnert, M. 1971. *Reverse Dictionary of Present-Day English*. Leipzig: VEB. *pp.* 86, 243, 244, 247.

Leitner, G. 1977. Zur Vorhersagbarkeit von Derivation: Teil-von-Nomen als Basen. In Brekle & Kastovsky (eds.), 140–54. *pp.* 62, 82, 85.

Levi, J. N. 1973. Where do all those other adjectives come from? *Papers from the Regional Meetings of the Chicago Linguistic Society* 9, 332–45. *p.* 184.

Levi, J. N. 1978. *The Syntax and Semantics of Complex Nominals*. New York, etc.: Academic Press. *pp.* 161, 184–6.

Lewicka, H. 1963. Réflexions théoriques sur la composition des mots en ancien et en moyen français. *Kwartalnik Neofilologiczny* x, 131–42. *p.* 48.

Lightner, T. M. 1975. The role of derivational morphology in generative grammar. *Language* 51, 617–38. *pp.* 5, 93, 132.

Lipka, L. 1975. Prolegomena to "Prolegomena to a theory of word formation", a reply to Morris Halle. In Koerner (ed.), 175–84. *p.* 170.

Lipka, L. 1977. Lexicalisierung, Idiomatisierung und Hypostasierung als Probleme einer synchronischen Wortbildungslehre. In Brekle & Kastovsky (eds.), 155–64. *pp.* 48, 55–7, 85, 158.

Ljung, M. 1970. *English Denominal Adjectives. A generative study of the semantics of a group of high-frequency denominal adjectives in English*. Gothenburg Studies in English 21. Lund: Acta Universitatis Gothoburgensis. *pp.* 68, 70, 85, 93, 99, 178.

Ljung, M. 1976. -ed adjectives revisited. *Journal of Linguistics* 12, 159–68. *p.* 93.

Ljung, M. 1977. Problems in the derivation of instrumental verbs. In Brekle & Kastovsky (eds.), 165–79. *pp.* 43, 48, 62, 85.

Lyons, J. 1963. *Structural Semantics: an analysis of part of the vocabulary of Plato*. Publications of the Philological Society xx. Oxford: Blackwell. *p.* 12.

Lyons, J. 1968. *Introduction to Theoretical Linguistics*. Cambridge: Cambridge University Press. *pp.* 9, 12, 14, 15, 33, 66, 94, 105, 106, 141, 157, 175, 183, 267, 279.

Lyons, J. (ed.) 1970. *New Horizons in Linguistics*. Harmondsworth: Penguin. *pp.* 12, 48, 267. *See also* paper by Matthews.

Lyons, J. 1977. *Semantics*. Cambridge: Cambridge University Press. *pp*. 5, 12, 20, 22, 27, 31, 32, 35, 47, 48, 49, 54, 56, 60, 63, 65, 141, 150, 154, 156, 191, 192, 195, 197, 243, 279.

McMillan, J. B. 1980. Infixing and interposing in English. *American Speech* 55, 163–83. *p*. 90.

Malkiel, Y. 1978. Derivational categories. In J. H. Greenberg (ed.) *Universals of Human Language. Vol 3: Word Structure*. Stanford: Stanford University Press, 125–49. *pp*. 38, 89.

Marchand, H. 1969. *The Categories and Types of Present-Day English Word-Formation*. 2nd edn. München: C. H. Beck. *pp*. 4, 5, 32, 37, 62, 64, 76, 77, 79, 82, 104, 105, 107, 108, 123, 124, 141, 155, 164, 199, 201, 202, 207, 208, 209, 211, 212, 213, 217, 218, 219, 220, 221, 222, 223, 224, 225, 226, 229, 230, 233, 243, 244, 250, 254, 267, 290.

Martinet, A. 1960. *Eléments de linguistique générale*. Paris: Armand Colin. *p*. 27.

Martinet, A. (ed.) 1969. *La Linguistique: guide alphabétique*. Paris: Denoël. *p*. 37.

Mathesius, V. 1975. *A Functional Analysis of Present Day English on a General Linguistic Basis*. The Hague: Mouton. Czech original published in 1961. *pp*. 91, 142.

Matthews, P. H. 1970. Recent developments in morphology. In Lyons (ed.), 96–114. *p*. 17.

Matthews, P. H. 1972. *Inflectional Morphology: a theoretical study based on aspects of Latin verb conjugation*. Cambridge Studies in Linguistics 6. Cambridge: Cambridge University Press. *pp*. 8, 9, 12, 13, 16, 20, 21, 32, 33, 106.

Matthews, P. H. 1974. *Morphology: an introduction to the theory of word-structure*. Cambridge: Cambridge University Press. *pp*. 12, 13, 14, 15, 16, 20, 27, 28, 30, 33, 36, 39, 41, 48.

Matthews, P. H. 1979. *Generative Grammar and Linguistic Competence*. London: George Allen & Unwin. *p*. 81.

Meys, W. J. 1975. *Compound Adjectives in English and the Ideal Speaker—Listener*. Amsterdam: North Holland. *pp*. 48, 74.

Miller, G. A. 1978. Semantic relations among words. In M. Halle, J. Bresnan & G. A. Miller (eds.) *Linguistics Theory and Psychological Reality*. Cambridge, Mass.: MIT Press, 60–118. *pp*. 70, 192.

Miller, G. A. & Johnson-Laird, P. N. 1976. *Language and Perception*. Cambridge, Mass.: Harvard University Press. *p*. 192.

Minton, A. 1958. *Sputnik* and some of its offshootniks. *Names* 6, 112–17. *pp*. 243, 265.

Mitchell, T. F. 1956. *An Introduction to Egyptian Colloquial Arabic*. London, etc.: Oxford University Press. *p*. 168.

Mitchell, T. F. 1962. *Colloquial Arabic*. London: The English Universities Press. *p*. 168.

Motsch, W. 1970. Analyse von Komposita mit zwei nominalen Elementen. In Bierwisch & Heidolph (eds.), 208–23. *pp*. 47, 48, 160–1.

Motsch, W. 1977. Ein Plädoyer für die Beschreibung von Wortbildungen auf der Grundlage des Lexikons. In Brekle & Kastovsky (eds.), 180–202. *pp*. 48, 59, 65, 83, 87, 96, 292.

Neuhaus, H. J. 1977. Wortbildungssemantik. In Brekle & Kastovsky (eds.), 203–9. *pp*. 182–4.

Newmeyer, F. 1970. The derivation of the English action nominalization. *Papers from the Regional Meetings of the Chicago Linguistic Society* 6, 408–15. *pp*. 5, 47, 186.

Newmeyer, F. 1971. The source of derived nominals in English. *Language* 47, 786–96. *p*. 186.

OED. The Oxford English Dictionary. 1884–1928. *pp*. 86, 87, 88, 89, 97, 120, 213, 243, 244, 246, 249, 251, 279, 289.

OEDS. Supplement to *The Oxford English Dictionary*. 1972– . *pp*. 35, 76, 217, 220, 221, 243, 252, 253, 254, 259, 268–9, 278, 279, 280, 282.

Ohala, J. 1974. Experimental historical phonology. In Anderson & Jones (eds.), 353–87. *pp*. 138, 296.

Bibliography and citation index

Orsman, H. (ed.) 1979. *New Zealand Dictionary*. Auckland: Heinemann. *p.* 277.

Pennanen, E. V. 1966. *Contributions to the Study of Back-Formation in English*. Tampere: Acta Academiae Socialis, ser. A. vol. 4. *pp.* 43, 64.

Pennanen, E. V. 1971. *Conversion and Zero-Derivation in English*. Acta Universitatis Tamperensis, ser. A. vol. 40. *pp.* 33, 229.

Pennanen, E. V. 1972. Current views of word-formation. *Neuphilologische Mitteilungen* 73, 292–308. *pp.* 5, 66.

Pennanen, E. V. 1975. What happens in back-formation?. In Hovdhaugen (ed.), 216–29. *p.* 230.

Pennanen, E. V. 1980. On the function and behaviour of stress in English noun compounds. *English Studies* 61, 252–63. *p.* 103.

Quirk, R. 1962. *The Use of English*. London: Longman. *p.* 44.

Quirk, R., Greenbaum, S., Leech, G. & Svartvik, J. 1972. *A Grammar of Contemporary English*. London: Longman. *pp.* 36, 62, 64, 228, 229, 230, 274.

Rex, R. 1975. The origin of *beatnik*. *American Speech* 50, 329–31. *pp.* 260.

Robins, R. H. 1964. *General Linguistics: an introductory survey*. Rev. edn. 1967. London: Longman. *pp.* 26, 31.

Roeper, T. & Siegel, M. E. A. 1978. A lexical transformation for verbal compounds. *Linguistic Inquiry* 9, 199–260. *pp.* 5, 163–74, 176–82.

Rohrer, C. 1966. Review of Lees (1960). *Indogermanische Forschungen* 71, 161–70. *p.* 160.

Rohrer, C. 1967. *Die Wortzusammensetzung im modernen Französisch*. Pub. edn., Tübingen, 1977. *pp.* 38, 47, 59, 149, 171, 184.

Rohrer, C. 1973. Some problems of wordformation. Prepublication draft. Stuttgart. *pp.* 149, 153.

Rohrer, C. 1974. Some problems of wordformation. In C. Rohrer & N. Ruwet (eds.) *Actes du colloque Franco-Allemand de grammaire transformationelle II*. Tübingen: Niemeyer, 113–23. Slightly revised version of Rohrer (1973). *pp.* 149, 150–7.

Romaine, S. 1981. The status of variable rules in sociolinguistic theory. *Journal of Linguistics* 17, 93–119. *p.* 252.

Rose, J. H. 1973. Principled limitations on productivity in denominal verbs. *Foundations of Language* 10, 509–26. *pp.* 62, 82, 85, 86, 87.

Rudnyckyj, J. B. 1959. Sputnik and -nik derivatives in the present language of North America. *Etudes Slaves et Est-Européennes* 4, 142–50. *pp.* 243, 259.

Sampson, R. 1980. Stress in English N + N phrases: a further complicating factor. *English Studies* 61, 264–70. *p.* 108.

Sapir, E. 1921. *Language*. London: Harvest. *pp.* 8, 9.

Sapir, E. 1949. *Selected Writings of Edward Sapir in Language, Culture and Personality*. Ed. D. G. Mandelbaum. Berkeley, etc.: University of California Press. *p.* 201.

Skousen, R. 1974. An explanatory theory of morphology. In Bruck *et al*. (eds.), 318–27. *p.* 101.

Soudek, L. I. 1978. The relation of blending to English word-formation: theory, structure and typological attempts. In Dressler & Meid (eds.), 462–6. *p.* 237.

Stein, G. 1976. Semi-productive lexical rules: a note on -*ed* adjectives. *Journal of English Linguistics* 10, 30–3. *p.* 93.

Stein, G. 1977. The place of word-formation in linguistic description. In Brekle & Kastovsky (eds.), 219–35. *pp.* 59, 68, 82.

Steinberg, D. & Krohn, R. K. 1975. The psychological validity of Chomsky & Halle's vowel shift rule. In Koerner (ed.), 233–59. *p.* 138.

Strang, B. M. H. 1968. *Modern English Structure*. 2nd edn. London: Edward Arnold. *pp.* 22, 27, 32.

Strauss, S. L. 1980. How abstract is English morphology?. *Glossa* 14, 89–112. *pp.* 136, 222.

Teleman, U. 1970. *Om Svenska Ord*. Lund: Gleerups. *pp.* 48, 67, 149.

Thiel, G. 1973. Die semantische Beziehungen in den Substantivkomposita der deutschen Gegenwartssprache. *Muttersprache* 83, 377–404. *p.* 46.

Thompson, S. A. 1975. On the issue of productivity in the lexikon. *Kritikon Litterarum* 4, 332–49. *pp.* 28, 62, 85, 94, 96.

Tietze, G. O. 1974. *Einführung in die Wortbildung des heutigen Englisch: Typen und Prozesse*. Anglistische Arbeitshefte 5. Tübingen: Niemeyer. *pp.* 48, 64, 78, 230.

Vendler, Z. 1968. *Adjectives and Nominalizations*. The Hague: Mouton. *pp.* 5, 47, 160.

Vennemann, T. 1972. Rule inversion. *Lingua* 29, 209–42. *p.* 136.

Vennemann, T. 1974. Words and syllables in natural generative grammar. In Bruck *et al.* (eds.), 346–74. *p.* 135.

Vos, A. L. 1952. *Stress in English Compound Nouns*. Unpublished Diploma dissertation, Department of Linguistics, University of Edinburgh. *pp.* 47, 103.

Ward, D. 1965. *The Russian Language Today*. London: Hutchinson. *pp.* 156–7.

Warren, B. 1978. *Semantic Patterns of Noun-Noun Compounds*. Gothenburg Studies in English 41. Lund: Acta Universitatis Gothoburgensis. *pp.* 48, 85, 105, 184, 202.

Webster's. 1966. *Webster's Third New International Dictionary*. Springfield, Mass.: G. & C. Merriam. *pp.* 86, 120, 243, 271, 278, 279, 289.

Wentworth, H. 1941. The allegedly dead suffix -DOM in modern English. *PMLA* 56, 280–306. *p.* 220.

Wheeler, C. J. & Schumsky, D. A. 1980. The morpheme boundaries of some English derivational suffixes. *Glossa* 14, 3–34. *pp.* 44, 296.

Whitaker, H. & Whitaker, H. 1976. Language disorders. In R. Wardhaugh & H. D. Brown (eds.) *A Survey of Applied Linguistics*. Ann Arbor: University of Michigan Press, 250–74. *pp.* 84, 296.

Whorf, B. L. 1936. The punctual and segmentative aspects of verbs in Hopi. *Language* 12, 127–31. *p.* 86.

Williams, T. 1965. On the "-ness" peril. *American Speech* 40, 279–86. *pp.* 81, 88, 164, 222, 225.

Winther, A. 1975. Note sur les formations déverbales en *-eur* et en *-ant*. *Cahiers de Lexicologie* 26, 56–84. *p.* 158.

Žepić, S. 1970. *Morphologie und Semantik der deutschen Nominalkomposita*. Zagrebacke Germanisticke Studije, Svezak 3. Zagreb. *pp.* 5, 59, 149, 184, 202.

Zimmer, K. E. 1964. *Affixal Negation in English and Other Languages*. Supplement to *Word* 20. *pp.* 3, 82, 94, 95.

Zwicky, A. M. & Sadock, J. M. 1975. Ambiguity tests and how to fail them. In J. P. Kimball (ed.) *Syntax and Semantics IV*. New York, etc.: Academic Press, 1–36. *p.* 187.

INDEX

Index

French, 12, 156, 194; compounding in 39, 46, 151, 152, 178n., 205; inflection in 25, 27, 28; Old French 76, 128, 138, 244; phonology 101, 102; prefixation in 37–8, 150; source of English words 45, 52, 225, 290; suffixation in 19, 23, 36, 40, 158, 223
frozen, *see* institutionalization
-fucking-, 89–91, 98
-ful, 62, 92, 122, 194, 195, 224
-fuld, 51
"full entry theory", 170

generative phonology, 4, 109, 121, 129, 132, 136
generative semantics, 140, 146–8, 153n., 154, 166, 171
German, 25, 62, 91; compounds in 37, 46, 53–4, 55, 67, 101, 151, 152, 178n.; gender in 15–16; prefixation in 38; suffixation in 36, 89, 92, 96
Germanic languages, 66–7, 71
gerund, 78, 203
government, 25
grammatical meaning, 189, 193
grammatical word, *12*, 24
grammaticality, 67, 68, 82–4
Great Vowel Shift, 52, 127–8, 129, 134, 138
Greek, 14, 54, 156, 213, 216, 225, 226

-heit, 36
hemi-, 67
homo-, 175
-hood, 36, 91, 112, 221, 222
Hopi, 86
hydro-, 213
hyper-, 215
hyponymy, 30–1
hypostatization, *85*, 143, 252

-i, 253–5, 266
-ia(c), 113
-ial, 113, 223–4
-ian, 112, 122, 268, 293
-iana, 113, 117, 221, 252
-ic: stress 51, 112, 113, 114–16, 119, 121, 122; syntax 69, 224, 240, 268; truncation of 271
-ical, 122
Icelandic, 9
ICF (Initial Combining Form), 214, 270, 271, 272, 273, 275, 276, 293
ideal speaker–listener, 132, 138, 170, 252
idiom, 61, 142, 178, 262
idiomatization, *see* lexicalization
-ie, 244
-ify, 122, 195, 198, 199, 222–3, 277

-iller, 223
in-, 214, 219
-in, 92
inalienable possession, 93–4
incompetent formation, 266
-ine, 268
infix and infixation, *18*, 90
inflection: exemplified 10; vs. derivation 22–9, 39–41
inflectional category, *10*, 12
inflectional paradigm, *see* paradigm
institutionalization, *48*, 53, 86, 88, 95, 199–200, 210, 274
inter-, 220
-ion, 92, 198
-isation, 23
-iser, 19
-ish, 23, 29, 71, 112, 182–4, 225, 268
-ism, 35, 120–1, 221
iso-, 275
-issage, 23
-ist, 36, 69, 71, 113, 122, 222, 250, 261, 268, 269
Italian, 10, 14–15, 17, 27, 39, 89, 94
-ite, 250, 261, 268, 269
item familiarity, *48*, 74
-itis, 112, 117
-ity, 82, 88, 91, 93, 95, 112, 113, 122, 134, 135, 138
-ive, 122, 124, 224
-ize, 69, 70, 91, 122, 135, 168, 198, 221, 222–3, 277

journalistic language, 42, 43, 63, 264, 266

langue, 252
Latin, 9, 12, 194; derivation in 39, 89, 92–3; inflection in 17, 25, 217; source of English words 54, 91, 125, 128, 197, 213, 216, 219, 225, 270; Vulgar Latin 20
learned words, 91
-lein, 89
-less, 81, 122, 224
-let, 23, 221
lexeme, *11–13*, 22, *33*, 35, 38, 71, 137, 142, 175
lexical address, *195*
lexical entry, *192–3*, 194–5, 196, 243, 245, 251, 257, 262, 267–8, 271, 285
lexical meaning, 189
lexical morphology, *see* word-formation defined
lexical restrictions on productivity, 93, 97
lexicalist and transformationalist approaches to word-formation, 5, 75–81

Index

primary defining characteristic, 95
pro-, 218
productivity, 18–19, ch. 4, 134, 139, 242,
292, 293; as a cline 97–9, 292; 'full' 88,
100, 221; syntactic 65–6, 83; vs. analogy
96, 295
Proposition, 144, 149, 162, 163, 172, 173,
174
Proto-Indo-European, 39, 45, 131, 132
pseudo-, 68, 125, 215
psycho-, 68
psychological reality, 123, 138, 200, 252,
295–6

-rama, 236
re-, 67, 68, 124, 179, 219
realization, *12*
received, *see* institutionalization
redundant formations, 95
recognizability, 267, 276
respiro-, 272
-ric, 93
Romance languages, 23, 54, 223
root, *20–2*, 28–9, *33*, 54, 175, 214, 290
root compounds, *164*, 171
Russian, 14, 23, 25, 28

-s, 14, 15, 18, 20, 23, 26, 138, 166
-'s, 8, 25, 38
-s-: in Danish 37, 101; in German 16, 53
-sam, 96
Sanskrit, 2, 30, 31
-scape, 221
-self, 212
semantic compositionality, 28, *58*, 95, 98,
169, 176
semantic restrictions on productivity, 93–4
semi-, 67, 68
semi-productivity, *27–8*, 74, 82–4, 100
"sentential source" analysis, 148–50, 156,
171
-ship, 94, 122, 221
simplex, *30*, 123, 190–2, 193, 226
socio-, 68, 215
-some, 225
spelling pronunciation, *53*
stem, *20–2*, 28, 38, 258
step-, 124, 218
Stress: as a conditioning factor 90; general
rules 116–17, 125; in compounds 50–1,
101, 102–12, 280, 293; in derivatives 101,
112–25; in French 101; in Icelandic 9; in
lexicalization 99, 107, 108, 192; in
sentences 103; influenced by consonant
cluster 117, 118; influenced by tense
vowel 117, 118; lexical conditioning of

107–9; semantic correlations of 107, 108,
210
stød, *51*, 102
style, 143, 185, 193, 217, 233, 244, 261,
265, 273, 286, 288–90
sub-, 125, 214, 220
subcategorization, 174, 177–82
subject nominalization, 285–91, 293
suffix and suffixation, *18*, 31, 112–23, 165,
175, 220–6, 243–70; recursiveness of
69–70; strings of 70, 92
super-, 29, 215
Swahili, 14
Swedish, 102
synonymy, 150, 287, 289–90
syntactic restrictions on productivity,
163–9, 293; no extrinsic ordering 168–9;
no medial variables 167–8; no phrasal
categories 163–5, 175; syntactic category
shift 165–7

tele-, 273
tense: verbal 150, 153–4, 157–8; vocalic
117, 118, 119
-ter, 79
-teria, 236
-th, 49, 55, 222
-tician, 23
-tion, 23
tone, 102, 192
-topia, 236
transformationalist, *see* lexicalist
transparent, *19–20*, 48, 49
truncation, *115*, 119, 120, 121, 176, 247,
251
-ture, 23
Turkish, 9, 14
type familiarity, *48*

-ual, 223–4
-um, 273
un-, 13, 18, 20, 68, 94, 176, 189, 214, 215,
217, 218, 219, 224, 279
underlying phonological
representation, 130
underlying verb in compounds, 47, 159–63,
184, 204
universality of word-formation
processes, 10, 86–7
"upside-down" phonology, 133–4
-ure: in English 222; in French 19

variable rule, 98, 252
velar softening, 91, 128, 138, 247
verbal compound, 170–4, 180–2
verbalization, 23, 222–3